MARGARET THATCHER

A TRIBUTE IN WORDS AND PICTURES

MARGARET THATCHER

A TRIBUTE IN WORDS AND PICTURES

EDITED BY IAIN DALE

FOREWORD BY CHARLES MOORE

The Daily Telegraph

WEIDENFELD & NICOLSON

Contributors

Foreword
Charles Moore

Margaret Thatcher is eighty years old this year, yet so much has she already been made part of myth and part of history that it is easy to forget the living, breathing woman. But I would argue that the impact of Mrs Thatcher as a human being, especially as a female human being, has been equal to the power of her deeds and ideas. As I work on her authorised biography, I find that my first question to the hundreds of people whom I interview is, 'What is your first memory of meeting Mrs Thatcher?' They almost always have one, and it is almost always illuminating. The story of the last meeting can be pretty good too.

Lady Thatcher is one of those people – other twentieth-century examples include Winston Churchill, Nelson Mandela, Diana, Princess of Wales, and Pope John Paul II – whose impact derives from more than their role alone. People often call it 'star quality', and that is partly right, for one of the statesman's necessary gifts is the ability to act. You will see that skill displayed in many of the pictures in this book, as Mrs T grabs a dog or a voter or Mikhail Gorbachev or Denis, and makes something startlingly good of the scene for the camera. But it is not only acting. For though she is superb at putting on a show, Margaret Thatcher is what the philosophers call an 'authentic personality'. Everything she says reflects what she believes, the way she is, the way she thinks and feels. If you meet her, you notice this, and you want to go home and tell your family about it.

As a result, Lady Thatcher generates a curious excitement in company which goes beyond the content of the particular conversation she may be having. This book records this excitement and communicates it to the reader.

I think that history will show that Margaret Thatcher was not necessarily original in her political ideas. Nor – for she is, as I say, human – was she always right, or always wise. But she is living proof of the force of personality in human affairs. Democratic government is by nature a diffused, sluggish thing, in which bureaucrats like to slow things down and elected politicians are more interested in the credit for doing something than in actually carrying it out. What was unique about Mrs Thatcher – as she was titled when she ran our affairs (the 'Lady' was part of the reward afterwards) – was her capacity to change this. Government became something dramatic – sometimes alarmingly so – and standards were high, and everyone, from the Cabinet Secretary to the doorman, jumped to it. She was a perfectionist, and political perfection, for her, consisted in actual achievement, not in pretence.

The effect was reinforced by the fact that she was the first woman Prime Minister and, with the notable exception of the Head of State, the only woman at the top of our public life. For more than eleven years in Whitehall and

Westminster, the word 'she' meant only one thing. This uniqueness added to the attention she received, the interest people felt, and the extent to which she could do things differently from anyone else. One of the most marked characteristics of men is our need to be esteemed by our chums. This strongly affects the way we run things. Margaret Thatcher loves admiration, of course, but she is shatteringly indifferent to that clubby solidarity which makes it more important to get on with one another than to get anything done. She would constantly complain, carp, go back over things, ignoring the *amour propre* of the Ministers, officials, even the world statesmen whom she met. This tendency did for her politically in the end, but it was actually one of her greatest glories. She liked to compare herself to the housewife who knows best and has to do all the work and never forgets the basic truths about life. What her colleagues eventually found unforgivable was that this comparison was both unflattering to them and essentially correct.

My theory is that almost everyone in Britain has his or her own Thatcher story. Often it is a funny one, for though Lady Thatcher is sometimes accused of not having a sense of humour, she has a readiness with words, a sense of occasion and a playful sense of self-parody which make her fun to be with. This tribute contains some of the best – funny (I particularly recommend John Whittingdale on the dead parrot) and serious. It would make a good present for anyone interested in the interaction of politics and human character. I like to think that it is a fitting birthday present for her, too.

Introduction
Iain Dale

This book has been a pleasure to compile and edit. I am indebted to the contributors whose anecdotes are entertaining, informative and, on occasion, quite moving.

The book contains anecdotes from world leaders, former Cabinet Ministers, Members of Parliament, journalists, civil servants and many other people who have experienced memorable encounters with the Iron Lady. We have also received co-operation from several leading publishers which has allowed us to reprint relevant passages from the memoirs of the late Ronald Reagan, Mikhail Gorbachev and the late Alan Clark among others. I thank them all for their co-operation.

I would also like to thank Morven Knowles from *The Daily Telegraph* whose support and encouragement during the book's long gestation period has been unstinting. My publisher at Weidenfeld & Nicolson Alan Samson deserves my continuing gratitude for having the courage to take the book on in the first place and remaining calm when I failed to meet the odd deadline, while Tom Graves, my picture editor, has done a magnificent job in sourcing many pictures with very little to go on. I hope I repay the confidence all three of them have placed in me and the book.

In the introduction to my previous book on Margaret Thatcher, *As I Said to Denis: The Margaret Thatcher Book of Quotations* (Robson Books, 1997), I said that an aim of the book was to give the reader insight into the character of Margaret Thatcher and her political views. It is even more the case with this book, and I hope it goes some way to destroying the myth of a hard, uncaring and ill-meaning politician. I hope that you, the reader, will enjoy the anecdotes in this book and will forgive me for setting the ball rolling with my own!

Margaret Thatcher is the reason I am actively involved in politics. She inspired me, as a sixteen-year-old, to join the Conservative Party and do my bit to help revive Britain. One of the tasks of today's political leaders is to provide a lead, to inspire, to motivate. Margaret Thatcher was able to do that in a way few politicians in this country have been able to emulate. My first tentative footstep into the political arena was to set up a Conservative organization in 1982 at the very left-wing University of East Anglia. Only a few months later followed my first encounter with Margaret Thatcher when she invited the chairmen of the various University Conservative Associations to a reception at Number Ten.

For a country boy like me, it was unbelievable to have been invited and it was something I had been looking forward to for months. Just to climb those stairs, with the portraits of all past Prime Ministers on the walls, was worth the trip on its own. And there at the top of the stairs was the Prime Minister. She had obviously perfected the art of welcoming people to receptions and as she shook you by the hand and wished you a good evening, she moved you on into the room without you even knowing she was doing it. Most of the Cabinet were there – I remember discussing with Cecil Parkinson the number of free running shoes he had been sent after a recent profile had announced to the world that he was a keen runner. He offered me a pair but it turned out his feet were much smaller than mine! We were constantly plied with wine and I made a mental note to stop at two glasses. But after the second glass was emptied I felt rather self-conscious without a glass in my hand so grabbed another. Just as the Prime Minister walked by I took a sip. All I remember is my stomach heaving and me thinking that I was about to throw up at the Prime Minister's feet, thus ending a glorious political career which had hardly got off the ground. Luckily I managed to control my stomach and all was well. It turned out that it was whisky in the glass, rather than white wine.

Later in the evening, as I was talking to my local MP, Alan Haselhurst, the division bell sounded. Although there were at least forty MPs there, none made a move to leave to go and vote over the road in the House of Commons. Mrs Thatcher started to look rather irritated and was obviously none too impressed. In the end she walked to the middle of the room, took off one of her shoes and

Margaret Thatcher's family home – the Roberts family corner shop in the town of Grantham in the county of Lincolnshire, where the future Prime Minister grew up.

banged it on the floor. There was instance silence. The Prime Minister then spoke. 'Would all Conservative MPs kindly leave the building immediately,' she instructed. 'And the rest of us will stay and enjoy ourselves!' Naturally we all laughed uproariously, enjoying the sight of the MPs trooping out of the room in a somewhat sheepish manner.

After I graduated I went to work at the House of Commons as a researcher for a Norfolk Member of Parliament. He was not a particularly well-known MP and never courted publicity. He had a marginal seat and devoted himself to his constituency rather than join the rent-a-quote mob. It served him well as he held his seat for the next two elections. If ever there was an MP less likely to be involved in sleaze it was him. But one day, a careless error by me left him open to charges of dirty dealing. We ran a businessmen's club in the constituency, called *The Westminster Circle*. It served two purposes – one to keep the MP in touch with local businesses, and secondly to raise a little money for the very poor constituency association. For £100 a year business people joined and were given a dinner in the House of Commons, usually addressed by a Cabinet Minister, and another dinner in the constituency, addressed by a more junior Minister. These clubs were common in all parties up and down the country. But in a publicity leaflet designed to attract new members I had used the phrase 'with direct access to government ministers'. By this I had meant that they would be able to meet and speak to a government minister at the dinner. In those pre 'cash for questions' days we were all rather innocent. But it proved to be my undoing – and very nearly my employer's.

Early one Tuesday afternoon he found out that at that day's Prime Minister's Question Time, the Liberal leader, David Steel, would raise this subject with the Prime Minister. He immediately went to see her in her office behind the Speaker's Chair. He must have been quaking in his boots but he later told me she had been brilliant. She sat him down, offered him a coffee and heard him out. She did not disguise her dislike for Steel and thought it typical of him to operate in this manner. She told him she would let Steel have both barrels, and of course she did! He returned to the Office after PM's Question Time and related the events of the day to me. I had been completely oblivious, which was just as well as I would no doubt have been having a premonition of what a P45 looked like.

A few months later I was having lunch with a couple of Tory MPs in the Members' Cafeteria. We had just finished our lunch when in walked Mrs T and her entourage. She grabbed a tray and chose a light lunch of Welsh Rarebit. Unfortunately, as we had finished, I did not have cause to hang around too much longer so left the room, cursing that we had decided to have an early lunch. A few minutes later I realised I had left some papers and magazines on the table in the cafeteria and returned to retrieve them. As luck would have it, the Thatcher group had sat themselves at the table we had been sitting at and Mrs T had her elbow plonked on my papers. I decided to summon up the courage and interrupt them to ask for my papers. Just as I had started I looked down at the pile of papers and to my horror saw that my copy of the new issue of *Private Eye* was on the top of them and the front cover had a particularly nasty photo of Denis Thatcher. Mrs

The young Margaret Thatcher with her sister Muriel in 1929.

Thatcher cottoned on to what I wanted, removed her elbow and gazed down at the offending magazine. My heart stopped. 'Oh, *Private Eye*, Denis loves it,' she gushed. To my eternal shame, I just picked it up, along with the rest of the papers, made my excuses and left. What a wimp.

In 1995 I took an American friend, Daniel Forrester, to the T E Utley Young Journalist of the Year awards at the Reform Club. Lady Thatcher had been invited to present the awards. She treated us to a half hour impromptu speech on political issues of the moment, which seemed to go by in about five minutes – quite an achievement as her entire audience had to remain standing throughout. After she had finished Daniel whispered to me: 'I have to meet her, what should I do?' Knowing her penchant for strapping, six-feet-tall, dark-haired American men I encouraged him to go and introduce himself. He suddenly got cold feet so eventually I dragged him over to where she was talking to several of the award winners. In typically American style he launched into a sycophantic introduction which immediately attracted her attention. 'Mrs Thatcher,' he began. I kicked him. 'Er, Lady Thatcher,' he hurriedly corrected himself, 'May I say how much our country misses your leadership ...' and he continued in that vein for a few seconds. While he was speaking, the diminutive figure of the Iron Lady (for she is much smaller in height than most people imagine) stared up at him, her eyes never leaving his. When he had finally finished having his say, Lady Thatcher hardly

Opposite: The young Margaret Thatcher (right) with her sister Muriel, her father, Alfred Roberts, and her mother Beatrice, pictured in the late 1930s. Alfred Roberts is wearing his chains of office. He was mayor of the family's home town of Grantham, Lincolnshire.

Pictured with her fiancé Denis Thatcher on 26 October 1951.

paused for breath. 'Your President, President Clinton.' She paused, heightening the drama for my American friend. 'He is a great communicator.' Up came the forefinger, almost prodding Daniel's chest. Then in a particularly contemptuous tone, came the pièce de résistance. 'The trouble is, he has absolutely nothing to communicate.' With that she was away. It was almost a flounce. Daniel eventually came down from whichever cloud he had been on – probably nine – and said, 'I'll remember that for the rest of my life' – and as a well-known critic of Bill Clinton, has been dining out on it ever since.

Another encounter came at a retirement party for ITN's much missed political editor Michael Brunson. My friend Alan Duncan, the Tory MP for Rutland, started a conversation with her and she suddenly asked where Denis had disappeared off to as they had to leave for a dinner. Being of diminutive stature, and me being over six feet tall, she asked me to scan the room. Both of them looked at me expectantly. To my horror I spied Denis on the other side of the room talking to Michael Heseltine. I summoned up all the courage at my disposal and explained where he was. Lady Thatcher's eyes became even bluer than normal and she exclaimed: 'Denis and I are having dinner with Cap Weinberger tonight. I think he's rather more important than THAT man, don't you?! If Denis isn't over here within one minute I shall go over and stare at them.' Luckily for Michael Heseltine, she didn't have to.

Early in 2005 I invited Lady Thatcher to come to a fundraising party to raise money for my campaign as Conservative candidate in North Norfolk. To my delight she accepted and on a cold March evening turned up on time to work a room of fifty friends and political acquaintances. And boy did she work! She was particularly pleased to meet the teenagers present, including one with a particularly eye-catching piece of metal face jewellery. My task for the evening was to guide Lady T around the room so she could meet everyone. It was a thankless task. The Iron Lady decided where she was going and no amount of me tugging at her elbow was going to persuade her otherwise!

What memories! What a woman! What a Prime Minister!

Iain Dale
Swanton Abbott, Norfolk
August 2005

Margaret and Denis on their wedding day, 13 December 1951. The dress was in royal blue velvet, the halo-styled hat was trimmed with ostrich feathers.

Margaret with her newborn twins, Mark and Carol, who were born on 15 August 1953.

Talking to dustmen during
the 1951 General Election
campaign in Dartford, Kent.

Left: The young Margaret Roberts attending a garden party in 1950.

Right: Conservative candidate Margaret Roberts, pictured on 24 January 1951, the youngest candidate for any party in the 1951 General Election, at work in a laboratory where she was a research chemist.

Below: Margaret Roberts on the hustings during the 1951 General Election, where she was standing for the Conservatives, aged twenty-four, in Dartford, Kent.

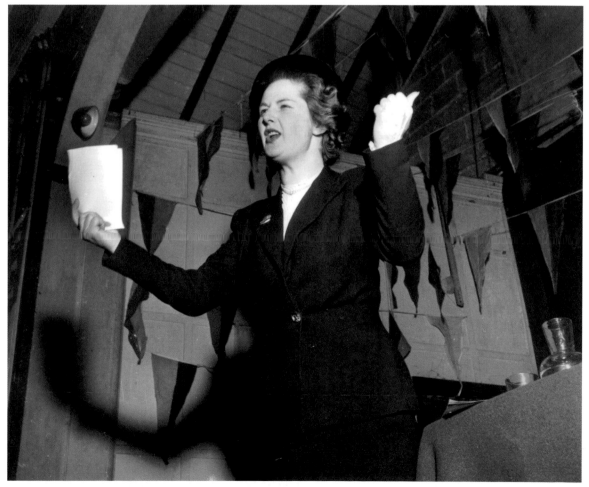

Sir Richard Body

CONSERVATIVE MP

Sir Richard Body was the Member of Parliament for Billericay from 1955 to 1959, then for Holland and Boston from 1966 until 1997, and from 1997 to 2001 for Boston and Skegness.

In court with Margaret

IT WAS IN 1949 WHEN I FIRST MET MARGARET ROBERTS, then with ICI at Manningtree in Essex. She came to help me as the Conservative candidate in the London County Council election when I was standing for Deptford.

Television was yet to dominate our electioneering; canvassing was limited and public meetings were held every day, indoor in the evenings and outdoor ones in the daytime.

Margaret came to speak outside New Cross station in the rush hour to scores of commuters on their way home, and I well remember her standing with microphone in hand beside the loudspeaker car.

The memory does not fade. It may have been her first open-air meeting, but any nervousness was difficult to detect. She spoke with modesty and sincerity and observers might have thought her demure and earnest. Her speech perhaps was rather too intellectual for a transient audience, yet quite a number delayed their journey home to hear the reasoned arguments.

In those days almost any meeting had a lively amount of heckling. It was in many ways a far more democratic form of electioneering than is the case now, because the speaker had to be on the ball and if unable to get the better of the heckler the audience would soon lose interest, whilst in open air meetings it would melt away. It is much to her credit that that was not the case on that evening outside New Cross station.

I much regret that we did not invite her to speak at one of the many indoor meetings we held throughout the constituency, as she was so obviously in command of her subject I have no doubt that she would have been a match for any heckler.

I met Margaret many times in those days. We were both YCs and Prospective Parliamentary Candidates and attended regularly the monthly meetings we used to have in the Candidates' Association. At one subsequent supper Ted Heath and she once sat beside each other. I remember he was cheerful to all while she was taciturn yet attentive to everything said around our table.

There were many other occasions too. I remember her as unfailingly considerate towards other people, whoever they were and whatever the circumstances.

We later went on to practise at the Bar and both of us became pupils to masters who were 'in crime'. In those days there were only five sets of chambers that were of criminal specialists with an aggregate membership of no more than sixty.

Now, it might be added, it is about twenty times that number.

Only four courts sat at the Old Bailey then with seldom a brief for a young barrister, so it meant going to London Sessions, by the Elephant and Castle. Going

> *'I remember her as unfailingly considerate towards other people, whoever they were and whatever the circumstances.'*
>
> **Sir Richard Body**

John Boyd Carpenter, the Minister for Pensions and National Insurance, greets Margaret Thatcher after her appointment as Joint Parliamentary Secretary to his Ministry on 12 October 1961.

down to grubby cells to take instructions from old lags was not to her liking. What was worse were the occasions when they sought a dock-brief. This required all barristers who could not escape the court to sit in the front row of counsel benches – usually there were about a dozen of us there, for other young hopefuls would crowd in – and the old lag would emerge from the cells and shuffle to the well of the court to stand in front of counsel clutching his £2.4s.6d. Then he would run his eye up and down the rank of newly made wigs, usually pointing his finger along the line as he looked and then cry out 'I will 'ave 'im' or in Margaret's case it would have been 'I will 'ave 'er.'

So naturally she turned her back on that sort of life and moved to the more intellectually congenial world of tax chambers.

In obtaining a seat for the 1955 General Election I had better luck than her, and when I decided to stand down from Billericay, choosing to concentrate on the Bar instead of Parliament, she applied to take my place in the constituency, despite my advice not to go there. She was one of the twelve chosen for interview, but fortunately rejected. She went on to be adopted for Finchley but had she been successful in Billericay her future might have been different, for a subsequent defeat in that seat would have been inevitable.

When hecklers stand up, I get a mental jump for joy.

Sir David Mitchell

CHAIRMAN OF EL VINO AND FORMER CONSERVATIVE MP

David Mitchell was the MP for Basingstoke from 1964 until 1983 and MP for Hampshire North West from 1983 until 1997, serving as a Minister in Margaret Thatcher's government. He is currently the Chairman of the wine company El Vino.

An act of kindness

I RECALL AN ELDERLY CONSTITUENT coming to one of my 'surgeries', as UK Members of Parliament like to call their constituency advice sessions. It was a Saturday morning, he was last in my queue and stayed on to recount his wartime experiences.

He had been shot down over the Channel coastline and burnt on his arms. At that time Basingstoke Hospital was the major burns unit in southern England. After some treatment there he was sent to Newcastle by train for further specialist treatment.

As the train stopped at Grantham the sirens sounded for an air raid. Shortly after the 'all clear' sounded it was announced that the train would go no further until morning. Everybody got out and organised themselves as best they could for a somewhat uncomfortable night.

An air-raid warden approached my bandaged constituent asking where he was spending the night, to which he gave the reply, 'I'm okay I've got a place on the ticket office floor.'

'No you haven't,' came the rejoinder, 'you are coming home with me.' This total stranger took him home, and he had a comfortable bed for the night.

Next morning breakfast was cooked by the blond pigtailed daughter in the house who then picked up her school satchel, kissed her parents good bye and left.

He had had his breakfast cooked for him by a future Prime Minister – and that tells you something important about the home in which Margaret Thatcher grew up.

It may be the cock that crows, but it is the hen that lays the eggs.

Margaret Thatcher pictured in 1970 in the kitchen of her Flood Street home in Chelsea, London.

Lord Harris of High Cross

FOUNDER PRESIDENT OF THE INSTITUTE OF ECONOMIC AFFAIRS

Raised to the Peerage in 1979, Lord Harris of High Cross is amongst the most respected political and economic thinkers of our time. He was a founder member of the Institute of Economic Affairs and of Buckingham University. He has published numerous works on economic policy and political economy.

No, Prime Minister

I HAD MET MARGARET THATCHER a time or two before, in the 1960s. Once was over dinner with a bevy of businessmen including a rather self-important Arnold Weinstock – whom she made seem pretty feeble. Another occasion was over lunch with a motley bunch of back-bench Tory MPs who were lamenting the difficulty of putting across the complex case for free markets – which she resolved brusquely by suggesting they should ask their constituents whether they would rather shop at Marks & Spencer or the Co-op!

But the first personal encounter I recall more vividly was in the twilight days of Ted Heath, at the Department of Education of which she was then Secretary of State. She had agreed to meet informally with a small deputation of academics, including Sydney Caine and Max Beloff, to hear about our plan to establish an independent university – once we could raise the first million or so for start-up costs!

A sudden Cabinet crisis over the Middle East prevented her prompt arrival so she had arranged for us to be met by a junior colleague named (Bill) van Straubenzee. Not for nothing was he nicknamed 'strawberry tea'. Beautifully turned-out in suit and matching waistcoat (probably with lapels), he received us in a slightly scruffy office, but with a contrived pomp and ceremony more suited to a state occasion. He invited us to sit around him in a small semi-circle and, with appropriate solemnity, launched into a discourse on the importance of higher education, periodically stretching out an elegant leg in order rather elaborately to adjust the crease in his immaculate trousers.

Suddenly, the door burst open and in rushed Margaret Thatcher, complete with handbag and a striking hat, which was allowed in those days. Explaining that she might be called away again in a few minutes, she perched on the edge of a chair and told the junior minister to carry on. He had hardly completed his opening statement – to the effect that there was 'no hostility' in the Department to the broad concept of an independent university – when the lady broke in: 'No, no, William, can I put that differently?' She then proceeded to declare with deliberate emphasis that there was positive enthusiasm for the idea of competition from an institution of respected academics independent of the state.

Leaving the deflated van Straubenzee with little better to do than contemplate the crease in his other trouser leg, she emphasised with a candour new to me from a politician, that we would not receive – nor should we expect – any subsidies or special favours. What she would promise was to remove any bureaucratic obstacles that discriminated against the new enterprise. (It was precisely such equal treatment which that famous social democrat, Shirley Williams, refused to grant

Pennies do not come from heaven. They have to be earned here on earth.

a few years later as Secretary of State for Education. Thus when one of Buckingham's first graduates applied for an army commission under a special system of graduate entry, Mrs Williams refused to support the appeal of Max Beloff, our first Principal, for equal treatment that was automatically granted to equivalent products of state universities.)

In 1976 when the University College of Buckingham was ready to welcome its first intake of sixty students, it was Margaret Thatcher who performed the opening ceremony and in 1983 it was her Government that awarded the institution its royal charter as the University of Buckingham, of which she was to become Chancellor in 1992.

My second, more personal memory of Maggie's decisive style was at Chequers just two weeks after her election victory in May 1979. My wife and I had been totally astonished to be invited for Sunday lunch and to find ourselves guests of the Thatcher family – Denis, Mark and Carol – plus Douglas Hurd and wife, Lady (Janet) Young and husband, who all lived nearby.

I was further amazed to find myself at the table placed on the Prime Minister's right and almost dumbfounded when she suddenly leant across and confided her decision to put me into the House of Lords. I managed to get out the words: 'Do I have any say in the matter?' to which she answered shortly, I thought almost sharply: 'No,' and with an impatient shrug of the shoulders proceeded to complain of the delays of official procedures before my name could be checked and formal marching orders issued.

I still recall the irritation, bordering on anger, with which she added: 'I sometimes think I'm the only one trying to get anything done.' I recall those exact words simply because they came into my mind so often thereafter as she struggled against Cabinet colleagues, departmental committees, civil servants, journalists

Education Secretary Margaret Thatcher and Prime Minister Edward Heath at the 1971 Conservative Party Conference in Brighton.

and no doubt many others, in her sometimes lonely mission to subdue the trade unions, check the money supply, curb government expenditure, and resist the rising tide of mischief from Brussels. I was therefore not in the least surprised that she saw off the Argentine junta and got Peter Walker to stand firm for months against Scargill's militant miners. I can think of no previous British PM this century, Churchill always excepted, who regularly stuck to his guns and displayed in Keith Joseph's words, 'such personal, moral courage'.

I had scarcely been introduced as peer in July when her PPS, the incomparable late Ian Gow, sounded me out (at a celebration party in his Eastbourne constituency) on whether I would consider quitting the cross-benches in the Lords to accept a ministerial appointment. I did not hesitate even for one second before replying: 'I'm afraid not, in no circumstances,' adding: 'I beg you not to put our friendship at risk by ever raising that dangerous question again.' Dangerous for me because I knew if I became Maggie's political leg-man, I would never be able to refuse her anything – even when I might think the great lady was, conceivably, in the wrong. Only my immediate family should be able to call on such absolute loyalty!

A more light-hearted memory, although second-hand, was told me with a chuckle by Geoffrey Howe in the days when he still basked in Maggie's favour. At an early Cabinet meeting, he had a strong impulse to smoke. Seeing no one else had lit up, he stealthily extracted a packet of cigarettes from his pocket, followed by a box of matches, before looking round to see if anyone was noticing. The Prime Minister leant across smiling and whispered: 'Go on, Denis smokes!'

Margaret Thatcher has fun on a ski run in Battersea Park with instructor Joe Hoki, 7 December 1962.

John Blundell
GENERAL DIRECTOR, INSTITUTE OF ECONOMIC AFFAIRS

John Blundell has been amongst the most prominent and influential thinkers on modern economics of recent years. He has worked for, and contributed to, numerous think-tanks both in Britain and the USA.

Early soundings

THE IEA (INSTITUTE OF ECONOMIC AFFAIRS) archive contains an interesting exchange. On 24 October 1969 the IEA Editorial Director Arthur Seldon wrote to Geoffrey Howe as follows: 'May we hope for better things from Margaret?'

Geoffrey Howe replied: 'I am not at all sure about Margaret. Many of her economic prejudices are certainly sound. But she is inclined to be rather too dogmatic for my liking on sensitive issues like education and might actually retard the case by over-simplification. We should certainly be able to hope for something better from her – but I suspect that she will need to be exposed to the humanising side of your character as much as to the pure welfare market-monger. There is much scope for her to be influenced between triumph and disaster.'

Drugs

One evening in the late 1970s a group of younger members of the Conservative Party took Lady Thatcher to dinner in a private room at the Café Royal to brainstorm policy ideas. Two of us were very firmly trodden on.

First I suggested that all council housing be given away to current tenants. I was a newly elected Lambeth Borough Councillor and I had figures to show we would be much better off if we could simply tell our Director of Administration and Legal Services to mail out every single deed. Just mail them out and get rid of them, I argued.

'People will not value it properly unless they at least pay something for it,' she observed, quickly moving on.

Next went a colleague destined for the Cabinet who said that she was putting too much emphasis on economic freedom and not enough on personal freedom.

'Take cannabis,' he said. 'It is available freely everywhere. Why not recognise reality and legalise it?'

'What do you mean by available freely everywhere?' she said in a tone of voice that should have told him to back off.

'Well, for example,' he ploughed on, 'my flat mate always has some and knows lots of places where he can get it!'

She turned her gaze on him.

'Peter (not his real name),' she said. 'My detective is standing outside that door. I want you to call him in now and give him your friend's details.'

I forget how Peter managed it, but he ducked and dived, weaved and wriggled, and she let him off the hook.

No, Prime Minister

In 1990 I was living outside Washington DC. It was early summer and I was

Aren't I working class? I work jolly hard, I can tell you.

People will not value it properly unless they at least pay something for it.

planning a trip to Munich and Moscow for early September. One day the mail brought an invitation to the Social Affairs Unit's tenth birthday party at the Reform Club. I was about to say no when I realised that I could fly Moscow to Vienna to London, go to the party and fly to DC the next day.

I turned up on time. As I walked up the steps in a lounge suit I realised Sir Antony Jay, co-writer of *Yes, Minister* and *Yes, Prime Minister,* was next to me in black tie. We fell into conversation and entered the event. An hour later we joined up again as Margaret Thatcher was working the room. She turned from the group next to us and spotted Tony in his DJ – the only one in the whole room.

'Ah Tony,' she said, 'you must be going somewhere important later!'

'No, Prime Minister,' he replied contritely. 'I mis-read the invitation!'

So I heard the author of *Yes, Prime Minister* say to the then Prime Minister, 'No, Prime Minister'.

When I became General Director of the IEA I found we had already published a collection of speeches by my predecessor Lord Harris under the title of *No, Minister.* So when Ralph turned seventy and I published the best of his articles, I had no hesitation in calling them *No, Prime Minister.*

Fifty birthday roses

When Michael Forsyth was national Chairman of the Federation of Conservative Students I was his national Vice Chairman responsible for publicity. Mrs Thatcher's approaching birthday seemed to me to be a wonderful opportunity for us.

About a week before the big day (13 October 1976) we started brainstorming in The Marquis of Granby, just off Smith Square, as to what we could/should do. Eventually we settled on the idea of turning up at her Flood Street home with a very very large bouquet of fifty red roses at about 7.30am. Michael would present these to her against a backdrop of enthusiastic young students that I would recruit.

Everything was quickly arranged and the media alerted. On the morning of the big day I first picked up Michael and then this huge display of roses from a florist in Berkeley Square. The arrangement could barely fit in the taxi and we lost several heads en route.

When we pulled up there was a massive bank of cameras and a solitary policeman, but not one student. 'Wait here,' I told Forsyth. I jumped out, scanned the street again and finally walked up to the policeman.

'I wonder if you have seen any students?' I asked.

'Oh yes, sir,' he replied, 'Mrs Thatcher saw them out here twenty minutes ago and invited them in for a cup of tea!'

'Should I say you are ready, sir?' he finished.

The students duly emerged and formed a cordon. Michael presented the roses and the photos went out all over the world.

Speak up, young man

I was at a round-table dinner of forty people with Lady Thatcher some years ago. After dinner we enjoyed remarks from a distinguished guest. Then came questions. Most present were fairly senior types from the media, the civil service, industry

Conservative Education Secretary Margaret Thatcher with a portrait of Prime Minister Edward Heath under her arm.

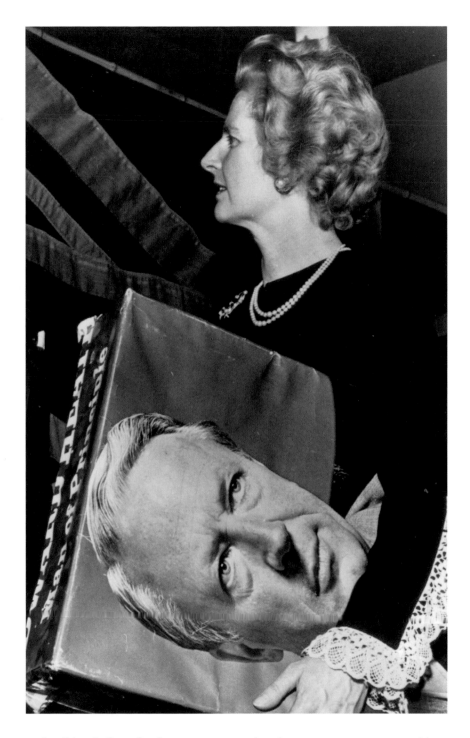

and politics. At forty-five I was pretty young but there was an even younger thirty-one-year-old representing his boss. To be accurate this young man was actually the leading expert in the room on our topic for the night.

Into the vacuum of space and time immediately following the guests' remarks the young man proffered an interesting question.

The problem was that nobody could hear what he was saying. 'Speak up, young man,' commanded Lady Thatcher.

He tried again but clearly did not measure up.

'SPEAK UP, YOUNG MAN,' she commanded again.

He started a third time. It still did not measure up. She glared down the table.

'Young man', she said. 'Stand up and throw your voice. We want to hear what you have to say.'

Turning bright red he stood; he threw; they listened and at the end they applauded.

Grace, you fool!

From March 1973 to March 1974 I was Chairman of the London Region of the Federation of Conservative Students.

My year finished just after the February 1974 General Election with a dinner at the House of Lords sponsored by the historian Lord Blake. My Guest of Honour was Margaret Thatcher. She had been invited nearly a year earlier as Secretary of State for Education. Now she was appearing before us as Shadow Secretary of State for the Environment.

Everything had been meticulously planned and at the appropriate moment the head table of eight trooped in. Some 200 people were standing staring at me as I thought to myself, 'We've forgotten something here. Oops, something's wrong. Why is everyone standing up. Why aren't they sitting down?'

Just as I was about to panic Lady Thatcher's left foot kicked, yes kicked, me on the outside right ankle.

'Grace, you fool!' she muttered.

Nobody had been lined up to say grace!

I stuck my head down, said grace, and we all sat down. Phew!

Over dinner she discovered that as retiring Chairman I had personally paid for the wine for the top table.

'Oh, I can't have that,' she said and quickly passed me some folded money under the table.

Nobody told me!

I was hosting a dinner once for a famous politician from overseas. Lady Thatcher's office asked if she and Sir Denis could attend and I replied yes.

On the night, Sir Denis failed to show and I faced having an empty chair at dinner.

I quickly recruited a Tory MP friend who is a generation younger than Lady Thatcher; tall, straight and, my wife tells me, handsome in a battered kind of way.

We sat down to dinner. I tapped on a glass to get attention and made a few announcements.

I concluded by saying that Sir Denis's place had been taken for the night by Mr X MP.

'Really,' said Lady Thatcher in an arch voice. 'Nobody told *me*!'

Stand up and throw your voice. We want to hear what you have to say.

Lord Fowler of Sutton Coldfield
CABINET MINISTER 1979–90

After a career in journalism, Norman Fowler became the MP for Sutton Coldfield in February 1974. He served in Margaret Thatcher's Cabinet from 1979 as Minister of Transport, subsequently becoming Secretary of State for Social Services and later Secretary of State for Employment. He was Conservative Party Chairman under John Major from 1992 to 1994 and a member of William Hague's Shadow Cabinet from 1997 to 1999.

Ministers decide

IN 1975 I WAS ALSO NOT AT ALL SURE whether Margaret Thatcher was electable. That was not because she was a woman. I had never regarded that as making any difference one way or the other in electoral terms. It was because in the mid 1970s she appeared to the public as aloof and most certainly not one of them. Although she had come up the hard way, she gave the impression that she was to the manor born. This was not an accurate picture of the woman but that was how she was seen. In the years after her election she was given media advice which she was wise enough to take, but above all she began to project her real self. A much grittier Margaret Thatcher emerged.

So what was the secret of a leader who had won three elections and survived crises that would have toppled a lesser person? Stamina obviously; courage certainly; but if I were to choose one factor, it would be professionalism. Her attitude to the televising of Parliament is a case in point. She was a strong opponent of televising the House. She thought it would change the character of Westminster and, I suspect, put more power in the hands of the media, including her *bête noire*, the BBC. At times I felt that she regarded me – a supporter of television and a former journalist – as personally responsible for this invasion. Yet when the decision was made and a majority, including half the Cabinet, voted for television she settled down to work. Most of the rest of us took the view that there was not much you could do. You would either come over well or not. Margaret Thatcher studied the angles of the cameras, considered how the pictures would be appearing in sitting rooms all over the country, and emerged as the undoubted star of Westminster. Whatever may have been Neil Kinnock's hopes of this new opportunity – and remember that Kinnock made his first national reputation on television – he lost. It was the same professionalism which took Margaret Thatcher from an Opposition leader without experience of foreign affairs to one of the world's best-known and most respected statesmen. It was the same professionalism which drove her into the early hours of the morning working on the multitude of red boxes produced by the departments of Whitehall. The same quality took her into the tea-room and the dining-room of the House of Commons, rather than taking the night off; and at party conferences she was tireless as she went from one function to another. She did not much like the annual trial of her speech at the Conservative Party Conference. She would sit there all week listening to her best lines being used by other speakers but knowing that the delegates would expect a sparkling performance at the end. With her speech writers she would be up half

I go for agreement – agreement for the things I want to do.

the night preparing her text. It was the price that the Leader of the Party had to pay and she paid it willingly. It was this complete professionalism which set her apart.

Margaret's family provided the indispensable background rock of support, and a clear and uncomplicated instinct about what was right and wrong provided the certainty of direction. She had a strong feeling of what was honourable and what was not. She was intensely loyal to the officials who most closely worked with her. If she ever lost her temper it was because of attacks on advisers like Bernard Ingham or Charles Powell. She regarded an attack on officials who could not answer back as basically cowardly. Critics were trying to get at her through her advisers. To her this was a despicable example of dishonourable conduct.

Her view of Ministers was more complex. She was loyal to them in the midst of a dispute and under attack but she also felt that they should be capable of looking after themselves. However close she might be to a Minister (for example, Nicholas Ridley), if the Minister insisted on digging himself into a hole then ultimately he had to live with the consequences. The interests of the Government took precedence over the interests of an individual Minister. The same is true in a rather less stark way of the frequent reshuffles. Ministers were moved out of jobs in the interests of keeping the Government's face fresh. In the process quite a number were roughly treated. Leon Brittan should not have been moved from the Home Office; Patrick Jenkin should have been moved from the Environment Department, not sacked; Peter Rees should not have had to suffer the entirely avoidable fate of reading about his demise in the papers for week upon week before it happened. All the Thatcher Governments would have benefited had Ministers stayed both longer in jobs and longer as Ministers.

Ultimately, however, success as a political leader is not measured by skill in the television studio or how you appear to your colleagues. It is about what you achieve. Political leaders have to win elections, but it is much more important that they win respect for doing the right things rather than an easy reputation for geniality. Margaret Thatcher's achievement was to take over a country which gave every appearance of being down and very nearly out and turn it round. The change was slow and at times painful but the chances are that much of the change is permanent. She took over a country which had been brought to its knees by uncontrolled trade union power and presided over a decade of reform. Any party which seriously tampers with that record does so at its electoral peril. She took over a country where too much industry and too much activity was controlled, not very successfully, by the state. Virtually no one today believes in widespread renationalisation and a reintroduction of controls. She took over a country where millions of people were excluded from home ownership. With the sale of council houses and wider share ownership important steps were taken to extend the traditional Conservative aims of one nation and a property-owning democracy. And she also took over a country where for decades tax rates had been too high but where it had become accepted that that was the inevitable way of things. Tax rates came down and my estimate is that most people in Britain would now like to keep them that way. These were real and substantial reforms which singled Margaret Thatcher out as one of the most successful political leaders this century.

'She took over a country which had been brought to its knees by uncontrolled trade union power and presided over a decade of reform.'

Lord Fowler

Sir Edward Du Cann

CONSERVATIVE MP

The distinguished former Conservative MP Edward Du Cann represented the constituency of Taunton for over thirty years. During that time he served in numerous positions within the Conservative Party and on many House of Commons committees. He received his knighthood in 1995.

Formidable

HAVING BEEN A STRONG SUPPORTER of Margaret Thatcher from the moment she became Leader of the Conservative Party in 1975 and Prime Minister four years later, I have a thousand clear memories of her.

Many people, MPs and others like me, will have watched her with admiration on public and semi-public occasions – standing resolute and indomitable at the dispatch box in the House of Commons, facing down the barrackers; evoking the enthusiasm of Conservative Party members at Party Conferences; and (how well I remember those occasions) her presence at meetings of the 1922 Committee, the backbench Tory MPs, where *prima inter pares* she solicited, deserved and obtained their loyal support all the years that I was their Chairman.

And, in her early days as Leader, and even when she won the General Election in 1959 and became Prime Minister, that wasn't always easy.

Her achievements as Prime Minister were formidable. The memories of her successes, which were also our country's successes, will endure to her credit.

There are a multitude of personal memories, also, which I sometimes recall. Most are private recollections, and should remain so. But not all.

I remember when we first met, at a meeting of Prospective Conservative Parliamentary candidates in 1950, a dominantly male group. All of us were recently demobilised after our wartime experiences in the armed services. The late Airey Neave, fresh from his duties as a prosecutor at the Nuremberg trials, was our secretary and convenor. Margaret was young and attractive. Naturally, she made a great impression on these lively men. And yet – she showed an exceptional keenness and capacity for self-advertisement, which was somehow daunting. Certainly it was untypical of her fellows.

Later, those of us who became MPs learned that her thrustfulness was one of her enduring strengths.

When I was a Treasury Minister, she came once to my constituency to open an old peoples' home. This was when she had her first ministerial appointment. I remember how my friends in Taunton were impressed by her seriousness, and slightly in awe of it. Here was a paradox which would endure: the truth was that she cared deeply about social issues, and yet that reality was not as widely believed as it deserved to be.

When she first became Leader of the Conservative Party, it took her a long while to settle into that position. The House of Commons then, like the Party, was also very much a masculine society. (Blair's babes hadn't yet been invented.) I am not sure how easy it was for her to fit into the smoke room camaraderie that was the style of the Conservative Parliamentary Party at that time. Nor did she always

Socialism and Britain go ill together. It is not the British character.

find it easy in those early days to shine in the House, but her determination, her chief characteristic, carried her through. Her hard work led to an apparently easy style to fell her argumentative opponents with her oratorical handbag, full of the notes of the careful preparation that was her habit.

I remember thinking in 1975 that it would reflect well on the Conservative Party to elect a woman as Leader, the first political party in Britain to do so; and even that it would be more creditable if she were to become Britain's first woman Prime Minister. (Not that the feminists in our society ever appeared to find her remarkable success attractive.) Her sex, on occasion, was an advantage to her. I have seen Tory MPs sit on their hands when Eden or Macmillan or Heath entered the room. When Margaret came in, they always stood up, to a man.

Sometimes she could be dictatorial – too often perhaps. In the end the Parliamentary Party revolted, following the example of one of her long-term Cabinet colleagues – who owed his career to her. It was his personal attack on her in the House that marked the beginning of the end. Gratitude is not often the hallmark of politics. (I often wondered why some of her close Ministerial colleagues were apparently supine under the criticisms which she never held back. She liked an argument. I suspect they found it hard to argue with a woman.)

She and her immediate predecessor, Ted Heath, were in one respect in the same mould: they could be aloof, even with their close colleagues, self-contained, in a way which their predecessors in my experience, Eden, Macmillan and Home, were not. My good friend Airey Neave, who had masterminded her election as Leader of the Conservative Party and became the head of her private office before his murder in the House of Commons by the Irish, told me, to my astonishment, that he was less close to her than he had expected. Leadership can be a solitary business.

As Chairman of the 1922 Committee, I was privileged to have a close relationship with her. Never was I received with anything but courtesy. Even when I had private advice to offer on matters of concern to the Conservative Parliamentary Party, including advice for which she did not care, she would hear me out with attention, take note, and, more importantly, take action.

There is one of our meetings, which I have most often looked back on, our last private meeting in the House, when I told her it was my intention, after thirty-one years, to retire as an MP. Typically generous, she pressed me to change my mind. I reflected aloud that it was sensible to retire early: perhaps then one's supporters might express regret; it would be foolish to wait to be pushed. I told her that she might consider this herself in due course. That advice, I remember, seemed to upset her. Now I wish I had pressed the point harder. Had she taken it in due course, she would have been spared the pain of her unpleasant dismissal by the electorate of Tory MPs. Matters could and should have been differently arranged.

She was badly counselled at that time. I hope that, while I had responsibility in the House of Commons, I never gave her poor advice: whenever we disagreed, which was rare, I still (after all these years) believe that I was right. Perhaps I learned that self-confidence from her. If so, it was a good lesson for a politician to absorb.

'Sometimes she could be dictatorial – too often perhaps.'
Sir Edward Du Cann

Margaret Thatcher with Sir Edward Du Cann (bottom left), Anthony Grant MP (top left) and Anthony Buck MP (top right).

Sir George Gardiner
CONSERVATIVE MP

Sir George Gardiner was the Conservative MP for Reigate from 1974 until March 1997 when he joined the Referendum Party. He is the author of *Margaret Thatcher: From Childhood to Leadership* (1975) and *A Bastard's Tale* (1999). Sir George died in 2002.

A cell of revolutionaries

THE 1975 THATCHER CAMPAIGN TEAM used to meet in a subterranean Committee Room below the Commons under the shrewd chairmanship of Airey Neave. Our task was to conduct a discreet canvass of how most of the 276 Conservative MPs intended to vote in the leadership ballot, all duly recorded by William Shelton. We were an odd bunch: backbench worthies like Julian Ridsdale, John Stokes, and Angus Maude; hard-hitters like Norman Tebbit and Nicholas Ridley; the lovable rogue Billy Rees-Davies, severely war-wounded and minus an arm; and a few like myself, products of the previous year's elections. Airey then reported to Margaret's sponsor, Sir Keith Joseph. We were as unlikely a cell of revolutionaries as ever you could find – yet did we realise quite what a hurricane force we were about to release on the British people, a woman who would break the miserable mould of post-war politics together with its complacent and stifling corporatism? Did we hell!

Few of us then could envisage a time when the mighty union leaders could no longer aspire to dictate Cabinet policy or indeed bring down governments. In a speech nine days after her election as Leader she dealt with the issue very cautiously: often when you find a solid rock blocking your path, she said, it was best not to charge it head on, but to move round or undermine it. What on earth, we asked, did she mean?

Not until we were into the following Parliament did we begin to get an inkling of what we had done. The first Thatcher manifesto, after all, was a pretty cautious document – new laws to curb picketing, slight tightening of the law on the closed shop, fresh curbs on immigration, more incentives through taxation – but not much more.

At the time the leadership election was called I was on Christian name terms with Margaret, but nothing more. Then a publisher asked me to write her biography, and she agreed to co-operate. So it was that in spring that year I went regularly on Saturdays to her flat in Chelsea's Flood Street with my tape-recorder. During these sessions I came to realise just how much her roots in Grantham meant to her. She was eloquent in describing her father, Alderman Alfred Roberts, the grocer's shop run by her family over which they lived, the local Methodist Church and its culture, and how the privations and hopes of World War II made her what she was. Only years later did she amplify this in her own memoirs.

From then until her downfall in 1990 I was one of her foremost backbench supporters, and for the final six years of her premiership saw her regularly as Chairman of the '92, a group of around 100 right-of-centre Tory MPs.

If you stood by Margaret in tough times she was supportive and loyal in return.

'Often when you find a solid rock blocking your path, she said, it was best not to charge it head on.'

Sir George Gardiner

But I am always amazed by the press caricature of her as an impetuous bully, happily handbagging everyone in sight. In fact, she was immensely cautious. So anxious was she to pacify the old Wets and supporters of her predecessor, Edward Heath, that after victory in 1979 she gave them preponderance in her Cabinet for eighteen months until she reshaped it more in the image of the Party as a whole. Peter Walker, who ran Heath's leadership campaign, was brought into her Cabinet, and even while he was delivering coded speeches attacking her policies she kept him there. Privatisation of the public utilities was barely heard of until just before the 1983 election. When miners' leader Arthur Scargill first challenged her on pit closures she backed off; not until she was equipped to beat him did she come back fighting.

Contrary to press myth, she was tolerant of other points of view, provided they were well argued. I flouted three-line whips many times, but never did she see this as an attack upon herself, nor did it affect our trusting relationship. The totalitarianism that crept into the Party after her downfall had no roots in her. In Opposition, when I was among those advising her twice a week in preparation for Prime Minister's Questions, I helped to organise a rebellion on the renewal of economic sanctions against what was then Rhodesia. We inflicted humiliation on the Tory Whips, yet when I turned up somewhat abashed to help advise her next day (along with Geoffrey Pattie, who had rebelled too) she was in teasing mood: 'What's the matter with you two? Have you lost your tongues?' She knew our rebellion was based on principle.

Never did she allow her high office to diminish her concern for her friends. Once, during her first Parliament as Prime Minister, I called one evening at Downing Street to compare notes with Ian Gow, then her PPS. I met him in her flat, where we watched the TV news. Our intention was to go on to his club for dinner – until Margaret arrived unexpectedly early. 'You two boys must be

Margaret Thatcher on the campaign trail with Conservative MP Winston Churchill, grandson of the wartime Prime Minister.

hungry.' Despite our protests she disappeared into the little kitchen, took chicken kievs, peas and carrots from the fridge – then insisted we sat at the kitchen table to join her for supper. Before we were finished Denis arrived, and he made coffee. Was there any other significant nation in the world, I asked myself, whose Prime Minister (or President, as the case may be) would insist on cooking supper for unexpected visitors?

When I was in hospital in 1992 awaiting bypass surgery she sent encouraging messages every few days. The weekend before my operation I wrote a leader-page article for the *Sunday Express*; no sooner was I out of my anaesthetic than there was a note from Margaret saying how spot-on my piece had been. When I was a lunch guest at Chequers one Sunday I watched her crouching beside Margaret Tebbit's wheelchair lifting food on a fork to her mouth. She felt it deeply that the IRA's Brighton bomb, which left Margaret Tebbit paralysed, was intended for her.

It often seemed that the media were determined never to present this human side to her character. There was the time I persuaded her to perform the official opening of the new East Surrey Hospital in my constituency. It was the first hospital she had ever opened; Geoffrey Howe, Kenneth Baker and I joined her, since the hospital served our constituencies; Health Secretary Norman Fowler and Reigate's Mayor were also there. The afternoon's itinerary was way behind as Margaret spent far more time than was scheduled at bedsides, listening to individual cases and sympathising. Likewise she spent far longer with staff than had been planned, asking and answering probing questions. Cameras followed her all the way. Yet what did the BBC report? Only that some trade unionist at a tiny demonstration outside had thrown an egg at her car! Big deal.

Her final downfall could not have been more brutal. Over the preceding year I and officers of the '92' often warned her of the dangers lurking, but she always believed she could face her critics down. Then Geoffrey Howe plunged the first dagger over European policy, opening the way for Michael Heseltine's challenge; Heseltine said he had a better alternative to the Poll Tax, which was deeply unpopular, and as the election drew near many Tory MPs were anxious.

She had a so-called Campaign Team, but there was no evidence of a proper campaign; utterly complacent, they gave her totally wrong advice. Worse still, she was in Paris for the election. Not until evening the day after the first ballot (which she led, though just short of an outright win) were I and others in the '92' able to get through to her. But by then it was too late; her resolution had been broken by Cabinet colleagues pledging support while telling her she could never win – 'treachery with a smile on its face', as she put it later. I will never forget her then, on the verge of tears as we pleaded with her to stay in the race, which I am convinced she would have won with a last-minute campaign worthy of the name.

I doubt whether we shall see the like of her as Prime Minister again. Yet the woman who sent packing the likes of Scargill, General Galtieri and the hooded assassins of the IRA, who restored pride to her country after years of creeping socialism, and who with President Reagan hastened the end of the evil Soviet Empire, was brought down by a clutch of her own MPs in a blue funk over a looming election, and by Ministers who owed her everything.

Our aim is to make tax collecting a declining industry.

Margaret Thatcher accepting the applause from the Conservative Conference in October 1982. Pictured with her are Deputy Prime Minister William Whitelaw and Conservative Party Chairman Cecil Parkinson.

Overleaf: Getting down to business.

Lord Bellwin

LEADER OF LEEDS CITY COUNCIL 1975–9

Lord Bellwin became a councillor for Leeds in 1969, serving as the Leader of Leeds City Council from 1975 until 1979 when he was raised to the Peerage. He was Parliamentary Under Secretary of State at the Department of Environment from 1979 to 1983. He was the Minister of State for Local Government from 1983 until 1984. Lord Bellwin died in 2001.

A true leader

I FIRST MET MARGARET THATCHER through my involvement in Local Government. This was in the late 1960s when I was Chairman of Housing on Leeds City Council. Together with Keith Joseph, she was co-chairing a small Party policy committee, looking into future housing possibilities.

I continued to meet her over the next few years, as a National/Local Government Leader and being the then Conservative Leader of the Council in Leeds. We had set up an informal liaison group which met with her three to four times a year.

The Ted Heath years did not produce good Local/National Government relationships. Heath was very remote and did not really want to listen to what his Party leaders throughout the country were saying.

As a contrast to this, Maggie, albeit not over enthusiastic about Local Government, was always thirsty for knowledge. Contrary to what is often said of her, in my experience she always listened, thoroughly questioned, and if convinced (not easy to do), she would take on board contrary views. She liked decisiveness and respected knowledge and practical experience, particularly if based on success.

She was invariably encouraging and whilst she expected loyalty, always gave it herself where she felt it was merited. She was, at all times, a serious, single-minded and focused person, quite formidable really. I always found her to be kind and considerate and certainly caring. She was never one for small talk. Even when greeting visitors at the top of the stairs in Downing Street, she would quickly go straight to the point of the meeting in question.

She first spoke to me about the possibility of my joining her future Government a year or so before the event. She asked me if I would like to do this and go to the House of Lords when, not if, but when we won the next General Election.

It was never mentioned again for a year or so, but when forming the Government over that first weekend in May 1979, she telephoned to ask if I remembered our conversation. This consistency of thinking was absolutely typical of her.

As an amusing aside, when the call came, my late mother-in-law, a dear lady then in her eighties, first answered the telephone. The operator, having confirmed the number, asked her to hold on to take a call from the Prime Minister. 'The Prime Minister,' said my mother-in-law. 'Just a moment I'll put my earrings on.' When I later told Maggie of this she said, 'How charming.'

Looking back, an abiding impression is the remarkable hours Mrs Thatcher

I owe nothing to women's lib.

'She asked me if I would like to do this and go to the House of Lords when, not if, but when we won the next General Election.'

Lord Bellwin

The new Conservative Leader poses in a glamorous olive green chiffon dress in 1974.

worked. She was always sprightly and immaculately turned out. Occasionally, whatever the lateness of the hour, she used to come into the Lords and sit on the steps to the Throne thereby giving support while listening to the debate. However tired she may have been, she never looked or acted it.

Unlike Tony Blair, she had a great respect for the House and its traditions. She always worked particularly hard in preparing for speaking in the Commons. Her in-depth briefing and preparation was thorough in the extreme. It was undoubtedly a major factor in the excellent performance she invariably gave at the Dispatch Box.

One amusing incident I recall, albeit after I had left the Government, is when she stayed with us at our home in Leeds. She had a 6am start in the City the following morning and therefore had to stay overnight. It was quite an experience in many ways. I arranged for my grandson, Danny, to stay with us overnight – when would he otherwise get the chance to meet a Prime Minister! I suggested to him beforehand what questions she might put to him and I got almost all right – he was well prepared and did well – he was fourteen at the time.

Although I had not seen her for some time prior to that overnight stay, on sitting down, her very first remarks were to ask what I had specifically meant by something I had said in the House of Lords a week or two beforehand – she had taken the trouble to read the Hansard.

A magic moment was when we had noted guards surrounding the house, part of the street blocked off, a bodyguard and secretary in the house and going to bed, my wife asked me if she should put the burglar alarm on!

Lunch on Sunday at Chequers was a memorable experience. It is a somewhat unusual place, not all that easy to find. We circled round looking for the entrance, eventually to be met at the door by the lady herself, on the steps, waiting to meet and greet visitors in her inimitable, dominantly cheerful way.

The morning was spent around the fire with the family, it being wintertime – all most congenial, pleasant, yet businesslike. When we walked into the dining-room, the prepared table layout was completely rearranged and everyone reseated by her so that she could be close and most easily converse with whoever she felt could most contribute to such topics as she wished to discuss.

My decision to leave Government was something of a wrench. Had I lived in London I would certainly have wanted to continue. She was not happy that I wished to go, but once I pointed out that it was 'not fair to the family' she was most understanding and wrote a typically gracious and kind letter which was published in *The Times*.

I could tell many stories of situations, amusing and otherwise, but always it comes down to my memories of her being a true leader in every sense of the word. Her courage and determination are now legendary – in my experience they have never been more deserved. Critics and opponents may choose to forget the appalling shambles Margaret Thatcher inherited from Labour in 1979. History will remind them.

'Unlike Tony Blair, she had a great respect for the House and its traditions.'

Lord Bellwin

Sir Peter Emery

CONSERVATIVE MP

Sir Peter Emery was first elected as the MP for Reading in 1959 and served there until 1966. He was Member for Honiton from 1967 until 1997 and for East Devon from 1997 to 2001.

Briefing Margaret

THERE ARE, OF COURSE, MANY STORIES. One of the least known was when she was appointed by Edward Heath to be the frontbench spokesman on Power, taking over from Sir John Eden and being the first woman to be given this appointment. At the time I was Vice-Chairman of the backbench committee on Power, of which she, as the frontbench spokesman, was Chairman.

I went to brief her in her flat one morning soon after her appointment. We discussed all matters that were dealt with by the Ministry, including iron, steel, gas, electricity, nuclear power and the coal industry. Towards lunchtime Margaret had to leave for a luncheon appointment, and I said that the only outstanding matter was the oil industry. I was then a director of Philips Petroleum UK and I said that I could fill her in on this whenever it suited her.

She turned to me and said, with a twinkle in her eye, 'Peter, you don't have to bother. I sleep with the oil industry every night.' Of course Denis was then a Director of Burmah Oil.

We are prepared to fight for peace.

At the 1975 Conservative Party Conference with Peter Morrison MP (left) and Sir Keith Joseph MP (centre).

Lord Jenkin of Roding

CABINET MINISTER 1979–85

Patrick Jenkin served in Margaret Thatcher's Cabinet from 1979 until 1985, initially as Secretary of State for Social Services, moving to the Department for Industry in 1981 and the Department of the Environment in 1983. He was raised to the Peerage by Margaret Thatcher in 1987.

Always Margaret

LET ME GET ONE THING CLEAR FROM THE OUTSET: never in all the fifty-odd years that I have known Margaret Thatcher have I, or any of her colleagues in the Party in either House of Parliament, ever called her 'Maggie'. Indeed, we never used the word, either when speaking to each other, let alone when speaking to her. She was always 'Margaret', or, in Cabinet, 'Prime Minister'.

I mention this because it is a stark illustration of the gulf that exists between the world of politics as portrayed by the populist media and the real world in which the players actually operate. Apart from seeing the word in print, where I suppose journalists were after a snappy headline, 'Maggie Swings Her Handbag Again', one remembers the left-wing demos where the marchers chanted 'Maggie, Maggie, Maggie, Out, Out, Out!' By giving a political leader a label like that, it becomes easier to build up a caricature that is further and further removed from the real person.

I once discussed this phenomenon with her, not because I myself ever had a media nickname (I was not important enough to merit that!), but I was experiencing what everyone in politics faces from time to time – a concerted press campaign of mockery and vilification which bears little or no relation to reality. Margaret's reaction was immediate and very clear: 'I never read the nasty things they write about me, because it would only upset me,' she said, 'and I strongly advise you to do the same!'

She was of course right; the press soon tire of pursuing one victim and go off to find another. I suppose that it sells newspapers but I wonder how many people who might make a real contribution to public life are put off, not because they fear becoming victims of what I recently heard described as 'tabloid crucifixion', but because of the endless denigration of all politicians.

Yet there is another side, and this story illustrates it. I was ending an election walkabout with our candidate in Monmouth when, just as I was getting into the car, a man came up, and in that wonderful lilting Welsh accent, said: 'Excuse me, Mr Jenkin, can I have a word?'

'Of course,' I replied, 'if you can keep it short.'

'Oh, it won't take long. I just wanted to tell you' (and his voice became very bitter) 'I hate your Party, I hate your policies, I hate everything you stand for!'

I replied, with a smile, 'It doesn't sound as if we are going to get your vote!'

'Oh, yes you will!' he said; 'she's the only one who knows what she wants to do!'

The chattering classes have never understood that phenomenon. Margaret Thatcher's appeal, over the heads of the political establishment and the media, to millions of ordinary men and women in all walks of life was remarkable and

Power is a trust and we must exercise it in that way.

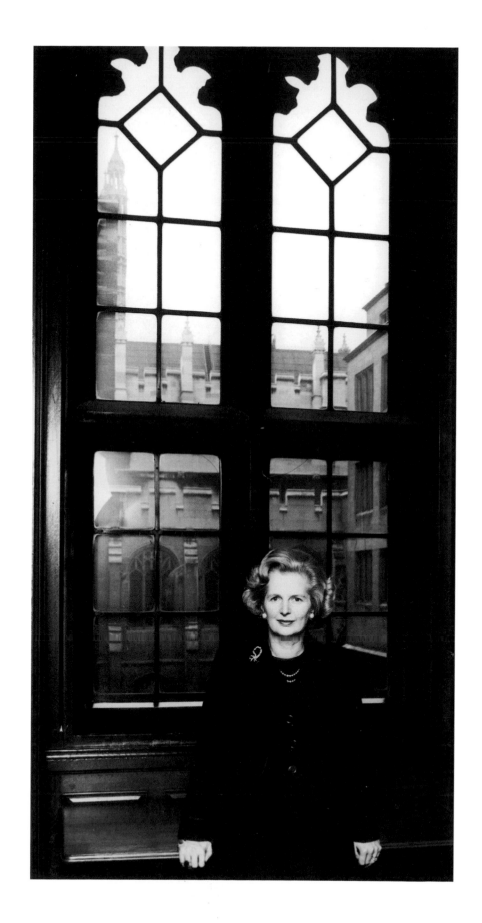

Prime Minister Margaret Thatcher, pictured in the Palace of Westminster in 1976, by Karsh of Ottawa.

was the foundation of her long spell as Conservative Leader and Prime Minister. Mr Blair sees himself cast in the same mould, but spin is no substitute for character and focus groups are no substitutes for conviction. It was the force of Margaret's character and the conviction with which she pursued her goals that won her the huge support of the people, and ensured that she won every general election she fought.

I have known Margaret for nearly fifty years. We met in the early 1950s when she and I served on the Executive Committee of what was then the Inns of Court Conservative and Unionist Society. She had joined the same set of Chambers in the Temple as I had though we worked with different barristers. She came with a rising reputation as a formidable politician: her election campaigns in Dartford in 1950 and 1951 had attracted the attention of senior MPs, including Iain Macleod, who had spotted a winner very early on.

I remember an early argument with Margaret over the future of the steel industry. I had spent a week campaigning in South Wales and had witnessed, in Ebbw Vale, the early effects of nationalisation on investment in new plant, and was unsure whether it would be wise to try to denationalise the industry. Instead, I argued for giving the workers a stake in the businesses through some form of co-partnership. Margaret was scornful; only the full rigour of market disciplines would ensure the industry's success, and we should not shrink from the inevitable political row. But when the next Conservative Government did denationalise it, it was followed by re-nationalisation by the next Labour Government. Thirty years after that argument with Margaret, as Industry Secretary in her first administration, I prepared British Steel for privatisation which was finally achieved during her period in office. She was of course right – but it took over thirty years for her wisdom to prevail.

Despite our long acquaintance, I was not sure that she was the right person to lead the Party after Ted Heath had been defeated in the 1975 leadership election and I voted for Willie Whitelaw. She was well aware of that, and though I was in the Shadow Cabinet, she asked Denis Thatcher if she could rely on my loyalty. He gave me a clean bill, and I retained my job as Energy Shadow. In January 1976 she asked me to take over shadowing the Health and Social Security portfolio. 'You have been in the Treasury and understand public finance. You must now experience the pressures on a major spending department,' she told me. However, she went on to impress on me the overriding need to avoid any new spending commitments at all. Indeed, I was asked to ensure that the DHSS would find savings to contribute to the cuts in public spending needed to finance tax cuts – and thereby hangs a tale.

In the run-up to the 1979 election we had committed ourselves to just two specific pledges in my policy area: we promised that we would not cut NHS spending, and we promised to protect pensions and other long-term benefits against rising prices. On health, where we were to inherit the three year projection of modest increases in spending (at constant prices), I realised that during the campaign I would be challenged as to what our pledge meant: did we mean no cuts but no increases, or did we mean that we would maintain the modest increases

I never read the nasty things they write about me, because it would only upset me.

planned by our predecessors? I was able to persuade Geoffrey Howe, the Shadow Chancellor, that I had to be allowed to say that it was the second of these, and I duly gave the pledge on a BBC *Newsnight* programme.

That did not stop the Treasury demanding cuts and in Cabinet, I came under pressure from other Ministers to find my share of the savings to which we were all committed. I read out the very specific pledge I had given on TV and Margaret at once, with no argument, agreed that that must be honoured – and of course it was.

We then came to Social Security. The Treasury demanded that we should allow no uprating of the short-term benefits in our first year, and uprate the pension and long-term benefits by less than inflation. I had earlier warned Margaret (in private) that I would feel obliged to remind colleagues of the words she herself had used in a radio interview. 'Of course, you must; we must have all the facts whatever we decide.' She had, of course, repeated the Manifesto pledge 'to protect pensioners against rising prices'. When I read this out, one colleague said, 'Well, that's it, isn't it? Next business.' Margaret made it clear that she would be willing to face the music if the Cabinet agreed with the Treasury's proposal, but, very wisely, her colleagues demurred, and we held to the pledge that she had given.

It is far too soon for history to form a balanced judgement on her reign as Prime Minister. The legends and the myths abound – of her abuse of colleagues, of her taking sides against her own Government, of her trying to force decisions before even hearing the Minister in charge; there was an element of truth in all this but of course it would be wholly wrong to think that it was the whole truth. She often showed that she had a sharper brain than most of the rest of us, and if she got her way it was because she had an amazing eye for detail. I will end with an illustration.

As Industry Secretary, I faced pressure from Sir Ian Macgregor, Chairman of British Steel, to allow him to close the loss-making Ravenscraig plant at Motherwell. However, this works had become a touchstone of the Scots' conviction that Mrs Thatcher 'did not care about Scotland'. I made it clear to Sir Ian that closure was not politically possible, and asked him to explore other options.

He knew the American steel industry well. He asked me to meet one of the American steel bosses and the three of us met over dinner at the Waterside Restaurant at Bray, not far from Heathrow. There, they put to me a scheme which involved British Steel, then still in the public sector, buying a quoted American company, Kaiser Steel, with a big works near Los Angeles in California. Ravenscraig would manufacture steel 'semis' – large slabs of steel – for shipment to California for Kaiser to manufacture heavy pipes for the then burgeoning oil fields in Alaska. This would be a new UK export market, which was too far from the big US steel makers in Chicago and Pennsylvania for them to supply competitively. I asked them to work it up, making it clear that this would need Cabinet approval.

Although the negotiations to buy Kaiser were difficult and complex, involving as they did the technicalities of the rules of the New York Stock Exchange, a way

'She often showed that she had a sharper brain than the rest of us.'

Lord Jenkin

Overleaf: Gazing into the future.

forward was devised. I had the firm support of the Scottish Secretary, George Younger, and of several other Ministers. It all came to a head at a late night meeting in the Cabinet room at which there were present, not only Treasury and Foreign Office officials, but also our New York investment bankers and lawyers. The Prime Minister questioned these Americans minutely, asking them to spell out exactly the several different stages in the acquisition process, concentrating on the issue of the precise point at which British Steel, and therefore the British Exchequer, would become committed. One of the answers caught me by surprise, and I did not immediately react as I could not see the way round it. It appeared that we would be bound at an earlier point than I had been advised, before we had had sight of the full documentation on Kaiser.

This was a moment of truth. Margaret had spotted a weakness in the arguments, and from that moment the discussion could lead only to a decision that we could not go ahead on the basis proposed, and we broke up long after midnight, very disappointed at this outcome.

The next day I discussed the decision with her and indicated that it might be very difficult to revive the project in a way that would get round the difficulty she had identified. 'When you did not respond immediately to the lawyer's point,' she told me, 'I realised that your Department had not thought of it, and that it would be too risky to go ahead on the basis you and George were proposing.'

Significantly, she had refused to allow Sir Ian to attend that meeting: 'He will bamboozle us all into supporting his scheme and I need to be certain that it would be safe to commit the Exchequer to the guarantee it would have to give.' I have no doubt that, as so often, she was right!

Most people who decide to go into politics have the perfectly laudable ambition of serving in office. I was very fortunate that six of my ten years on the Government Front Bench were in Margaret Thatcher's Cabinets. Although she and I had several monumental rows during these years, I will always look back on those six years as the high point in my political career. When I retired to the backbenches in 1985, the *Guardian* chided me for an excess of loyalty to her. All I can say in response is that she earned it, and I have no regrets!

Michael Brunson
ITN POLITICAL EDITOR 1986–2000

Now a freelance broadcaster and journalist, Michael Brunson is best known for being ITN's face of current affairs for fourteen years.

Have you got that, Mr Brunson?

MY FIRST-EVER ENCOUNTER with Margaret Thatcher, a little over a year before she became Prime Minister, was explosive, and therefore memorable. I had just returned to the United Kingdom after a spell as ITN's Washington correspondent, and I had already been told that I would be the reporter assigned to cover her eventual General Election campaign.

In January 1978, as Leader of the Opposition, she gave a wide-ranging television interview, during which she was asked about the issue of immigration. She replied with what she later described as some 'extremely mild remarks'. What she actually said was this: 'People are really rather afraid that this country might be rather swamped by people with a different culture.' Others immediately found her remarks, and particularly her use of the word 'swamped', as anything but mild, hearing in them an echo of Enoch Powell's notorious 'rivers of blood' speech almost exactly ten years earlier.

The following day, Mrs Thatcher was due to conduct a morning's campaigning for the Conservative candidate in a by-election in the Ilford North constituency to the east of London. I immediately suggested to the news editor at ITN that I should go and cover it. The Conservative campaign headquarters for the by-election turned out to be an old café, the former, though still appropriately named, Seven Ways Restaurant, since it was right next to the massive Gants Hill roundabout. The news conference was to be held in a large and unusually depressing room, hung from floor to ceiling with the faded maroon curtains which had presumably once been the establishment's glory in its heyday.

The news conference was surprisingly poorly attended, with no more than five or six other journalists present. I was therefore able, at an early stage, to ask about the previous evening's interview, and I thought it perfectly natural to ask whether she had not regretted having raised the issue.

A volcanic eruption followed. She had not raised the matter. How could I possibly say that she had raised the matter? She had simply been asked a question, and she had replied to it in a perfectly honest and straightforward manner. What on earth was I talking about? How could I possibly put such a question to her?

Stunned into silence, I left it to others among the equally astonished press corps to take up the running, and they quickly turned to local matters. The news conference drew to a close and I assumed that that was the end of the matter. But I was wrong.

During some closing remarks, the volcano erupted again. Mrs Thatcher announced that she wished to say a word or two about the media. As she did so, what President Mitterrand is once said to have called 'the eyes of Caligula' swivelled menacingly in my direction. She wanted journalists to know that she always did her homework, and that if we were to be regarded as true professionals,

People are really rather afraid that this country might be rather swamped by people with a different culture.

Britain is no longer in the politics of the pendulum, but of the ratchet.

she expected us to do ours. Of course, she wanted good relations with the media, and she was perfectly prepared to answer any and every question. She always had, and she always would, with one proviso. They had to be accurate questions, properly based on facts. Had we got that? Was that quite clear? The tirade delivered, she swept from the room.

Blimey! Was this the woman that I would have to deal with during the rigours of a General Election? I soon realised, however, that it had been an exceptionally useful experience. It gave me, at our very first meeting, a clear insight into the way Margaret Thatcher operated. Above all, it showed me how strongly she believed in the old adage that the best form of defence is attack – seizing, that morning in Ilford, for example, on the tiny technicality of whether or not she had raised, or had simply responded to, an issue in order to defend herself. It was all to stand me in good stead not just during the 1979 campaign, but during the many times over the following years when we were to meet again.

Addressing a Conservative Party rally in 1977.

Matthew Parris

BROADCASTER AND COLUMNIST

After working for the Conservative Research Department and in Mrs Thatcher's Private Office, Matthew Parris became the MP for West Derbyshire in 1979, a position he held until 1986. Since then he has worked as a broadcaster and most famously as a parliamentary sketch writer for *The Times*.

I have never dared ask …

WHEN I WAS A BRANCH CHAIRMAN of South Battersea Conservative Association we welcomed Margaret Thatcher, as Leader of the Opposition, on an official visit to our neighbourhood. I and others were deputed to guide her on a walkabout down the Northcote Road (a little market) for the local press. This was about 1978.

She spotted a council workman driving a motorised street cleaner. After speaking to him she began to climb into the driver's seat crying: 'Show me how this thing works and I will clean the street. Only a woman knows how to get into corners men cannot reach.'

* * * * *

In 1978 the RSPCA asked Mrs Thatcher to present me (at the time I was her Correspondence Secretary) with their award for bravery in rescuing a dog from the River Thames.

The ceremony took place on Westminster Bridge in the presence of a number of officials, the dog (Jason) and some photographers. Privately, Mrs Thatcher thought I had been mad to rescue the dog. But she was a kindly employer and no doubt spotted a good photo opportunity too.

During the ceremony the dog began (as little male dogs too often do) to mate with her elegantly-stockinged leg. She took absolutely no notice and carried on smiling for the cameras. To this day I have never been quite sure whether she realised what was going on down below, and have never dared ask her.

> *If you want anything said, ask a man. If you want anything done, ask a woman.*

Handing out cups of tea to waiting journalists outside her Flood Street home.

Sir Alfred Sherman

ADVISER TO MARGARET THATCHER

Sir Alfred Sherman co-founded the Centre for Policy Studies with Sir Keith Joseph and Margaret Thatcher in 1974 where he acted as a formative influence on Thatcherite political and economic thinking. He served as a speech-writer and aide to Margaret Thatcher from 1974 until 1983.

All that is real is rational

THOSE WHO REACHED THE TOP of the greasy pole this century can be counted on your fingers; identifying qualities which brought them to the top where many others failed remains infinitely challenging. I had personally identified Margaret Thatcher as a potential successor to Heath under certain circumstances back in Autumn 1973, when asked by two friends, Basil (now Lord) Feldman, a leading party figure, and Barry Rose, publisher and one-time Conservative council-leader. Basil called this far-fetched. How right he was. That it came to pass does not make it any less so. That an almost unknown middle-aged lady from a lower middle-class background whose political career had been unspectacular could within sixteen months reach the top in the Tory interest seemed inconceivable. Nor were her chances of leading her Party to electoral victory, once precariously established as Leader, rated highly until the Callaghan government's last few months, beset by difficulties of its own making. Yet in a short time she became one of the few twentieth-century leaders of whom it could be said that she 'bestrode our narrow world like a colossus'. But per Hegel: 'all that is real is rational'; there must have been valid reasons for her achievement.

When I forecast that Margaret might receive the mandate of Heaven, I had never met her, and only once even seen her. What struck me then was the fervour of her beliefs. The Spanish political philosopher, José Ortega y Gasset, distinguished between ideas and beliefs, complaining that historians and political writers over-emphasised the importance of the former at the expense of the latter. Current sensitivity among Conservatives about what they pejoratively dub 'ideology', by which they mean ideas or conceptual frameworks, reflects the fact that for generations Conservatives managed on the basis of implicit beliefs incorporating practices which had evolved over time and ideas derived from classical philosophy and Protestant Christianity. As Nigel Lawson was later to argue in a CPS pamphlet, Conservatives had managed quite well without a structure of explicit ideas until Liberals and Labour elaborated theirs, following which the Conservatives had no alternative but to match them. MT filled the gap by her Conservative beliefs: the puritan ethic; personal responsibility; patriotism. Conversion of these beliefs into ideas as a basis for policies was left till later, too late.

I did not meet her till the spring of 1974, under Keith Joseph's auspices, after he had accepted my outline for the 'we were wrong' Upminster speech in June, which was to become the first in his series on 'Reversing the Trend', rejecting Butskellism and advocating radical Tory counter-revolution. The speech was designed to launch his new think-tank (soon to be named the Centre for Policy

Economics are the method: the object is to change the soul.

Margaret Thatcher asking for support during the 1979 Election Campaign.

Studies) which Heath had suggested after Keith had declined the Shadow Cabinet portfolio offered, in the hope that it would keep him busy and out of mischief expounding Butskellism and Europhilia, but which I had persuaded him – I am still not sure how – to devote to expounding radical Conservatism, which eventually became known as Thatcherism.

He decided to offer Margaret Thatcher the deputy-chairmanship. She was then fifty, with grown-up children, but there was then something girlish about her: her enthusiasms; the simplicity of her beliefs; her trusting nature. She reminded me of nineteenth-century explorers, aware that their ambiance was strange and dangerous but unquestioningly confident in themselves. At the time, she believed strongly that Keith should become Party leader, and that only Lady Joseph's reluctance to give him full support was preventing this. Since Keith had always been the antithesis of a leader, this convinced me that she was a bad judge of character.

She was unapologetically aware that her grasp of ideas, politics and economics was insufficient for the role in which she was subconsciously casting herself, and had no hesitation in casting me as a second John the Baptist after Keith.

When we first met, her chosen persona was as an upper-middle-class Tory lady in twin-set and pearls. But her first reactions to Keith's epoch-making 'we were wrong' Upminster speech, praising it for its 'economy with words', suggested to me an alternative persona, the puritan grocer's daughter, bringing faith and common sense to the convoluted world of public affairs and economic controversy: 'economics is Greek for running a household'. Peel's dictum that a Prime Minister must be 'an uncommon common man' was relevant. Her outward demeanour as a housewife shopping at Marks & Spencers reassured many who are basically suspicious both of politicians and of political ideas, believing that politics and government ought to be much simpler.

In opposition, and to some extent in government, we worked closely for hours on end, often à deux, sometimes with her PPSs. During the day, we worked in the Leader of the Opposition's office, overlooking Boudicca's statue, evenings and weekends we worked at her home in Flood Street, Chelsea, in the dining-room, with a typewriter on the table. When we had progressed, she would go into the kitchen to prepare food, giving instructions though the linking door, exemplifying her dual roles. In her flat at Number 10 – living over the shop – she was in and out of the kitchen, as no other premier ever was.

It is not easy for labourers in the vineyard to get into the minds of the great, who achieve greatness precisely because their mind and spirit work distinctively. I found that she possessed a razor-sharp mind and great application, but because they had been honed in natural science and the law her thinking was linear rather than lateral. But it was her will which marked her out. Though power wrought its effects on her in time, she remained free to the end from the side and self-importance which it inflicts on so many politicians. I remember an occasion when I had arranged to bring an American to see her, who ran a media-monitoring unit, which I believed we should emulate. As we waited in the ground-floor reception at Number 10, she suddenly appeared in the doorway in stockinged feet and took

Economics is Greek for running a household.

us up to her study. Conversely, she never fully acquired the art of suffering fools gladly, so essential in democratic politics. It was her body language rather than her politics which so enraged Geoffrey Howe that he steeled himself to resign his benefice and stab her in the back.

In the course of time her enthusiasm for ideas seemed to lapse, while the ironclad self-confidence, which had been so essential when she was an outsider storming the citadel, became an impediment. The leadership election, which she had lost by four votes, epitomised the personal dimension in her trajectory. Had she stayed and fought it, personally meeting waverers and lukewarm supporters, and impressing on enthusiastic supporters not to disqualify their vote by writing slogans on their ballot paper, and hence spoiling it, she would have come home comfortably. Instead, misled by naive canvass reports which took voting promises at face value (since many MPs, characteristically, backed themselves both ways) and hankerings after the glory of the prestigious Paris end of the cold war summit which coincided with the leadership contest, she went to Paris and left re-election to look after itself. Her fall, like her rise, was the stuff of which cautionary fables are made.

As I argued earlier, Margaret Thatcher's rise to power had come about by the interplay of chance and 'necessity' (Hegel's rendering of the Greek *ananke*) between the accidental, incidental and inherent, per Aristotle. I had been catalyst to this process. When, after her 1983 election victory (which looked much larger than it actually was), Margaret Thatcher was persuaded to dispense with people and ideas which had brought her to power in the first place, it was not apparent to her that she might be eroding the ideal cement of her own power base, that her native hue of resolution might depend on the ideas which had fed into Thatcherism. In the event, de-Shermanisation of the CPS and its milieu, which had been the seed-bed of Thatcherism, set in motion de-Thatcherisation, leaving her bereft of a lodestar and vulnerable to her colleagues-cum-enemies. Legend and literature contain many such instances.

Alexander Haig

NATO SUPREME ALLIED COMMANDER IN EUROPE 1974-9

General Alexander M. Haig Jr is Chairman of his own international advisory firm, Worldwide Associates Inc, based in Washington DC. He was White House Chief of Staff for President Richard Nixon, Supreme Allied Commander in Europe (NATO) and President Ronald Reagan's first Secretary of State.

Giant among leaders

MARGARET THATCHER IS A GIANT among contemporary world leaders. She is a woman of conviction, courage, and principle.

I first met her in the mid seventies while I was serving as the Supreme Allied Commander in Europe (SACEUR). I recall being urged by one of Great Britain's leading conservative political leaders to meet with an upstart conservative lady who believed she could be the next Prime Minister of Great Britain. He urged me to meet her in Brussels and brief her on the European security situation, adding that her intellectual well was somewhat dry on such things. Because of the position of the caller, I agreed and after spending approximately one hour with this attractive, bright, and enthusiastic political hopeful, left with the impression that my contact's assessment had been an accurate one as it applied to European security issues.

I saw Margaret Thatcher six or eight months later at a point when she had become the nominee of the Conservative Party. In the brief intervening period between our two meetings, she had acquired a level of military knowledge that was both remarkable in scope and the match for a professional with years of European security background. During the remainder of my time as SACEUR I met frequently with the then Prime Minister, and remained in awe of her military and geopolitical acumen.

Some years later, as America's 59th Secretary of State, I came to know Margaret Thatcher in an environment where the vital interests of both of our respective nations were at stake on several important occasions. Perhaps the most difficult of those occurred at the end of my service in the Reagan Cabinet during the Falklands War. In my first book entitled *Caveat: Realism, Reagan, and Foreign Policy* I described this remarkable woman in the following brief paragraph:

In the Falklands, the West was given a great victory by Great Britain. I do not mean the defeat of Argentinian soldiers by British soldiers. Every man who fell on either side represented a loss to the free world. British arms prevailed, but principle triumphed. The will of the West was tested and found to be equal to the task. The rule of law was upheld. The freedom of a faraway people was preserved. For this, the free world may thank the men of the British task force and Mrs Thatcher, who was by far the strongest, the shrewdest, and the most clear-sighted player in the game. In times of acute national crisis, a leader will always hear advice that clashes with his inner convictions. Easier courses than the right course will be thrust upon him. It is the leader, who knowing where the true interest of the nation lies, resists such counsel and perseveres in his principles, who deserves the name of statesman. Margaret Thatcher belongs in that company.

I know nothing about democracy, but I know I want certain things for Britain.

'Mrs Thatcher ... was by far the strongest, the shrewdest, and the most clear-sighted player in the game.'

General Haig

A 1979 portrait of Margaret Thatcher by Karsh of Ottawa.

Mark Prisk

CONSERVATIVE MP

Mark Prisk is a surveyor and a former National Vice Chairman of the Federation of Conservative Students. He was elected as MP for Hertford and Stortford in 2001, and is a Conservative Whip.

Ask not what your country ...

OVER THE LAST TWENTY-SEVEN YEARS I've had many encounters with Lady Thatcher. She was originally one of the main reasons I came into politics, because she showed that an individual can make a real difference. Ideologically she inevitably helped shape my views, though I've not always agreed with her. Yet it is perhaps my first meeting with her which helped me form my view of the woman behind the ism.

I first met the then Mrs Thatcher in Truro City Hall, in the run up to 1979 General Election. I had recently become Chairman of Cornwall Young Conservatives and was determined to meet our Party's Leader. The hall was packed, yet somehow when she entered at the back everyone sensed it and turned. Not great in stature she bustled in to the hall and strode towards the platform, her support team trailing behind. She spoke with energy and clarity, and as she did so she dominated the audience. Yet it wasn't her speech which I remember most. There were two other incidents which showed a hint of her true personality.

During her speech a photographer, perched on a high stand, fell quite heavily. She stopped speaking and made sure that he was OK. Most politicians ignore such things, but she seemed genuinely concerned – when she might perhaps have been annoyed at the interruption.

Then after speaking, as she was leaving I collared her and asked what a Conservative Government would do for young people. She turned and simply said, 'Do for you? Shouldn't we let you get on with it for yourself?' Momentarily I was taken aback. Had I blown it with the Leader? Yet it wasn't intended as a rebuke, just an honest response, which saw through the question to the assumption beneath. It reflected that unsentimental part of her character, which was often caricatured as uncaring. All she was expressing was the same notion President Kennedy has previously been lauded for, 'Ask not what your country can do for you, ask what you can do for your country.'

In watching her since I have often found these two incidents instructive. A woman genuinely concerned for others' welfare, but able to distinguish between care and sentimentality. In this age of hand-wringing emoting, it's a quality much missed.

One is an ordinary person – and don't you forget it!

A 1979 Conservative Election Poster. The caption reads: 'Don't just hope for a better future, vote for one.'

Andrew Rosindell

CONSERVATIVE MP

Andrew Rosindell is a former national chairman of the Young Conservatives and chairman of the International Young Democratic Union. He was elected MP for Romford in 2001.

Inspiring the young

IT WAS MARGARET THATCHER that made me want to get involved in politics. Even though I was only in my early teens, somehow our new Prime Minister seemed to represent all the things that my instincts had told me were right. At last, Britain had a leader who was prepared to fight to restore our nation's confidence and pride and demonstrate the bulldog spirit that some thought we had lost.

As Prime Minister, Mrs Thatcher was first and foremost a patriot. She loved her country and believed in everything British, but knew the country had to change economically and saw it as her mission to drive forward reforms that would bring long-term prosperity for our people.

Difficult and dangerous times lay ahead of Margaret Thatcher when she entered 10 Downing Street in 1979, but nothing would deflect her from doing what she knew was her duty to the nation. Her deep sense of patriotism was always the driving force that kept Maggie going!

The 1982 Party Conference at Brighton was my first encounter with Mrs Thatcher. I was introduced to the PM by the late Ian Gow who was her PPS during her first term in office. As a very young YC, I watched her address the Party Conference with the theme of 'The Resolute Approach'. Having liberated the Falkland Islands and restored a sense of self-belief to our country, Margaret Thatcher was stronger than ever.

There was always a Union Flag on the platform at Party Conference when Margaret Thatcher was Leader and we always sang the National Anthem at the beginning and end of conference. She understood that patriotism was one of the Conservative Party's greatest strengths. Not for her the shallow short-termism of the politically correct and today's so-called 'modernisers'.

On the night freedom was restored to the people of the Falkland Islands, crowds gathered outside Number 10 to cheer Mrs Thatcher and as she greeted the crowds, the spontaneous singing of 'Rule Britannia' echoed all around. It was precisely that spirit which characterised her years as Prime Minister. Standing firm for Britain is something that has always come naturally to Margaret Thatcher and how we have missed that characteristic in our leaders since then.

As Chairman of the National YCs in 1993, Margaret Thatcher came to a conference I had organised for young political leaders from across Europe. This was the first YC event she attended since standing down as Prime Minister. What surprised our guests from the continent was the reaction of the UK YCs who greeted Lady Thatcher as if she was still leading the Conservative Party. She was adored by the younger generation within the Party and was so much more in touch with their views, ideals and aspirations than those who had succeeded her. Central Office were horrified that I had organised an event with the former Leader.

Margaret Thatcher pats Andrew Rosindell's bull terrier Buster.

There is no such thing as Society. There are individual men and women, and there are families.

I did it again in 1996 when for EYC (European Young Conservatives) and IYDU (International Young Democrat Union), I asked Lady Thatcher to address the Freedom Dinner at the Britannia Hotel in Docklands.

This time young people came from all over the world. Many spoke passionately about why they owed so much to the Iron Lady who, together with Ronald Reagan, had led the world towards freedom. The most moving statements came from a young girl from Poland who spoke of how Margaret Thatcher had represented a beacon of hope for the people of Eastern Europe and a young leader from Argentina who thanked the former Prime Minister for standing up to dictatorship, which had led to the restoration of democracy in Argentina too.

Union Jacks were draped around the room and patriotic songs were sung by everyone. It was a truly memorable occasion, but at 10 o'clock is was time for Lady T. to depart, although we had not reached the point when the National Anthem was to be sung. We were way behind schedule. Lady Thatcher refused to go until we had all stood to sing it. 'I am not leaving before the National Anthem,' she said to me and so, to the delight of everyone present, Lady T. remained until the end.

In 2001, Lady Thatcher made Romford her final stop of the General Election campaign. Having arrived in Romford Market, she was greeted by hundreds of cheering people, not just Party activists, but ordinary local residents who loved her for what she had done for our country and admired her like no other.

'Spike', my Staffordshire Bull Terrier, was the first to welcome her, dressed in his Union Jack waistcoat and wearing his 'I love Maggie' badge. When Lady Thatcher came to Romford again in March 2005, my new dog 'Buster', also a Staffie, was there wearing his Cross of St George waistcoat. It came as no surprise that Lady T. soon made friends with both Spike and Buster. Somehow, all three of them seemed to represent the true spirit of Britain, the bulldog spirit!

Margaret Thatcher sits at the feet of former Prime Minister Harold Macmillan on 7 February 1979 as they converse on his eighty-fifth birthday at the Carlton Club.

Sir Ronald Millar

MARGARET THATCHER'S SPEECH-WRITER

Sir Ronald Millar was an accomplished playwright and film-script author. He began writing speeches for Prime Minister Edward Heath in the early 1970s. He was then invited to continue as speech-writer firstly to Margaret Thatcher and then John Major. He was the author of a phrase that has entered our language – 'The Lady's Not for Turning'. Sir Ronald died in 2000.

Lincoln's address

MARGARET THATCHER WAS ELECTED Leader on 11 February 1975 but stubborn loyalty to her predecessor was still with me when, six days later, I was summoned to meet her in the House of Commons. At this first meeting her attitude to me was guarded as was mine to her. I had the feeling she was thinking: What sort of writer is this who worked for Ted? Not one of us, that's for sure. I was thinking: she must have something special or they wouldn't have made a woman Party Leader, but I wasn't clear what it was and in any case not at all sure that I wanted to be further involved politically.

I had heard that she was intent on change and fine, I thought, change is not only inevitable, it's desirable, but let's not wipe out yesterday like a wet sponge cleaning a blackboard. No one had said she intended this but the word was that she was a force to be reckoned with, a woman with all the determination of a man and therefore, in all probability, up to no good. However, seeing her in daylight for the first time, and suppressing one of those cliché assessments that were to dog her throughout her political life, there was a kind of senior girl-scout freshness about her that was rather appealing, as though she had stepped straight out of *The Sound of Music*, though I doubt if 'soft woollen mittens and whiskers on kittens' were ever her favourite things.

She offered me a chair and a coffee and said she had inherited a five minute Party Political Broadcast that was to have been given by Mr Heath and she understood that I helped with these broadcasts, was that right? 'Helped' was an understatement, but I nodded. Well now, would I consider doing this one for her? I explained that my play was opening in a few days' time and I was completely taken up with final rehearsals. She said she understood but that the broadcast only required a five-minute text. Couldn't I find time to squeeze it in?

I pointed out that a five-minute text took rather more than five minutes to write and in any case I'd no idea what she wanted to say. 'Just set out my stall in general terms. There won't be any time for more than that. My politics aren't quite the same as Mr Heath's, you know.' Yes, I did know that. I also knew that as well as strong views she had a sense of mission and people with missions could be difficult to work with.

'Well?'

Assuming I could find the time, exactly when did she want it?

Could I manage a draft by tomorrow morning say, about eleven? This really

Let our children grow tall, and some taller than others.

'…there was a kind of senior girl-scout freshness about her that was rather appealing, as though she had stepped straight out of The Sound of Music.*'*

Sir Ronald Millar

was rather tiresome. Reluctantly I said I would see what I could do.

'Thank you. Till tomorrow, then.'

A polite smile, which I returned. There had been no instant meeting of minds, rather, on my part, a feeling of irritation at being diverted from something more important to me, if not to the charismatic new Leader of the Conservative Party. I too could be stubborn on occasion. I really shouldn't have agreed so easily. I hurried away from the Palace of Westminster and sat at the back of the stalls in the Haymarket, my eyes on the stage and the actors and my mind concentrated nine-tenths on the play. During the lunch break I scribbled a few thoughts in my Rymans notebook but couldn't think of an ending. If stuck, 'go for a quote' is a cliché but it's not a bad fall-back position. I managed to remember some lines from a speech attributed to Abraham Lincoln, his most memorable after Gettysburg, which I had learnt once for an audition.

Next morning at eleven I returned to the new Leader's office. 'May I have it?' she held out her hand. On a sudden impulse I said, 'May I read it to you?' She seemed surprised but indicated a chair some way from her across the room. Then she sat down and half covered her eyes with her left hand. Was the light troubling her or did she fear the worst? 'It helps me concentrate,' she said. 'Go ahead. I'm listening.'

When I had done there was a total silence. I thought, well, that went down like a sack of potatoes. I'm off the hook. Glory hallelujah! But then she took her hand from her eyes and reached into one of these large holdalls in which nowadays women carry everything but the microwave. From this receptacle she produced a handbag. Out of the handbag came a wallet and from the wallet a piece of yellowing newsprint. All this was done very slowly and methodically without a word being uttered. Finally she got up and came across the room to me and handed me the piece of newsprint. 'It goes wherever I go,' she said. It was the Lincoln quotation.

'This time the smile was more than polite. It was a dazzler.'

Sir Ronald Millar

There are moments in life when something goes 'click' in what one assumes to be the brain and you find yourself without warning on the same wavelength with a total stranger. This appeared to be just such a moment. I started to explain that I'd turned to Lincoln because I hadn't really had time for a peroration, my mind had been up there on stage with the actors. She said: 'If that's what you can do when you're not really trying, what will it be like when you are?' And this time the smile was more than polite. It was a dazzler.

Margaret Thatcher with her infamous handbag.

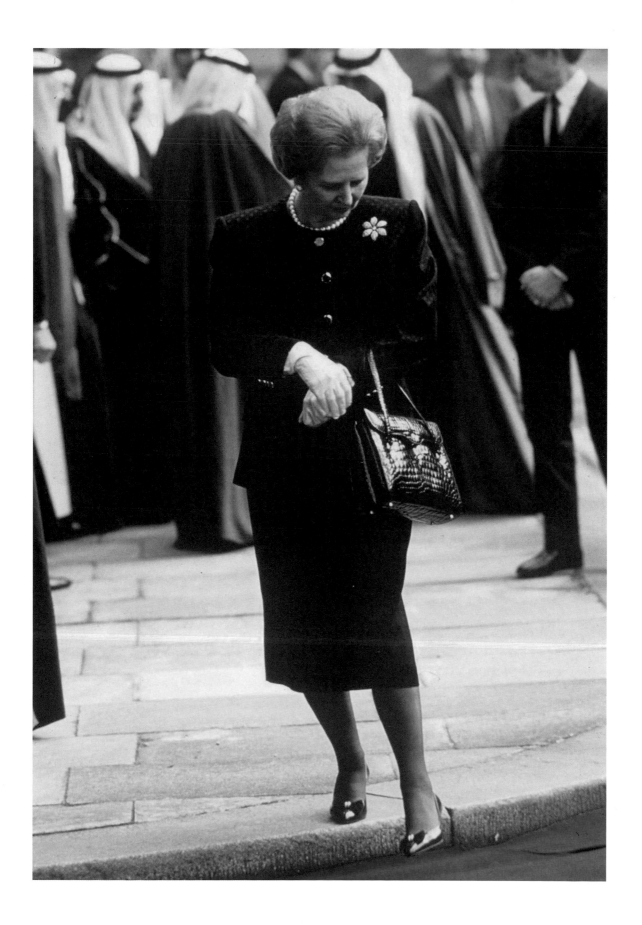

Sir Teddy Taylor
CONSERVATIVE MP

Sir Teddy Taylor was an MP from 1964 to 2005, initially for Glasgow Cathcart then from 1980 for Southend and from 1997 to 2005 for Rochford and Southend East. He served in Margaret Thatcher's Shadow Cabinet as Spokesman on Trade and then later as Spokesman on Scotland.

The Thatcher Shadow Cabinet

ONE OF MY EXCITING TIMES in Parliament was when Mrs Thatcher invited me to join her Shadow Cabinet in the post as Spokesman on Trade and Industry and then as the Spokesman on Scotland.

I have always had the feeling that one of the main reasons why I was appointed at all was because of my position towards devolution in Scotland and, happily, the Party turned from its previous commitment to devolution under Mrs Thatcher's leadership. It has always been argued that devolution was the only way to undermine the growth of the Scottish National Party who believed in full independence for Scotland, and both Mrs Thatcher and I thought that far from undermining the Nationalists, devolution would simply provide them with an opportunity to grow. Happily, by taking the Nationalists head on without the devolution commitment we were able to virtually wipe them out in the 1979 Election. The only personal problem, of course, was that by wiping out the SNP vote I lost my own seat in Cathcart in Glasgow and returned to Parliament a few months later as MP for Southend East in a by-election. I think I will never forget the fact that although Mrs Thatcher won the election and was on her way to Downing Street, she nevertheless found the time to phone me the morning after the election to offer her sympathy.

The discussions we had in the Shadow Cabinet when I was a Member were truly exciting because instead of endeavouring to make political propaganda we seemed to spend most of our time considering detailed and fundamental issues which were to be the basis of the Thatcher Administration. Amongst the most important issues we had to consider were the curbing of trade union abuses, the reduction of levels of taxation and the promotion of privatisation. Papers were constantly brought before the Shadow Cabinet and Mrs Thatcher always appeared to like having someone putting forward a contrary view which was subject to real discussion. If she won the argument she always expected everyone in the Shadow Cabinet to accept the decision and to go along with her, but if she lost the argument Willie Whitelaw had a habit of stepping in to suggest that the matter should be referred to a sub-committee and that was the end of the issue.

I will always remember Jim Prior, who was one of those who was constantly putting forward strong arguments against some of the fundamental changes in policy, but was always amongst the most loyal and most co-operative Members of the Shadow Cabinet in giving full support for decisions once they were reached. I enjoyed taking part in all these discussions and expressing my opinions.

The Conservative Shadow Cabinet led by Margaret Thatcher, pictured shortly before their victory in the 1979 General Election. Included in the picture are: Lord Carrington (3rd from left); William Whitelaw (4th from left); Margaret Thatcher, Sir Keith Joseph (6th from left); Francis Pym (8th from left); Norman St John Stevas (at the end of the table in the red tie); John Nott (8th from right wearing glasses); Sir Geoffrey Howe (5th from right wearing glasses); Lord Hailsham (4th from right); and Michael Heseltine (extreme right).

'…the most important issues we had to consider were the curbing of trade union abuses, the reduction of levels of taxation and the promotion of privatisation.'

Sir Teddy Taylor

Mrs Thatcher ran the Shadow Cabinet like a teacher in a school and because of my strong views on the EU I was constantly endeavouring to persuade the Shadow Cabinet to adopt a more aggressive policy on the issue. I can well remember an occasion when she reached across the Shadow Cabinet table, smacked my hand, and with a smile on her face said: 'Do not mention the EU again today, Teddy,' and there was laughter throughout the gathering.

I think the most impressive aspect of the Shadow Cabinet discussions for me was that under her leadership we looked with care and seriousness at problems which she felt had been neglected in Britain for far too long, and because these policies were implemented during her administration Britain was able to overcome many of the problems which other European nations still suffer from. I certainly think she was the greatest of all the politicians I have seen in Parliament in my long service here and she certainly did a great job for the country as a whole.

A Government that did less, and therefore did better, would strengthen its authority.

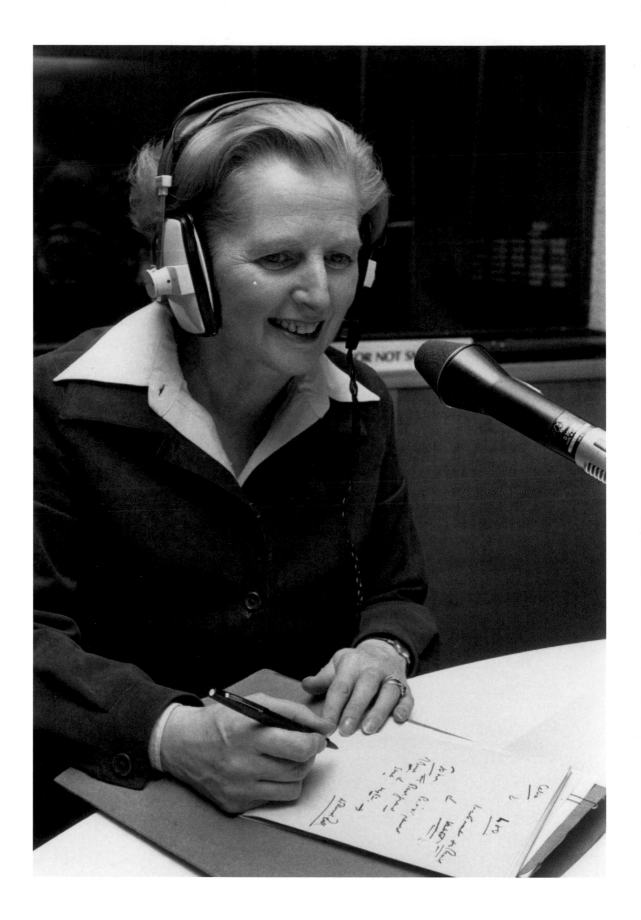

Lord Coe of Ranmore
ATHLETE AND POLITICIAN

Sebastian Coe's athletics career saw him beat twelve world records, win two Olympic gold medals and receive numerous other awards. He became the MP for Falmouth and Camborne in 1992, serving until 1997. He was Private Secretary to the Conservative leader William Hague and was raised to the Peerage in 2000. He led the successful British Olympic bid in 2005.

Prime Minister, you're wrong

THE ENDURING IMAGE OF MARGARET THATCHER is of an incredibly strong-minded woman with equally strongly held opinions. It was often written during her premiership that she had little time for those who disagreed with her. My own experience of her, long before I became a Member of Parliament or even entered active politics, was not altogether the same.

It was in 1988, in the run-up to the Seoul Olympics. I was invited to a reception at 10 Downing Street at which there were many distinguished people drawn from all walks of British life, not just athletics. Mrs Thatcher was a consummate professional at such events, moving round the room and chatting to her guests. She came up to me and asked how my preparation for the forthcoming Olympics was going. She knew I was expecting to be defending my title for the second time and I told her I thought it was all going really well (little realising that, in the event, the selectors had other intentions!). Her questioning then moved to how long in advance I would be going out to the region to acclimatise for the games and I realised I was getting in to a more detailed conversation than I had anticipated. Perhaps naively, I hadn't expected the Prime Minister to have thought about the preparations athletes make. Most people think you turn up, run, and come home. I explained I would be going out to Australia to train, on the same time zone as Seoul, and then fly directly to the Olympic holding-camp a few weeks beforehand.

'Oh, you don't need that length of time,' she said. 'Well, I think you do,' I ventured in response.

And so our conversation continued, both of us convinced of our point of view. Our discussion became quite detailed with Lady Thatcher increasingly focused on winning me over to her point of view. The rest of the room was, for a while, denied her attention as she pinned me to these questions. For some minutes, there was no other issue that mattered to her. The best efforts of various private secretaries to guide her on to the next person had no impact as our conversation became more and more animated.

Eventually the Prime Minister looked me in the eye and said, 'Mr Coe, I think you're wrong, and I am a research chemist.' To which I replied, 'Prime Minister, I think you're wrong – and I'm a double Olympic Champion.' For a moment, I thought my training would start sooner than I had planned but instead her natural, slightly stern expression melted and she laughed. 'Right,' she said, 'I am going to instruct our ambassador in Seoul to give you the complete run of the Embassy. You must have everything you need.'

Young people ought not to be idle. It's very bad for them.

Mr Coe, I think you're wrong, and I am a research chemist.

Margaret Thatcher in her pre-premiership days getting her message across on the *Jimmy Young Show*.

Henry Kissinger
INTERNATIONAL STATESMAN

Dr Henry Kissinger served as National Security Adviser and Secretary of State during the Nixon and Ford administrations. He is a prolific writer and broadcaster.

Meeting the Lady

THE ULTIMATE TASK OF A LEADER is to guide a society's transition from where it is to where it has never been. Conventional wisdom understands best what has already been experienced. But societies flourish by testing possibilities rather than celebrating achievements or wallowing in frustrations. To walk this lonely road requires, above all, courage and character. Great leaders inspire their people to discover and to explore their potential. Margaret Thatcher is such a person.

It is impossible for me to think of Lady Thatcher in terms of birthdays. To me, she is timeless; she will always be in my mind as she was the day I first met her, over thirty years ago. When just elected leader of the Opposition, she called on me at Claridge's Hotel. Jaunty, exuding vitality and assurance, she proceeded to explain her philosophy of leadership. She disdainfully dismissed the conventional wisdom that political contests were about winning the centre. In such a political system, the parties would look vapid and, what was worse, indistinguishable. The public would soon tire of electoral uniformity and, in time, despise leaders avoiding their responsibility of charting the future. Her faith in democracy based on drawing sharp distinctions would leave the centre in play, but it would have to choose between sharply defined alternatives. She was confident she would win the next election and govern on that basis.

History vindicated that vision. Lady Thatcher was elected and re-elected twice.

I saw her often in the years of her incumbency as well as in her retirement. Her buoyancy has never flagged, and her faith in her verities has remained constant: resistance to tyranny, alliance with America, insistence on a society shaped by free decisions and not the state, suspicion of supra-nationalism.

In 1981, I visited London during the Falklands crisis to celebrate the 200th anniversary of the founding of the Foreign Office. At a lunch at the Admiralty, various senior officials outlined possible compromises based on a mediation proposal by Alexander Haig, then U.S. Secretary of State. At tea with Lady Thatcher, I tried to explore her views on these schemes. She refused even to discuss compromise. She was, in fact, so irate at the very idea of it that I protected my lunchtime interlocutors by assuming responsibility for their ideas.

Lady Thatcher has had her prejudices. One of these was the possible ambitions of Germany to achieve domination on the continent. At a dinner, I was quoting Bismarck to the effect that the best a statesman could do was to grasp the hem of God's cloak and walk with Him a few steps. Lady Thatcher, who had not been paying full attention, asked what hem of what cloak I proposed grasping. I said that it was not meant literally; it was a famous quote from Bismarck. 'Bismarck, the German?' asked Lady Thatcher. When she heard the affirmative reply, she

> *'Great leaders inspire their people to discover and to explore their potential. Margaret Thatcher is such a person.'*
>
> Henry Kissinger

ended conversation on the subject with, 'Time to go home.'

But German leaders told me after unification that when they examined the files of the defunct East German foreign ministry, they found that Lady Thatcher had said nothing behind their back that she had not said to their face – an assertion they could not make of some other allies.

So I will conclude by emphasizing how much I have learned from Lady Thatcher, including that greatness must not be confused with complexity. She has been inspirational, above all, because she incarnated unshakeable faith in the power of free peoples to shape their future. It has been an honour to be her contemporary.

When you stop a dictator there are always risks. But there are great risks in not stopping a dictator.

Lord Biffen

CABINET MINISTER 1979–87

John Biffen, now Lord Biffen, served as a Cabinet Minister under Margaret Thatcher from 1979 until 1987, initially as Chief Secretary to the Treasury then later as Secretary of State for Trade, Lord President and Leader of the House of Commons and finally as Lord Privy Seal.

Unbending leadership

THE CAREER AND CHARACTER OF MARGARET THATCHER will fascinate historians for decades to come. Her achievements and limitations will bear constant re-interpretation. This short piece would not seek such an academic task, but only offer a personal recollection.

Her actions never betrayed the trivial or banal. She was puritanical and committed to the work ethic. She despised the worldly and cynical politics of many Tories. I suspect she looked upon the Macmillan period with some unease and felt that his sunset years, from Profumo onwards, showed the consequence of a lack of political purpose. Her decision to stand against Edward Heath for the Conservative leadership in 1975 was an example of cool courage. No member of Heath's Cabinet, and more particularly William Whitelaw, was prepared to stand against him. She, alone, broke rank, although Keith Joseph might have done so had he possessed the suitable temperament. Margaret Thatcher was not foolhardy in her venture. She had self-confidence and a deep sense that the Conservative politics of the Heath Government needed reversing. Thirty years later it is difficult to recapture how demoralised the Tories had become by U-turns and ineffective trade union legislation.

Doubtless this inspired Margaret Thatcher to convert a defeated party into a government in exile. Rarely have policy groups worked so assiduously to propose measures 'proof against U-turn'. The trade union plans were recast to avoid the ignominy of the unenforceable Industrial Relations Act of Geoffrey Howe and Robert Carr. A host of City executives and academics, and notably Arthur Cockfield, toiled to produce a fiscal and monetary policy that would restore liberal economics and escape the thraldom of price, income and exchange control. The technical financial skills accumulated in Opposition fully matched the resources of the Treasury under Denis Healey.

Margaret Thatcher was not a commanding Commons speaker, certainly not equal to James Callaghan, but she was a formidable Party Leader. For her politics was not a game for amateurs: everything was played in earnest. This austere drive inspired the Parliamentary Party, and even more raised the morale of the Conservative activists in the country. Her rhetoric became sharper and more effective as she was able to tone down her natural shrillness. The Soviets dismissed her as 'the Iron Maiden'. She grasped the epithet and turned it into a compliment. The irony was that in many ways her commitment to firm government was reminiscent of her predecessor whom she had toppled. 'Ted Heath in drag' observed Denis Healey; but she was determined to succeed in economic and trade union policies where he had been ill served by fortune.

I don't notice I'm a woman. I regard myself as the Prime Minister.

'She had self-confidence and a deep sense that the Conservative politics of the Heath Government needed reversing.'

Lord Biffen

William Whitelaw and Margaret Thatcher – 1979 Conservative Party Conference.

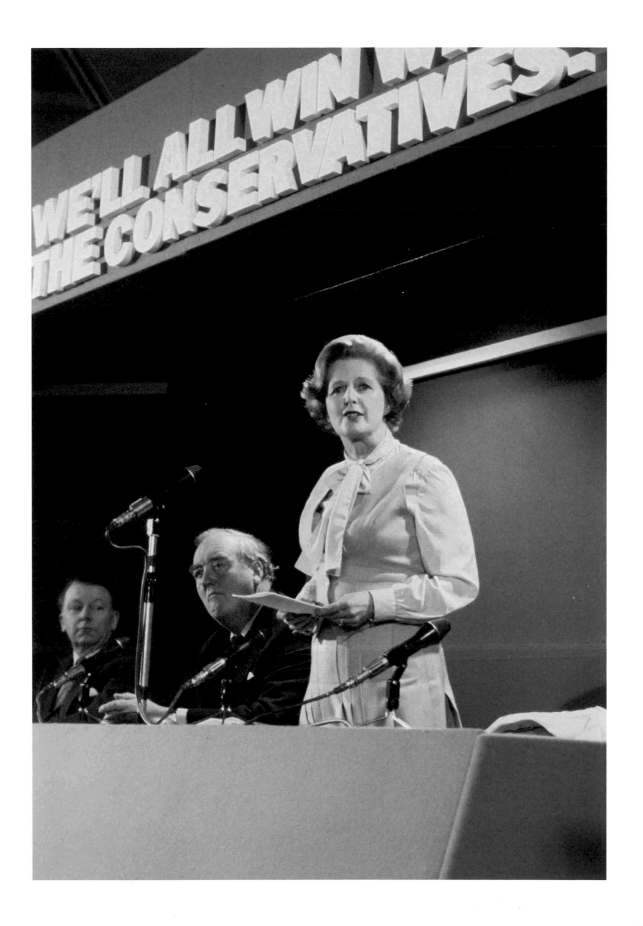

The redoubtable character of Margaret Thatcher became increasingly apparent in the early years of her premiership. Britain had a premier in a hurry. She was calculating and determined, placing her known supporters in the key Treasury and economic posts. The relative isolation of the pragmatists – later derided as 'Wets' – was a high-risk strategy; but it paid off. There were no resignations on account of policy, and the Cabinet was gradually reshaped with younger and more sympathetic members. Her Chancellor, Geoffrey Howe, loyally carried out the essential tenets of the new liberal economics. Exchange controls were abolished along with regulated prices and incomes. Public spending was stabilised and taxation was changed to enable income tax reductions to be financed by increases in Value Added Tax. It is no disparagement of Howe to say that he could not have achieved such major changes without the full-hearted support and prodding of his Prime Minister. No Cabinet cabal of spenders could prise apart the Downing Street partners. Alas it was not always to be the case.

Margaret Thatcher's single-mindedness was best demonstrated in the latter half of 1981. Unemployment had risen sharply; there were the usual government 'mid term blues'; the academic world was almost unanimous in calling for 'moderation' and a return to some kind of Keynesian economic policy. She persisted with her plans despite her growing adverse reputation for stubbornness. The sobriquet coined by Ronnie Millar, surely the decade's most elegant spinner, was 'the lady's not for turning'.

This view of her determined courage was emphasised by the Falklands dispute with Argentina. That conflict has been well documented. The task of recapturing the islands was a logistic nightmare. Success has subsequently created the false impression of comparative ease. Margaret Thatcher knew only too well the hazards of distance to the South Atlantic and the ambivalence of some of our NATO allies. Politically the campaign was conducted by a small inner Cabinet. There was general domestic political support for the venture but it would have been dissipated if there had been defeat or misfortune. Margaret Thatcher knew this and kept her nerve. There was no shortage of those who vainly sought a compromise settlement. If victory goes to the brave she certainly deserved her triumph. In the Commons, Enoch Powell – no stranger to courage and purpose – commented, 'Is the Right Hon. Lady aware that the report has now been received from the public analyst … It shows that the substance under test consisted of ferrous matter of the highest quality, that it is of exceptional tensile strength, is highly resistant to wear and tear and to stress, and may be used with advantage for all national purposes?'

There can be a nemesis which may mock the quality of determination and courage. Self-confidence becomes self-righteousness, and commitment becomes stubbornness and a vision becomes an obsession. Furthermore, as Churchill discovered, the British electorate is often short on gratitude. It was an experience that Margaret Thatcher suffered unhappily in her premiership between 1987 and 1990. One particular measure focused growing hostility – the community charge, popularly described as the 'Poll Tax'. The radical agitators took to the streets and incensed members of the middle classes bombarded Tory MPs with hostile

'The sobriquet coined by Ronnie Millar, surely the decade's most elegant spinner, was "the lady's not for turning".'

Lord Biffen

correspondence. Undeterred Margaret Thatcher pronounced the tax as the 'flagship' of Government policy and planned that it should raise more revenue than the rating system it was scheduled to replace. Such a reaction had panache but little electoral guile, ostensibly it was firm government but it lacked political touch.

We live too near the events to judge properly the various factors that impelled Margaret Thatcher to lose control of the Conservative Parliamentary Party. My instinctive judgement is that the Poll Tax was the major issue, not least because it had a lightning conductor attraction for other items of lesser discontent. Of course there were also major matters including the poor relations with the Chancellor, Nigel Lawson, and their divergent economic views. Her unhappy years with Geoffrey Howe over Europe have been well chronicled, and, though important, were not decisive in balancing Tory opinion in the Commons. At any rate a Prime Minister, however iron her resolution and fearless her politics, is unwise to quarrel simultaneously with her Chancellor and Foreign Secretary. The outstanding qualities of course that Margaret Thatcher bestowed upon the Conservative Party in the mid 1970s-80s simply had to be adjusted to meet Britain's changing economic and social circumstances. 'Not for turning' was no longer a compelling Thatcher slogan. Of course this reluctance to bend meant a somewhat poignant epitaph to her premiership, but it can never deny the overall quality of courage and perseverance that distinguish her politics.

Lord Mackay of Clashfern

LORD CHANCELLOR 1987–97

After a distinguished legal career in Scotland, James Mackay was raised to the Peerage in 1979. He served as Lord Advocate from 1979 until 1984 and then as Lord Chancellor from 1987 until 1997.

An offer I couldn't refuse

I HAD THE PRIVILEGE of being appointed to serve as Lord Advocate in Margaret Thatcher's first administration in May 1979. We had never met and my appointment was offered and accepted over the telephone. I was privileged to continue as Lord Advocate into her second administration when I became a Judge of the Supreme Courts of Scotland. On her recommendation I was appointed a Lord of Appeal in Ordinary, one of the two Scottish full-time judges in the House of Lords in October 1985.

In October 1987 I was listening to a debate in the House on the Criminal Justice Bill after the judicial sitting had terminated when I received a message from the Secretary of the then Leader of the House, Viscount Whitelaw, to ring urgently the Prime Minister's Private Secretary. That I did and was invited immediately to come over to meet the Prime Minister.

I duly went over to Number 10 thinking the Prime Minister had an inquiry of some kind that she wished me to undertake. Whenever I arrived at Number 10 I was ushered into the Prime Minister's study. She arose to welcome me, immediately asked me to sit down and sat in the chair opposite. She informed me that Lord Havers, the Lord Chancellor, had come to see her a little earlier that day and had tendered his resignation as Lord Chancellor on the grounds of ill health. She asked me to become Lord Chancellor in succession to him. As you can imagine, this was an extraordinary surprise and I answered that she knew my commitment to Sunday as a special day, to which she replied that she was also of the view that it should be a special day and that there would be no difficulty on that score. I then said that I would need to consult my wife but the Prime Minister knew better than any that when one is in an important public office there are profound effects for wife and family. She said 'Certainly, please go and ring her up', so I was duly presented with the telephone at the other end of the table from that at which we were sitting and I telephoned home, only to find that my wife was out. The Prime Minister said, 'We are very anxious to put the news out tonight of the new appointment along with Lord Havers' resignation and therefore I am very keen to have your answer as soon as possible.' I left promising to let her know as soon as I could.

As you can imagine, I kept ringing home to Edinburgh at frequent intervals and eventually my wife came in and when I told her my message she said, 'Oh well, you can hardly refuse that offer.' I duly telephoned to the Prime Minister's Private Secretary but he declined to take the message and put me through to the Prime Minister herself. I told her my wife's reply and in view of that reply I was happy and honoured to accept her invitation. She kindly said that she was delighted and that arrangements would be made for the intimation as soon as

Overleaf: Relaxing over a Prime Ministerial 'Red Box' in the Downing Street flat.

possible. The intimation was in fact made on the seven o'clock news that evening.

Shortly thereafter my wife was in London and we met the Prime Minister in Speakers' House. When we met I said to the Prime Minister, 'This was the lady for whose reply we were waiting the other day.' And with that charm and grace which was so characteristic of the Prime Minister she gave a very nice bow and said to my wife: 'We were very delighted with your reply.'

In the order of precedence which is established for State occasions the Lord Chancellor takes precedence immediately after the Archbishop of Canterbury, before the Archbishop of York and before the Prime Minister. I hope it is easy to imagine that I felt very embarrassed, and so did my wife, at the idea of preceding the Prime Minister. Again, her charm and grace always showed and on such occasions she would always encourage us to take our proper place in front of her, making it a lot easier for us to do so than if we had not been shown that charm. I remained as Lord Chancellor during the remainder of the tenure of Margaret Thatcher as Prime Minister and she was always most respectful and very clear about the importance of the Executive not interfering in the work and affairs of the judiciary.

Margaret Thatcher in 1980 striding past a military base in Cambridgeshire.

Baroness Cox

CONSERVATIVE PEER

Caroline Cox worked as a sociologist and in nursing education before being raised to the Peerage as Baroness Cox of Queensbury in 1983. She has been a Deputy Speaker of the House of Lords since 1986.

Surprise call

IN DECEMBER 1982 I received a telephone call 'out of the blue' asking me if I could spare the time to come down to Downing Street to meet the Prime Minister. With a mixture of excitement and terror, I asked if I might have some idea of the purpose of the meeting. With the prospect of meeting this formidable lady, I said that I would be very happy to come with an open mind but preferred not to come with an empty mind! I was advised that it was not possible to indicate the reason for the meeting but would I please be at Downing Street at 4.45pm the next day. Knocking on the black door with the golden 10, my knees were shaking; by the time I reached the waiting-room my mind was a 'white-out'. The only possible reason I could think for this invitation was a furious letter I had written to my MP about nurses' pay. At that moment I could not even remember a ward sister's annual salary!

Suddenly the doors opened and a charming man said, 'The Prime Minister will see you now.' I steered myself through the doors into 'the Presence'! Margaret Thatcher welcomed me graciously. She then said, 'Please sit down. I will come straight to the point because I believe in coming straight to the point.' I braced myself and she said, 'I am drawing up a list of names to go to Her Majesty the Queen for recommendations for life peerages. May I have your permission to put your name on that list?' It was a good thing I was sitting down or I would have fallen over backwards with astonishment.

She then said, 'In the Lords, I hope you will support us on education; I know you do not always agree with us on health. However, you always have freedom to speak and to vote according to conscience.'

She then said, 'I must ask you to treat this conversation in confidence until there is a press release next week. However, I expect all your family know you are here. You had better think of something to tell them. Why don't you just say that we had a little conversation about education?' She added, 'But you can tell your husband about the peerage, because spouses are different!'

I appreciated her thoughtfulness, thinking of the reception committee waiting for me at home. My children, their friends and neighbours all knew I had been to Downing Street and would be waiting eagerly for my return.

Lady Thatcher's anticipation of this situation enabled me to forestall the persistent questioning from my family. And by telling my husband I was able to come to terms with the shock of this offer which would transform my life.

I always profoundly respect Margaret Thatcher's principle of granting me the freedom to speak and vote according to conscience. Subsequently I took her at her word and not infrequently spoke and voted against the Government's policy. I believe that this principle is essential for the effective fulfilment of the role and

Please sit down. I will come straight to the point because I believe in coming straight to the point.

A 1983 portrait by June Mendoza.

responsibilities of the House of Lords as a refining and a revising Chamber. Without it, it becomes merely a politicised rubber stamp for the House of Commons.

I hope that present and future Prime Ministers will follow Lady Thatcher's example and respect the principle of the spirit of independent thinking and voting, for without it the importance and fundamental significance of the second Chamber is so profoundly diminished that its raison d'être will be destroyed!

We should back the workers, not the shirkers.

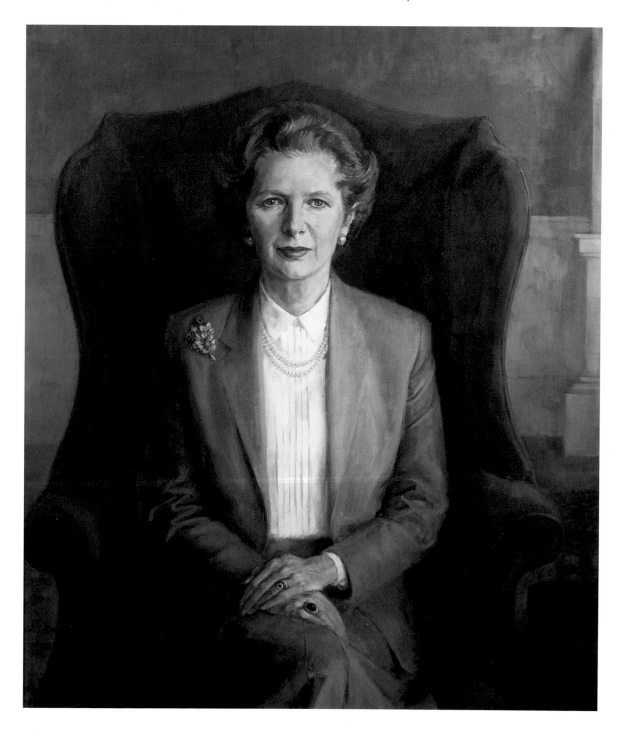

Javier Perez de Cuellar
SECRETARY OF THE UNITED NATIONS 1982–92

Javier Perez de Cuellar was Secretary General of the United Nations for a two-term period of office from 1982 to 1992.

The Baroness Thatcher

DEALING WITH A WOMAN at the height of power in a great European nation was something which immediately brought to my mind the great Elizabeth I, and was somewhat of a challenge for a newly appointed Secretary General of the United Nations.

My first acquaintance with the Prime Minister was on the occasion of the serious problem which arose in April 1982, following the Argentinian occupation of the Falkland Islands. Immediately I assumed that the Prime Minister would be concerned by the fact that the Secretary General of the United Nations was South American; I therefore made it a point of honour, as was my duty according to the Charter and my own conviction, to show total independence and impartiality.

From the beginning the Secretary of State, Alexander Haig, offered his good offices to both parties and kept me continually informed of the progress made. However, as is customary in the UN Secretariat, I decided to set up a small preventive working group comprising my immediate collaborators to put forward ideas to the parties involved, if necessary. When the endeavours of the United States proved fruitless, the British and Argentinian representatives agreed to continue within the framework of the United Nations. During this time it was clear that on the British side the Prime Minister was personally in charge of the British endeavours and we maintained indirect contact throughout. Although we were no more successful than the State Department, the rigorously technical manner in which the Secretary General contributed towards finding a peaceful solution to the difference of opinions was proof of the organization's complete impartiality, and I believe it was recognized as such by the British side.

I have to mention that when a military confrontation became unavoidable I received an unexpected telephone call from Mrs Thatcher, during which she asked me to do all I could to keep 'my boys' from being killed. I was moved to hear the voice of a mother. I must add that through various interviews with the Prime Minister I was able to appreciate her extraordinary intellectual capacity, her profound knowledge of the long-standing and arduous international problems affecting the international community, such as those of the Near and Middle East, and although we did not always agree, I admired the clarity of her position, at times inflexible, and her willingness to listen to the arguments of her interlocutors. She was indisputably a great stateswoman. Finally, let me say that I treasure the very kind letter she sent to me on giving up her office as Prime Minister, which I was so honoured and proud to receive.

In my view dictators do not surrender. They have to be well and truly defeated.

'I received an unexpected telephone call from Mrs Thatcher, during which she asked me to do all I could to keep "my boys" from being killed.'

Javier Perez de Cuellar

On a surprise visit to the Falklands in January 1983 Margaret Thatcher visits 'Y' Company of the 1st battalion of the Royal Hampshire regiment at Goose Green.

Sir Rex Hunt

GOVERNOR OF THE FALKLAND ISLANDS 1980–85

After an eventful colonial and diplomatic career, Sir Rex Hunt became the Governor of the Falkland Islands. He was present at the Argentinian invasion in 1982, removed by them and returned after liberation.

A welcome visit

THE LAST OF THE SERVICE CHIEFS to visit us in 1982 had been the Chief of Air Staff, Air Chief Marshal Sir Keith Williamson. He stayed in Government House and, on the first morning, asked to see me alone in my office. There he disclosed that the Prime Minister intended to visit the Islands from 8 to 12 January and handed me a letter from Sir Robert Armstrong, then Secretary of the Cabinet and Head of the Civil Service. Written in his own hand, with paragraphs and lines thoughtfully lettered and numbered to ease reply, Sir Robert stressed that security must be maintained and that the only person with whom I should discuss the programme was the Military Commissioner, Major General David Thorne. If news of the visit leaked out, it would be cancelled. He sketched a possible outline for a four-day visit, finishing with a postscript: 'The PM does not like much spare time on visits like this.' David and I mapped out a provisional programme and I sent it back in a handwritten letter to Sir Robert. He wrote again with a few further comments and told me to reply only if we disagreed. That was that. It was the easiest VIP programme I had ever arranged. Normally, and particularly where the military were concerned, such visits entailed weeks of preparation and discussion, with voluminous programmes and numerous printed revisions. For the Prime Minister, three handwritten letters sufficed.

It was not, of course, quite as simple as that for David, who was responsible for the Prime Minister's protection. On a strict need-to-know basis, he and his staff prepared a contingency plan 'for the visit of a VIP to the Falkland Islands'. No names or dates were mentioned, but it was planned for a Saturday arrival and Wednesday departure. The give-away was that one of the party was shown as 'VIP's wife/husband'.

As no announcement about the visit could be made beforehand, the journalists who would normally have accompanied the Prime Minister were to follow twenty-four hours later. There was a BBC television team in the Islands, led by Nicholas Witchell, but it had been there since before Christmas and was due to leave on 5 January, three days before the Prime Minister's arrival. That morning, I received a call from Bernard Ingham, the Prime Minister's Press Secretary, telling me to keep the team on the Islands but not to disclose the reason. I rang Nicholas at the Upland Goose, where he and his colleagues were happily packing, and asked him to come to my office. There I explained that something was likely to happen over the next week that he might wish he had stayed for and my advice was for him to postpone his departure. He said that must mean that we were expecting someone we wanted to see or someone we did not want to see; either way, he would stay (at the time, there were rumours that an Argentine intended to bring some next-of-kin to the Islands to pay homage to their dead). I think he guessed that the Prime

Freedom under the rule of law must never be taken for granted.

With Sir Rex Hunt, Governor of the Falklands, on her first visit to the islands in January 1983.

Minister was coming but, to his credit, he kept it to himself.

I told Mavis, of course, about our forthcoming guests, but we had to pretend to the staff that they were preparing for a party of journalists who could not be accommodated at the Upland Goose. In the village atmosphere of the Falklands, the slightest hint of an impending visit by the Prime Minister would have been flashed round the Islands by 'diddle-dee radio' within minutes and Don, for all his excellent virtues, would have been one of the first on the air. I hoped that he would forgive me for denting his reputation as a reliable newsmonger. I warned Patrick Watts and other local journalists to be at the airport by 4.30pm on Saturday, 8 January, but did not tell them who was coming.

As soon as Mrs Thatcher stepped off the Hercules, Patrick telephoned the FIBS studio, which interrupted its normal programme to announce her arrival. In the twenty minutes that it took Don to drive along the four miles of pot-holed airport road, the Stanley townsfolk flocked out of their houses and gathered along the route to welcome the Prime Minister. At her request, Don stopped at various points and she and Mr Thatcher got out and shook hands with scores of people. She said to one group, 'You were all marvellous,' to which Mike Bleaney, who was standing with young Daniel on his shoulders, replied, 'You didn't do too badly yourself, Ma'am!' As we passed near Harold Bennett's house, he came to the taxi window and handed Mrs Thatcher a single rose. His eyes were moist and he was too choked to speak. He turned away but the Prime Minister told Don to stop, jumped out of the taxi and hurried after him. I followed and introduced him. He still could not speak and I could see that Mrs Thatcher, too, was deeply moved as she thanked him for the rose. All along the route, the crowds had gathered. It seemed that the whole of Stanley had come out to greet her. For a normally undemonstrative community, it was a remarkable display of affection – spontaneous, sincere and from the heart.

The Prime Minister's party consisted of the Chief of Naval Staff, Admiral Sir John Fieldhouse, who had been the commander of the Task Force operations from April to June 1982, based at Northwood; her Principal Private Secretary, Robin Butler, who was later to take Sir Robert Armstrong's place as Secretary of the Cabinet and Head of the Home Civil Service; a Private Secretary, John Coles, who was seconded from the Diplomatic Service, Press Secretary Bernard Ingham and a duty clerk, Alan Logan. There was no security officer or personal detective. I showed Mr and Mrs Thatcher to their room and pointed out the Argentine bullet-holes in the ceiling. The Prime Minister elected to sleep in the bed beneath them. As she tidied up, Mr Thatcher came down to the small drawing-room and stood warming himself in front of the peat fire. Our first engagement was a briefing at HQ BFFI and I was surprised to see that he made no move to get ready. 'Oh, I can't come,' he said, 'I've not been security cleared.'

I ran through the programme with him and the secretaries who had now joined us, and pointed to one or two items that might be omitted if they thought that we had given the Prime Minister too much to do. I got a few rueful smiles in response and an assurance that she would fulfil every bit of the programme, and probably more. At the briefing, it was interesting to see the close rapport between the Prime

'You didn't do too badly yourself, Ma'am!'

Mike Bleaney

Minister and Sir John Fieldhouse and the detailed grasp that she had of military matters. Afterwards, we had a small dinner party at Government House with a few of the leading Islanders. There were only seventeen in all, but even this was a bit of a crowd for the small drawing-room. Nevertheless, that was where we stayed because the Prime Minister decided that she preferred it (as we did) to the main drawing-room. After the other guests had gone, she naturally gravitated to Mavis's chair beside the peat fire, kicked off her shoes and relaxed with a whisky and soda – a practice she was to follow each evening.

Sunday started with a visit to Stanley airport to see the RAF units and to visit the engineering works at the nearby quarry. The Royal Engineers were producing thousands of tons of crushed stone to build roads from the airport to the coastal sites along the Canache. The first coastel had arrived from Sweden in December on the *Ferncarrier*, a semi-submersible heavy-lift vessel, and we had hoped to have it in position in time for the Prime Minister to open, but the wind and tides had to be exactly right and the correct combination did not occur until the evening of her departure.

In the latter part of the morning, the Prime Minister attended a joint meeting of Executive and Legislative Councils, followed by lunch at Government House with councillors. They each expressed their thanks and undying gratitude to Mrs Thatcher for sending the Task Force and reiterated their loyalty to the Queen.

This picture was hung on the wall of Margaret Thatcher's Chesham Place offices. It depicts the final march on Port Stanley.

Looking to the future, they emphasised that Islanders had no wish to resume negotiations with the Argentines for as long as the Argentines equated negotiations with the transfer of sovereignty. They were grateful to Britain for providing the necessary security and for responding generously to Lord Shackleton's recommendations: they recognised that it was now up to Islanders to make the most of the opportunities thus created. Councillor Tony Blake urged the break-up of more of the larger farms and Councillor Tim Blake pressed for the development of the Islands' deep-sea fisheries by using the 150-mile protection zone in which to license fishing. Tim also explained the work of the Select Committee, of which he was chairman, on revising the constitution and the electoral procedure for the Islands and expressed the hope that proposals would be forwarded to HMG by July.

After lunch, the Prime Minister visited the Rookery Bay minefield and the Camber, where the Gurkha engineers, RAF Search and Rescue and several Royal Navy units were based, and then flew back across the harbour to see the Port Squadron of the Royal Corps of Transport, finishing a busy afternoon with a visit to the Field Post Office and the bakery. The latter was, literally, a museum piece. Used in the First World War, it had been taken out of an army museum and transported to the Falklands, where it performed magnificently until the troops moved to the Canache, after which it was returned to the museum. Parked under canvas between two FIC warehouses, it was a popular place to visit not only because of the appetising smell of freshly baked bread but also because it was the warmest place in town.

Before evensong in the cathedral, the Prime Minister laid a wreath at the cross of sacrifice for those Falkland Islanders who had lost their lives in the two World Wars. She had brought a number of wreaths from England, all beautifully made with flowers rarely seen in the Falklands. David was host for dinner that night in Britannia House.

Monday was, if anything, busier than Sunday. We visited four settlements in East Falkland and two in the West. At each place the Prime Minister gave speeches to the Islanders and to the troops and spoke to a large number of them individually. In order that she might meet as many Islanders as possible, David had kindly arranged for helicopters to bring them in from outlying settlements, so there was a large crowd (by Falklands' standards) wherever we went. Local journalists and the BBC team were joined by others from Britain who had flown in on the Sunday. Microphones and cameras were thrust in front of the Prime Minister at every opportunity and she sustained the barrage with unfailing good humour and patience. We travelled in a Sea King, with a Chinook for the Press and the infantry escort. Mrs Thatcher was welcomed with tremendous warmth wherever we landed, but none more so than at Goose Green, where the men, women and children who had been incarcerated in the community hall gave her three resounding cheers and gathered round to shake her hand and offer their personal thanks.

Brook Hardcastle and Eric Goss took us to the grave of Lieutenant Nick Taylor RN, where Mrs Thatcher laid one of her wreaths and Eric assured her that the

I am not wearing wellingtons to Captain Hamilton's grave.

people of the settlement would tend the grave with loving care for evermore. We then visited 'Y' Company of the 1st Battalion, the Royal Hampshire Regiment, accompanied by the battalion commander, Lieutenant-Colonel Hastings Neville. Sited near the remains of the old schoolhouse between Goose Green and Darwin, theirs was the first camp to be provided with Portakabins and was well on the way to completion. The Prime Minister was concerned about the welfare of the garrison and hoped that David's objective of having most of them out of tented accommodation by the onset of winter would be achieved.

From Goose Green we flew to Port San Carlos, where Alan Miller and his small band were sharing the settlement with the RAF Chinook detachment, the Harrier forward operating base and a platoon of the Royal Hampshires, and thence to San Carlos to lay a wreath at Blue Beach cemetery. Pat and Isabel Short provided lunch for the Prime Minister's party: after so many VIP visits they were becoming expert hosts. Indeed, I never ceased to admire Isabel for the seeming ease with which she adapted to the changed circumstances. Before the war, she had been extremely shy and retiring, but now she chatted easily to all and sundry, from the Prime Minister down. This I noted was a heartening characteristic of Islanders in general: they rose to the occasion, whether at home, like Isabel, or the UN, like John Cheek, or in London, like Lewis Clifton.

San Carlos Water was still protected by Rapiers, the crews of which lived in dug-outs reminiscent of the trenches in the First World War, but their morale could not have been higher, as the Prime Minister discovered. At Kelly's Garden, across the bay from San Carlos, the Royal Engineers were busily constructing a camp, which was intended to house the Chinook detachment and the headquarters of the ground air defence battery. Like most of the camps under construction, the biggest enemy was mud. We wore wellingtons as we splashed from hut to helicopter.

The Prime Minister refused to wear wellingtons for our next port of call, which was Port Howard cemetery. In fact, she was quite indignant when I suggested on the aircraft that she should put them on. 'I am not wearing wellingtons to Captain Hamilton's grave,' she said firmly, and promptly donned her best shoes. A Gurkha guard of honour presented arms as she walked through the mud to lay a wreath on Captain Hamilton's grave. I followed in my wellies, wondering whether a male Prime Minister would have been so sensitive.

After chatting to the people in the settlement, we flew from Port Howard to Fox Bay East, where Islanders from Fox Bay West, Port Stephens and Chartres had assembled. It was also the base for 'A' Company, the Royal Hampshires, whose camp was taking shape a little way up-river, at Doctor's Creek. Returning to the triangle after so many take-offs and landings, and so long in a noisy helicopter, I think that we were all feeling tired; within half-an-hour, however, we were changed and heading for a public reception at the Town Hall. On the short journey from Government House, I warned the Prime Minister that we had a surprise in store. Councillors had decided to confer upon her the freedom of the Falkland Islands, a unique honour in that only the freedom of Stanley had been awarded before (and that only to the Royal Marines and the West Yorkshire Regiment, which had been based there in the Second World War). Harold Rowlands, as the most senior kelper in the FIG, had been chosen to present the scroll; I would introduce him and we would both speak for no more than two minutes. She would be expected to say a few words in reply, but not to make a long speech.

The Town Hall was packed. There must have been 600 or more there, in a room normally considered crowded with 200 (indeed, the Director of Public Works was concerned that the floor might not take the weight). The atmosphere was electric and the Prime Minister perked up as soon as she entered: she was engulfed in a sea of grateful well-wishers and it took the best part of an hour to guide her through the crowd to the stage at the other end of the hall. I introduced Harold and stuck to my allotted two minutes. Harold was equally brief: describing the occasion as the greatest moment in his life, he said that he was echoing the sentiments of all Falkland Islanders in expressing his pleasure at being able to thank Mrs Thatcher in person for their liberation and pledged Islanders to build a better future to ensure that the war had been worthwhile and that British lives had not been lost in vain. He read out the formal proclamation, presented the scroll and then brought the house down by kissing the Prime Minister. Clearly elated, Mrs Thatcher made what many of the audience told me afterwards was the best speech they had ever heard. It lasted for twenty minutes, without notes or briefing (none of us had prepared any material for her), and touched exactly the right chord. She received the most enthusiastic reception ever witnessed in the Falkland Islands. The biggest cheer came when she said, 'Today again the Union Jack flies over Port Stanley, and may it ever fly there.' This had of course particular significance for me, for it was here in the Town Hall that General Garcia had told me that the Argentines would stay 'forever'. It was an intensely moving experience for us all, including the Prime Minister's party. Bernard Ingham came up afterwards and smothered me in a huge bear-hug. Dinner that evening was a lively affair, with all the day's fatigue banished. Indeed, though well past midnight, Mr Thatcher had difficulty in persuading the Prime Minister to go to bed.

Tuesday was largely a nautical day but, before flying to HMS *Antrim*, the Prime Minister visited the junior and senior schools, the hospital, the post office, the power station, PWD, the Brewster houses and the FIGAS hangar, where the Beaver was being reassembled. At sea, she went from HMS *Antrim* to the RFA *Fort Grange*, the *Stena Inspector* and HMS *Charybdis*, returning in the evening to give interviews to the *Penguin News* and the local radio. David was host at a tri-service dinner that night, which lasted until after midnight. Relaxing in front of the peat fire before going to bed, the Prime Minister suddenly said, 'I haven't seen a penguin. I must see a penguin before we leave.' As she was due to depart at 8am that morning, there was not much time to arrange a visit to a penguin colony. Then she added, 'And I should like to walk over Tumbledown.' I groaned inwardly. 'It will mean getting up at five, Prime Minister,' I said. 'That's fine,' she replied. After she and Mr Thatcher had retired, David organised a helicopter and I got hold of Ian Strange. We agreed that we should be able to fit in both Tumbledown and Seal Point before breakfast.

It was a miserable morning, blowing and raining. Undeterred, the Prime

Minister jumped into the Sea King and we landed in the wet on Tumbledown. Mr Thatcher urged her to put a scarf over her head, but she would have none of it. Although the dangerous ordnance had been removed, there was still plenty of evidence of the battle, sangars and foxholes festooned with bits of webbing, tattered clothes and the inevitable tubes of toothpaste. Surveying the difficult terrain in the wind and the rain, the Prime Minister marvelled that the Scots Guards had been able to storm the Argentine positions. From Tumbledown, we flew down to Seal Point, on the tip of Port Harriet, and the jackass penguins obliged the Prime Minister by coming out of their burrows and eyeing her curiously. Thanks to the helicopter, we were back at Government House and having breakfast by 7.15am.

Everything had gone without a hitch up till now; we had even managed to keep the Prime Minister's departure a secret. To convince the Press that she would not be leaving until the following day, one of the crew of her Hercules had been told to stay up late drinking with the journalists (who were sharing the Upland Goose with them). He played his part so well that, when the rest of the crew climbed out of their bedroom windows at 4.30am, he failed to surface and had to be quietly spirited away by his colleagues. Most of the Press had accepted an invitation to be flown on a wildlife tour for the day and were on their way to a penguin colony

Margaret Thatcher leans out of the window of Conservative Central Office, acknowledging the cheers of supporters on election night, June 1983.

when we escorted the Prime Minister to the airport. We bade our farewells and the Hercules door closed at precisely 8am. As it was raining hard, David and I sought shelter in the helicopter and sat waiting for the Hercules to take off. We were congratulating ourselves that everything had gone well when the intercom crackled and our pilot reported that the Hercules was taxiing back. Apparently all four engines had lost power as the pilot opened the throttles. There was no danger because he had scarcely started his take-off run; but it was worrying. David and I dashed out of the helicopter and across the apron to be at the foot of the steps again as the Prime Minister and her party disembarked. We waited in the Station Commander's Portakabin while the RAF decided what to do. The Prime Minister was naturally perturbed about losing precious time; her programme was as full as ever, with a big reception at Ascension on her way home (she had passed through unknown on the way down) and she wanted to be back in London for Question Time in the House of Commons the following afternoon. The choice lay between checking the faulty engines, which might have taken several hours, transferring the special caravan which had been fitted into the Prime Minister's aircraft, into the Press Hercules, or taking the Press Hercules as it stood. As switching the caravan would also have taken several hours, the Prime Minister elected to go in the Press Hercules, without trimmings. After almost an hour's delay, we said farewell a second time and breathed sighs of relief as the heavily laden Hercules lumbered off the runway and disappeared into the overcast skies. We had thoroughly enjoyed the visit, but another day at that pace would have been hard to bear. 'Early night, tonight, David,' I said, as we flew back to the triangle, with which he heartily concurred.

Before she left, Mrs Thatcher said that she had been deeply touched by the warmth and kindness of the welcome she had received everywhere she went and from everyone she had met. She knew that what was being expressed to her was the loyalty of the Falkland Islanders to Britain and their gratitude for the professionalism and gallantry of the Task Force in freeing them from the domination of a military invader. But that was only part of the story. What in truth the Islanders were expressing was their gratitude to Mrs Thatcher for sending the Task Force and never wavering in her determination to liberate the Islands. They believed that, had she not been the Prime Minister at the time, the Task Force would never have sailed and they would have been under Argentine domination 'forever'.

In coming 8,000 miles to meet the Islanders, the Prime Minister boosted morale as nothing else could. The citizens of shabby, shell-shocked Stanley needed a tonic and the Prime Minister's visit was the perfect medicine. It was fitting that she should come in the month that marked the 150th anniversary of continuous British settlement, the date by which the Argentines had determined that they would achieve sovereignty over the Islands. Her clear, unequivocal commitment to the Islanders both reassured them and instilled confidence in the future. Whatever other politicians or the Foreign Office might do or say, Islanders knew that they had a staunch champion at the helm in London.

Ronald Reagan

PRESIDENT OF THE USA 1981–9

After his career as a film actor and as Governor of California, Ronald Reagan became President of the USA in 1981 and held the office for two terms until 1989. His great friendship with Margaret Thatcher and their shared political priorities cemented relations between Britain and the USA throughout the 1980s.

Moral duty

ON A TRIP TO ENGLAND IN 1978 I bumped into Jason Dart, one of the Californians who'd been in my Kitchen Cabinet, and he said he wanted me to meet a friend of his who had recently been elected the first woman to head the British Conservative Party.

I'd been planning on spending only a few minutes with Margaret Thatcher but we ended up talking for almost two hours. I liked her immediately. She was warm, feminine, gracious and intelligent and it was evident from our first words that we were soul mates when it came to reducing government and expanding economic freedom. At a reception that evening, an Englishman who had heard about our meeting asked me: 'What do you think of our Mrs Thatcher?'

I said I'd been deeply impressed. 'I think she'll make a magnificent Prime Minister.'

He looked at me out of the corners of his eyes with a kind of mocking disdain

Above: The Reagans on a visit to Downing Street in June 1989.

Below: Margaret Thatcher and Ronald Reagan meet for the first time in the House of Commons in 1976.

that seemed to suggest the idea was unthinkable: 'My dear fellow, a woman Prime Minister?'

'England once had a queen named Victoria who did rather well,' I said.

'By jove,' he said. 'I'd quite forgotten about that.'

* * * * *

Throughout the eight years of my presidency, no alliance we had was stronger than the one between the United States and the United Kingdom. Not only did Margaret Thatcher and I become personal friends and share a similar philosophy about government, the alliance was strengthened by the long special relationship between our countries. The depth of this special relationship made it impossible for us to remain neutral during Britain's war with Argentina over the Falkland Islands, although it was a conflict in which I had to walk a fine line. After the landing on South Georgia island, Margaret Thatcher called me and said that Britain would never submit to a takeover of one of its crown colonies. She asked me to telephone Leopoldo Galtieri, President of the military junta that ruled Argentina, to urge him not to proceed with the invasion and to say that Britain would use whatever force was necessary to keep her colony. I spoke to Galtieri but couldn't budge him.

The junta misjudged not only Margaret Thatcher's will but the strength of our ties to England. We assured Margaret Thatcher that we were fully behind Britain. Margaret Thatcher, I think, had no choice but to stand up to the generals who cynically squandered the lives of young Argentinians solely to protect the life of a corrupt and iron-fisted totalitarian government. She did so, I believe, not because, as was speculated in Britain, her government might fall if she did not, but because she believed absolutely in the moral rightness of what she was doing and in her nation's obligation to guarantee the handful of people living in the Falklands the right of self-determination.

I am an undiluted admirer of American values and the American dream.

Left: Ronald Reagan and Margaret Thatcher take a press conference.

Right: Taking the salute with President Reagan on a visit to Washington DC in 1988.

Overleaf: Lady Thatcher reaches out to touch the flag-draped coffin of former US President Ronald Reagan as he lies in state in the rotunda of the US Capitol, 9 June 2004.

Major General Julian Thompson

BRIGADE COMMANDER DURING THE FALKLANDS CONFLICT

Julian Thompson served with distinction in the Royal Marine Commandos for many years, eventually rising to the rank of Major General. He is currently a Visiting Professor of War Studies at King's College.

And the lady loves …

FOLLOWING THE MARCH PAST of the representatives of the Falklands Task Force at the Mansion House in the City of London in Autumn 1982, a luncheon was held in Guildhall, hosted by the Lord Mayor of London attended by sailors, marines, soldiers and airmen of all ranks. After lunch, the Prime Minister, Mrs Thatcher as she was then, rose to speak. Before she began, there was a prolonged, spontaneous standing ovation, cheering and clapping for her, led by the junior ranks in Guildhall without any encouragement or lead being given by the officers present, but quickly taken up by all of us with the greatest enthusiasm; we wanted to show our affection for her. I was sitting opposite some of the members of her Cabinet, who were open-mouthed in astonishment. We adored her, and would have done anything for her. In all my years' service, I have never seen anything like it. In the last hundred years, I can think of no politician except Winston Churchill who struck such a chord with servicemen, who usually have no time for politicians.

Some years later, Margaret Thatcher, still Prime Minister, attended an exercise involving the SBS boarding a 'target' ship. There was an advertisement around at the time featuring a man overcoming a series of difficult obstacles, all with the aim of carrying a box of Cadbury's Milk Tray to his lady love. I decided that the SBS would follow his example, and they entered into the plot with enthusiasm. The storming of the target was a great success, culminating in an SBS operator stepping forward, unzipping the top of his wet suit, and presenting the Prime Minister with a box of Cadbury's Milk Tray. She was surprised but delighted, and when one of her aides tried to take it off her, she rebuffed him, saying that the chocolates were for her, and no one else. We all loved her for calmness in the face of one or two potentially unnerving moments on that particular exercise, her enthusiasm, and, dare one say it, because she is an extremely handsome lady. We appreciated that too.

Enjoying a joke in *Anyone for Denis?* at the Whitehall Theatre, 1981

Left: Taking control of a tank on a visit to Germany with Helmut Kohl.

Viscount Tonypandy

SPEAKER OF THE HOUSE OF COMMONS 1976–83

Secretary of State for Wales under Harold Wilson, the distinguished parliamentarian George Thomas was elected Speaker of the House of Commons in 1976. After his resignation in 1983 he was created First Viscount Tonypandy and sat in the House of Lords until his death in 1997.

Test of her mettle

IN MID 1982 THE QUEEN GAVE A STATE BANQUET for the Reagans at Windsor Castle, where I renewed my acquaintance with Mrs Reagan, whom I had met at the wedding of Prince Charles and Lady Diana the year before.

The banquet itself was a considerable strain for Mrs Thatcher and those of us who knew that there had been very heavy losses in Bluff Cove as Welsh Guardsmen were being landed prior to the taking of Port Stanley on the Falklands. The news had not yet been released and that was the only time I saw Mrs Thatcher show any real sign of strain during the whole Falklands campaign.

I think that had a man been Prime Minister, he would probably have lost his nerve long before. Any man would have gone back to the United Nations to make sure he was not going to be ostracised by the world community, in much the same way as the Opposition were putting themselves in the clear if things went wrong. Britain would have lost all influence in international affairs if Mrs Thatcher had submitted to the pressures and gone back to the United Nations. It would have meant that never again would Britain take any decisive action to defend her

> *I am not a consensus politician. I am a conviction politician.*

Margaret Thatcher's new Cabinet in June 1983.

The Prime Minister on a factory visit in 1985.

people. The Prime Minister showed remarkable courage and determination throughout the whole of the tragedy, and she knew tragedy was inevitable once the islands had been invaded by Argentina. But by her action she saved the good name of Britain.

The whole exercise showed that British youth, who never thought they would have to do that sort of thing again, could respond magnificently to the challenge. The Falklands affair reinforced my belief that the British character has not really changed, despite all the troubles that we face with violence and sometimes appallingly selfish behaviour. We are still a tough little race, and now the world knows it.

Lord Armstrong of Ilminster

SECRETARY TO THE CABINET 1979–87

Robert Armstrong joined the Civil Service in 1950 serving in numerous senior positions both within the Treasury, Home Office and Cabinet Office, eventually rising to be Head of the Home Civil Service in 1981. He currently sits as a cross-bencher in the House of Lords.

A call from the White House

ONE AFTERNOON IN MAY 1982, during the war in the Falkland Isles, the telephone rang on my desk. It was the National Security Adviser in Washington: would I please set up the 'hot line', as the President wanted to speak to the Prime Minister? I told the Prime Minister's Private Secretary that the President would be calling to speak to the Prime Minister, activated the 'hot line', and went through to Number 10 for the call.

The conversation began with the usual exchange of pleasantries about health and weather, customary even in such high level conversations, and then the President asked how things were going in the South Atlantic. This was something that the Prime Minister had at her fingertips, and she spoke well and fluently for about a quarter of an hour. Then the President began to speak. After two or three sentences he asked another question. The Prime Minister took the opportunity of dealing with a few points which she had not been able to cover in her first exposition and responded, once again speaking well and fluently for another fifteen minutes. She then thanked the President for his call, expressed her gratitude to him and to the United States Government for their help and support, promised to keep him posted on future developments, said good-bye and replaced the receiver.

Not long afterwards I met the National Security Adviser, and I said that we had been a little mystified by the President's call and did not quite know what it was all about. He laughed, and said: 'We shan't try that again.' 'What do you mean?' I said. He said: 'Well, we had a message to convey which we thought that the Brits would find unhelpful, so we figured that it had better be conveyed by the President to the Prime Minister. The trouble was, the President couldn't get a word in edgeways.'

Many years later I happened to meet another American official who had been one of those who were in the Oval Office when this exchange took place. He told me that, during the Prime Minister's second exposition, the President had taken the receiver away from his ear and held it out in front of him so that they could all listen, saying as he did so: 'Isn't she marvellous?'

I think – though she never said as much – that the Prime Minister had a shrewd suspicion that the President was calling in order to convey some unpalatable message, and was not averse to the thought of making it difficult for him to do so.

> *'Well, we had a message to convey which we thought that the Brits would find unhelpful, so we figured that it had better be conveyed by the President to the Prime Minister. The trouble was, the President couldn't get a word in edgeways.'*
>
> Lord Armstrong

Margaret Thatcher entering Number 10 Downing Street in May 1979.

Lord Hamilton of Epsom

MARGARET THATCHER'S PPS 1987–8

Archie Hamilton was Member of Parliament for Epsom and Ewell from 1978 to 2001. After serving as a Government Whip and as Parliamentary Under Secretary of State for Defence Procurement he became Margaret Thatcher's Parliamentary Private Secretary (PPS) in 1987, remaining with her until 1988 when she made him a Minister of State at the Ministry of Defence. He was raised to the Peerage in 2005.

Life with the leader

I FIRST MET MARGARET THATCHER when she came as Leader of the Opposition to support me in my by-election in 1978 when I was first elected as MP for Epsom and Ewell.

At the end of a full day of walkabouts and opportunities to meet my prospective constituents, we had a press conference. The questions from our local newspapers were not exactly challenging and the last one was particularly sycophantic.

'Mrs Thatcher, it looks very much as if you might win the forthcoming General Election. If you do, will you find a place for Archie Hamilton in your government?'

I was expecting a reply that, while being non-committal, would sing the praises of the candidate hoping to enter Parliament. Not a bit of it.

'Oh no! It's much too early to consider that.'

Knowing her as I now do, I suspect that she was much more concerned about appearing to take the outcome of the forthcoming election for granted, than being committed to having Archie Hamilton in her government.

* * * * *

I was PPS to Margaret Thatcher as Prime Minister for the fifteen months following the 1987 Election.

We were sitting one evening in her rooms in the House of Commons and she raised the question of women priests in the Church of England. Although brought

Obviously one isn't indestructible – quite.

Electioneering in May 1983, Margaret Thatcher buys some paté saying, 'I hope there's no garlic in it!'

up a Methodist, she had become an Anglican and was troubled that ordaining women would split the Church.

I took issue with her and argued that as a woman Prime Minister she really could not be seen to be against women entering the priesthood.

'Anyway,' I said, 'I don't know why you are so worried. I think women are capable of greater spirituality than men and also they are less inclined to succumb to sexual temptation.'

'Oh, I don't know about that,' said the Prime Minister.

As with so many arguments, she would never cede any ground and, on occasions, one was left wondering whether one had gone too far and upset her.

It was a week later that I read a short excerpt in the paper, headed 'Thatcher backs women priests'.

* * * * *

Weekdays in Number 10 started with a meeting to discuss forthcoming events and what was in the newspapers.

Staff in Bernard Ingham's press office must have got up very early to produce an extraordinarily succinct summary of all the stories in the newspapers on a couple of sides of foolscap. Closely argued articles from the broadsheets would be reduced to three lines.

I asked Margaret Thatcher one day whether she ever read the daily papers.

'Oh no!' she replied. 'They make such hurtful and damaging remarks about me and my family, that if I read the papers every day, I could never get on with the job I am here to do.'

Some years later, when John Major was Prime Minister and having serious problems with the press, I repeated Margaret Thatcher's remark to him.

He did not respond but just gave me one of those pitying looks that people reserve for the feeble-minded.

* * * * *

Margaret Thatcher did not read the daily papers but she invariably studied the Sundays during her weekends at Chequers.

She always took great heart from Woodrow Wyatt's articles in the *News of the World*.

Monday morning meetings with Cabinet colleagues often started with the Prime Minister saying 'Did you see Woodrow's marvellous article in the *News of the World*?' Many Cabinet Ministers found that it became almost compulsory to add the *News of the World* to their Sunday morning reading.

* * * * *

As her Parliamentary Private Secretary, I used to sit behind Margaret Thatcher at Cabinet meetings, on a chair against the wall.

On the whole, Cabinet meetings were rather formal and dull affairs, and policy formulation was reserved for smaller ad hoc meetings with Cabinet Ministers and Cabinet sub-committees.

At these meetings the Prime Minister dispensed with preamble and launched into the contentious elements of the policy paper, often with the help of a briefing from the Policy Unit, in which she had highlighted the most significant passages.

On one occasion, a heated argument ensued between her and a favoured Cabinet Minister. This prolonged and acrimonious discussion left everyone exhausted and some rather bruised.

Finally, she announced: 'Of course, I agree with everything you are trying to do here. I just wanted to play devil's advocate to ensure that you were prepared for all the counter-arguments.'

* * * * *

Margaret Thatcher was always known to be an avid listener of the *Today* programme, which she had on the radio whilst she got up.

I remember her telling me that the coverage of *Today* regularly infuriated her husband Denis, and she used to hear him shouting 'Bastards!' as he lay in bed, listening to the programme.

* * * * *

Margaret Thatcher had a rather odd belief that it was impossible to write a speech for the Party Conference until the conference itself was underway and the 'atmosphere' of the gathering had been accurately assessed.

The result was that most of her conference speech had to be written at the end of a series of hard days among the Party faithful and would stretch on until the early hours of the morning. Contributions came in from all and sundry but invariably only small bits were selected with the rest being torn up by the Prime Minister amid cries of 'Nothing fresh here!'

* * * * *

There was an occasion when one of Margaret Thatcher's Cabinet Ministers had asked himself to Sunday lunch at Chequers. The Prime Minister did not want to be subjected to unremitting pressure from this man for most of her Sunday, so she asked me, as her PPS, to join the two of them, plus Denis, for lunch.

I gladly accepted the invitation, although slightly worried that I was neglecting my family at home.

A few days later, the Prime Minister realised that her invitation might have disrupted a family weekend.

'Why don't you bring your wife Anne too?' she asked.

'The problem is, Prime Minister', I replied, 'that she has our three teenage daughters at home that weekend.'

'Bring them all,' she said.

Later on, life was made even more complicated when it became apparent that my youngest fourteen-year-old had also invited a friend home from school.

'I am afraid Prime Minister that my youngest daughter has invited her friend Abigail for the weekend as well.'

'Bring her too!'

I admired the Secretary of State who arrived for what he imagined was to be a tête-à-tête with the Prime Minister only to be confronted with the Hamilton family and a row of teenage girls. It must have resembled a scene out of St Trinians. Not a flicker of emotion crossed his face; he was charm itself.

Conversation at the ensuing meal was somewhat strained. The Minister struggled in vain for a hearing, as one daughter, in that uncompromising teenage mode which is determined not to be overawed, rolled up her sleeves, and putting her elbows on the table, embarked on what seemed an interminable anecdote. The PM drummed her fingers on the table, while another daughter, benefiting from the adult distraction, dipped her finger in the jug of cream. Her friend Abigail sat immobilised as if she were a rabbit caught in the headlights.

It crossed my mind that Mrs Thatcher might have regretted her generous invitation.

* * * * *

To understand the exceptional qualities of Margaret Thatcher as a politician, one should think of her as an evangelical.

She was born a woman with immense powers of concentration, a prodigious memory and an exceptionally analytical mind.

What made her one of the greatest Prime Ministers of the last century was the conviction with which she drove her policies and the way she was prepared to risk serious short-term unpopularity for doing things which she knew were right in the long-term.

Although prepared ultimately to compromise, she always dragged the argument further than most into her own territory.

I often wondered whether her determination to press her own point of view could be attributed to the fact that she was a woman. All I do know is that all the men I have met and worked with in politics have shown themselves more ready to compromise than she.

With Foreign Secretary Sir Geoffrey Howe at the launch of the 1984 Conservative manifesto for the European parliamentary elections.

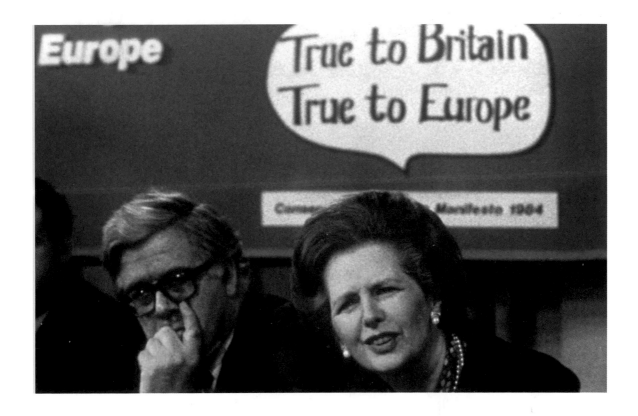

Edward Pearce
AUTHOR AND JOURNALIST

Until recently, a columnist for the *Scotsman* and former Commons sketch writer for the *Daily Telegraph*, Edward Pearce has published twelve books including *Machiavelli's Children*, *The Lost Leaders* and a biography of Denis Healey.

Personal kindness and public outburst

PERSONALLY, UNLIKE MOST CONTRIBUTORS to this book, I am not a fan of the Lady – too rigid, too narrow, too full of animus, a sort of Protestant ethic gone rogue. Oddly, she was so much better with what we inadequately call 'ordinary people' than with coadjutors. There is a nice story about custard. At a Cabinet dinner, a very inexperienced and frightened young waitress spilt a great dish of custard all over Geoffrey Howe. Instead of berating her, or going all steely silent, Margaret threw her arms round the girl and said 'My dear, you mustn't cry. Anyone could have an accident,' and to Geoffrey Howe, who was ineffectively sponging away at his suit, 'Geoffrey! Stop making such a fuss.'

It could be, of course, that the victim being Geoffrey, between whom and herself there was something of a sympathy deficit, charitable feeling came very easily. But it shows her very nicest side and wasn't the only example.

When her chauffeur died, she didn't send a card, she went to the funeral in person. Contrast, under the next Conservative regime, the death of Giles Shaw. He was a Minister of State, a former serious candidate for the Speaker's chair and very widely liked. The only sitting MP at his funeral in Yorkshire was Tam Dalyell!

I saw most of Margaret Thatcher in Opposition and really rather liked her. Pity about the politics. Actually I mean that seriously. She did behave well enough and pretty nicely away from politics. The excesses came with the Party struggle. After all, Neil Kinnock isn't a communist, but Maggie thought he was and said so in the Commons. 'He is a Marxist, a crypto-communist.' It was an unbelievable remark, but instructive. The good nature and manners of ordinary life would regularly be swept away in the political context, but so was all sense, sophistication and judgment.

The same is true of that outburst on TV, instantly recalled and apologised for – 'drooling and drivelling about the poor'. It is one thing to be hard-headed, but that spoke a partisan rage beyond party, directed rather at a class. Would she ever have embarked on the Poll Tax which fell so heavily on the claimant, canned beer-drinking, football-watching, undeserving part of mankind if the 'drooling and drivelling' outlook hadn't been an underground stream in her nature? Like I said, a Protestant ethic gone rogue.

Class was central with her and I'm not alone in noticing. At a seminar at Durham about five years ago I set out before lunch the notion of Margaret Thatcher, class warrior. Alan Clark, her great fan, breezed in on time for what he would have called 'pudding', and afterwards launched himself onto the thesis. 'It's

My job is to stop Britain going red.

'My dear, you mustn't cry. Anyone could have an accident,' and to Geoffrey Howe who was ineffectively sponging away at his suit, 'Geoffrey! Stop making such a fuss.'

Margaret Thatcher

Margaret Thatcher looking suitably trenchant at the 1980 Conservative Party Conference.

all absolute crap, of course, to talk about liberal market theory. What Margaret is on about is the Class War.'

I don't mind the fierceness. Where Blair cringes, she bops and when she does, sometimes you find yourself at the other end of the telescope approving!

I was at a dinner for her in 1985 where Charles Moore was attacking the new Anglo-Irish agreement, 'Robert Armstrong's revenge' as some of us called it. 'What about the Protestants?' he asked in the odd Orange way of so many English Catholics. She leaned into the table and in her best, taut, intense, Puff the Magic Dragon way, said 'Yes, Charles and what about the Catholics?' She had heard John Hume's great speech not long before she was actually listening to people like Armstrong. Consequently all the fierceness which she would misuse in hating the Germans and despising the unemployed, was turned towards getting a decent equity for the minority. It was wonderful.

'Am I no a bonny fighter?' asks Alan Breck. Yes indeed but too much so in Margaret Thatcher's case. For she started fighting her own side. When a leader of a party creates factionalism, as she did in her last two years – and during the term of her successor when she called in backbenchers to bully them into voting against the Tory whip – it is simply ruinous. For a head of government to summon a seminar to collectively analyse the character faults of a notably friendly neighbour, Germany, was to do something against reason. And in politics, whatever the joys of raging conviction, reason has its uses.

She was 'the little girl with a curl, right in the middle of her forehead'. And you know how that ends.

With Chinese premier Deng Xiaoping in the Great Hall of the People in Beijing, before signing the Anglo-Chinese Agreement on the future of Hong Kong in 1984.

John Redwood
CONSERVATIVE MP

After a successful career as an academic and then in banking, John Redwood became the head of Margaret Thatcher's Policy Unit in 1983 and remained there until 1985. In 1987 he became the MP for Wokingham, rising rapidly until he joined John Major's Cabinet as Secretary of State for Wales in 1993. He resigned in 1995 to fight for the leadership of the Conservative Party, a position he fought again for in 1997.

Testing the argument

I ALWAYS REMEMBER MY FIRST ENCOUNTER with Margaret Thatcher. As Leader of the Opposition she had heard that I had set out a number of proposals to privatise Britain's unprofitable, unhelpful, unfriendly, lumbering nationalised industries. I was added to the guest list for one of her lunches in the Shadow Cabinet Room at the House of Commons. The main intellectual dish of the day was devolution. Margaret was about to go to the House to raise just this issue. I watched as a range of constitutional experts told her their thoughts, only to see her more than a match for them, well briefed, deadly in her questions. Now I realise she was fired up and a little nervous before appearing in the House. Then it was quite a spectacle to see such a powerful senior politician in full flight, clearly the mistress of her brief, able to deal with professors and advisers with forceful points and searching questions.

I steeled myself for the challenge. I knew my turn was to come soon. After what seemed like an age discussing devolution, where I kept well out of the fray, she turned to me to hear my thoughts on privatisation. I had soon grasped from watching and listening to the previous conversation that you had to be quick and make your best points while you still had the chance. Once you allowed your flow to be interrupted and the questions to begin you were going to be thrust on the defensive. I marshalled my best points. I was sure the position I had adopted was proof against the most forceful of counter-attacks. The questions soon came thick and fast and I held my ground. I was beginning to enjoy it, realising that if you could withstand the barrage you might even shift her position. As the nerves went and the determination increased, Margaret Thatcher decided she had had enough as it was not the subject of the day. With a crushing 'That's all very well, Mr Redwood, but they'll never let me do that,' I realised my time was up and we were on to the next question.

That first encounter fascinated me. Whilst I could see what many saw, that here was a strong-minded lady who was powerful in argument and gave no quarter, it also struck me very forcefully that here was someone really interested in the issues who was learning by the clash of different opinions. It was, to adapt a phrase she made famous about someone else, 'someone I could do business with'.

I went away realising that if privatisation was to turn from the dream of a few to the reality of the many, we needed to create a climate of opinion in which Margaret Thatcher's political judgment sensed it was possible or safe to do it. Here was a canny, cautious, even defensive politician who often judged the mood of the nation well and was only going to lead them up to a point. Like all great leaders she

We Conservatives do not accept that because some people have no choice, no one should have it.

knew that on many occasions she had to follow rather than lead. In a democracy the leader has to accept that there are limits to how far he or she can take the people, and an absolute prohibition on leading them in certain directions at all.

This first encounter had prepared me well for many meetings, arguments, debates, discussions and exchanges which I had with Margaret Thatcher when I became her Chief Policy Adviser after the 1983 General Election. It was satisfying to put to her a memorandum saying that in her second period as Prime Minister she now had the political strength and the financial and economic necessity to get on and privatise large chunks of the public industrial and service sector. It was a pleasure to find that now a lot of the caution and the worry had abated. Now the issue was not 'will the public buy it?' but 'how can we do it technically?' By 1983 Margaret Thatcher rightly sensed that the main problem was no longer public opinion, which was ready for some drastic changes to get Britain on the move again, but opinion in the City which was extremely cautious.

Doing business ... Margaret Thatcher meets Mikhail Gorbachev at Chequers for the first time in 1984.

When I went round the City trawling opinion from my Number 10 base it was a disappointment to discover that many in the City strongly held the view that to sell something worth several billion pounds on the Stock Market was a technical impossibility. They believed that equity issues could not be larger than a few hundred million pounds and were strongly against selling shares in British Telecom. They preferred the idea of bonds to finance it in a different way. I proposed to Margaret Thatcher that we could overcome these difficulties with a new structure, selling shares direct to the public by mail order and newspaper advertisements, and selling to overseas interests at the same time as selling some of them through the conventional brokers and banks in the City. She saw the point and became excited by the possibilities and gave me the backing I needed at the Treasury and in the City.

The whole privatisation story illustrated Margaret Thatcher at her best. At first her caution was demonstrated by tough argument. She believed in testing people out, almost to destruction, to see if they could stand their ground. She knew that she would have to stand her ground in a very public way and wanted to make sure that those advising her really did believe in the idea and had thought it through.

It showed her brutal honesty in judging the public mood and judging what the obstacles were at the time. Finally, it showed that she was indeed prepared to change her mind as others helped her make the case and overcome the obstacles.

Throughout the years that I worked for Margaret Thatcher in one capacity or another, the thing that never ceased to amaze me, apart from her remarkable energy, was her constant striving for the truth and her constant willingness to change her mind. It could take months to get her to make a decision on a big issue. She would be argumentatively indecisive for long periods. It was because she knew that with her style of politics once she had committed herself to something and went public she had to fight it through all the way. She combined caution with radicalism in a quite remarkable way which enabled her to stay at the top of British politics for so long. It also meant that when people come to write the history of Britain in the twentieth century, with the benefit of some perspective they will see that, unlike many other Prime Ministers, she did have a general vision, a sense of direction, and she did find the measures and the men to help her carry it through in many important respects.

Privatisation may well go down as her greatest success. From modest beginnings it took off after the sale of BT. It spread around the world. The most unlikely people became converts, from the Labour governments of New Zealand and Australia, through the former communist states of Eastern Europe, to Fidel Castro's Cuba. It even eventually permeated the UK Labour Party, where a UK Labour government is now privatising Air Traffic Services, a bridge too far for the Conservative administration.

Margaret Thatcher came to see the connection between privatisation, wider ownership and every man a shareholder. She came to enthuse over it, as she had over her very successful campaigns to sell council houses to their tenants. It was a pleasure to take her such an idea, it was exhilarating to argue it through with her, and exciting to see it come to fruition.

Lord Deedes

JOURNALIST

W F Deedes is a veteran *Daily Telegraph* journalist and columnist. Sir Denis Thatcher was one of his best friends. He was a Cabinet Minister in Harold Macmillan's Government.

Diplomatic incidents

ON THE NIGHT OF 19 MAY 1982 Margaret Thatcher as Prime Minister gave a dinner at 10 Downing Street for the Duke and Duchess of Kent and Prime Minister Muldoon of New Zealand, who was paying us a friendly visit. It was the eve of the contentious Falklands war. On our arrival just before 8pm, both Mrs Thatcher and her then Foreign Secretary, Francis Pym, were unsurprisingly missing.

'Talk to Muldoon,' Denis Thatcher ordered me, 'and keep talking.' Dinner was late, awaiting our hostess. I sat between Mrs Thatcher and the renowned singer, Kiri Te Kanawa, an easy companion because we shared an interest in golf. The Prime Minister engaged Muldoon, who was sitting on her right.

As the main course arrived, a long message was brought to Mrs Thatcher. She read it, pencilled some notes and returned it. 'Awkward,' she said to me. 'United Nations will be on the telephone at 9.45pm. It will interfere with the speeches.' She sent a message suggesting that UN call at 10.30.

The only sign of her abstraction was that her wrist watch had stopped. She had forgotten to wind it. Then, putting UN on one side, she resumed talking to Mr Muldoon about figures they liked and disliked on the international scene. Muldoon had just returned from Dublin, where he visited Ireland's Prime

> *'The only sign of her abstraction was that her wrist watch has stopped. She had forgotten to wind it.'*
>
> Lord Deedes

Caddying for Denis at Chequers in 1980.

Denis and Margaret enjoying a local brew, with Malcolm Rifkind in the background.

Minister, Charles Haughey. His government had declined to support sanctions against the Argentine. It was not Haughey's wish, he explained to Muldoon, but his people 'had insisted on it'. From Mrs Thatcher's face I judged Charles Haughey stood in low esteem.

With the coffee, a message then arrived at our table from UN in New York. They would call at 10.30pm. Margaret Thatcher rose and delivered a polished speech of welcome to the Prime Minister and her royal guests. The Foreign Office had given her the date of our first import of lamb from New Zealand. This was the only note she used.

Prime Minister Muldoon rose to the occasion. This was a family business, he declared, and spoke of our good fortune in having the right leader at the right time. He would make his nation's contribution and pledged the gift to us of a destroyer – a gesture not universally approved back in New Zealand, we learned subsequently. It went down well in the company assembled at Number 10.

In the distant past, I reflected, I have occasionally sent flowers to my hostess in return for dinner. Presenting a destroyer was original, probably unique. Duty fulfilled as hostess, Margaret Thatcher retired with her Foreign Secretary and chiefs of staff to deal with UN.

I admired the steely self-control of her performance that evening, the more because I knew that along with it there lurked an altogether softer side to her nature. We saw it a couple of years later, after the IRA had attempted to murder her at Brighton by blasting her hotel during the Party Conference of 1984.

One Sunday soon afterwards, a beautiful autumn day, Margaret Thatcher emerged from church in tears. 'It went through my mind,' she said by way of explanation, 'that this was a day I was not meant to see.'

Marxists get up early to defend their cause. We must get up even earlier to defend our freedom.

Lord Butler of Brockwell

CABINET SECRETARY 1988–98

Robin Butler served in numerous positions in the Home Civil Service from 1961 onwards but is best remembered as the Principal Private Secretary to Margaret Thatcher from 1982 until 1985, and as Cabinet Secretary and Head of the Home Civil Service from 1988 to 1998. He currently sits as a cross-bencher in the House of Lords.

'It's what they would want'

MY DOMINANT RECOLLECTION of working with Margaret Thatcher was the certainty of her instinctive reactions. When the IRA bomb exploded in the Grand Hotel Brighton at ten to three in the morning on the last day of the Conservative Party Conference in 1984, I was with her in the sitting-room of her suite at the Grand Hotel. She had just finished her conference speech and I had given her a paper on which a decision was needed by start of business next morning. Denis had gone to bed next door.

When the bomb went off, I thought it was a car bomb outside. I said to her, 'We should move away from the windows.' As we went across the room we could hear the noise of collapsing masonry through the bedroom door.

Without hesitation she said, 'I must see if Denis is alright.' She opened the bedroom door, whereupon the noise of structural collapse became louder, and she disappeared into the darkness. I paused in the sitting-room, wondering what I should say to the tribunal of inquiry if she was killed by the collapsing building. To my relief she and Denis emerged almost immediately, Denis pulling on some clothes over his pyjamas.

We then moved into the corridor. Miraculously the lights had stayed on. (Thereafter Margaret Thatcher carried a torch in her handbag in case the same thing happened again – she always learned from experience.) Some others joined us and we began to debate what we should do next. I suggested returning to London – only one hour away.

Margaret Thatcher said, 'I'm not leaving the area.' The decision was then taken out of our hands by the arrival of a fireman who – after one false start – led us down the main staircase and out of the back of the hotel, not without Margaret Thatcher breaking off to ask whether all the staff in the foyer were accounted for.

We were taken to the training accommodation at Lewes Police Station where the Thatchers were allocated bedrooms. At that stage I did not know that the bomb had been in the upper part of the building or that anyone was missing. I lay on the bench in the day room at 5am. At 5.45 the telephone rang. It was John Gummer, then Chairman of the Party. He said, 'It's worse than we thought. The Tebbits, the Wakehams and others are trapped in the collapsed building.'

I decided not to wake Margaret Thatcher but turned on the television to watch the news, including Norman Tebbit being brought out. Margaret Thatcher appeared just after 8; she had seen the news on a television in her room. 'We must make sure the Conference re-starts on time,' she said. I was appalled. I said, 'Surely you can't go on with the Conference when your colleagues and friends are

I went to Oxford, but I've never let that hold me back.

Margaret Thatcher at Battersea Power Station in 1988.

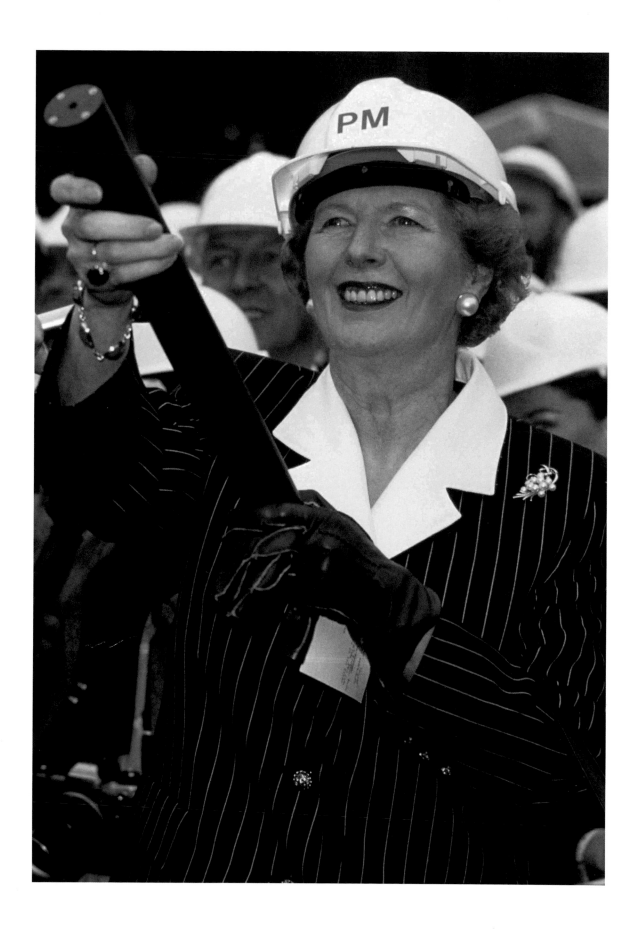

being dug out of the rubble.' 'It's what they would want,' she said. 'We can't allow terrorism to defeat democracy.'

Another quality is that she never seemed to waste energy by looking back and worrying about whether she had done the right thing. What was done was done. The only thing worth using energy on was what to do next. I remember travelling back with her from a lunchtime engagement in the City during a bad moment in the coal miners' strike, when the dockers were for a short time also on strike and the prospects of importing the energy supplies needed were threatened. On this journey back we suffered another blow, learning that the Government had lost its case in the High Court over the banning of the GCHQ unions. Margaret Thatcher was faced with making a statement in Parliament in front of a jubilant Opposition. She was immediately clear about what she would do. 'I will make clear that we will appeal the GCHQ case to the House of Lords and, if we lose, we shall accept the judgement of the court. We cannot fight for the rule of law in one area if we don't accept it in another. Now back to the miners' strike.' The Government won its appeal in the House of Lords.

The legends about Margaret Thatcher's physical toughness and stamina are justified. In December 1984 she went to Beijing to sign the Hong Kong agreement and then went on to Hong Kong to reassure opinion there. Believing that Ronald Reagan was in the Western White House in California, the Foreign Office suggested that she should visit him on the way home following his re-election as President. Even if this information had been correct, the geography would have been dubious since it is a shorter distance from London to California than from Hong Kong. In fact, Ronald Reagan was in Washington and the visit involved a 24-hour flight from Hong Kong on the VC-10 but only a 12-hour time change. While the staff decided that we would get what sleep we could, Margaret Thatcher announced that she would stay awake and study the Anti-Ballistic Missile Treaty and Cap Weinberger's speeches in preparation for her talks with Ronald Reagan on the Strategic Defence Initiative.

> *'The eyes would light up and the thoroughbred would be pawing the ground before the off.'*
>
> Lord Butler

She did this to such good effect that, faced with the President and the US defence establishment at Camp David, she persuaded them to accept the four principles which preserved the principle of nuclear deterrence. We returned home in time for Christmas Eve having flown right round the world. The full trip had lasted five and a half days or 130 hours, of which 55 hours had been spent in the air. I had occasion to telephone her on Christmas Day and asked whether she felt tired. 'Certainly not,' she said. 'Why ever should I?'

On another occasion she had a dental appointment in the morning. On her return, I asked her whether she had had any trouble. 'I'm afraid the dentist said that I had to have my impacted wisdom teeth out,' she said. Later that day, at the end of the usual round of meetings and engagements, I asked when she would like an appointment made with her dentist for the removal of the wisdom teeth. 'He did it this morning,' she said.

What was the secret of Margaret Thatcher's energy? Apart from the certainty of her instincts and her physical stamina, she seemed to have an inexhaustible supply of adrenalin. No occasion was too trivial for her not to take seriously, whether it was a school prize-giving or a confidence debate in the Commons. All were the subject of intense and detailed preparation. As Principal Private Secretary, I regarded one of my many jobs as being the regulation of the adrenalin flow. For the most part this involved calming and reassurance. But just occasionally, after lunch, I felt that she was a bit too tranquil for a great performance at Prime Minister's Questions in the House of Commons. On those occasions I would say 'Prime Minister, I think you are really vulnerable if the Opposition raise such and such a point.' That always did the trick. The eyes would light up and the thoroughbred would be pawing the ground before the off.

On the evening of the day when Margaret Thatcher left Downing Street, I invited her and Denis to a farewell party in my office with some of the civil servants I knew she regarded most highly. I said, 'When we are very old the thing which our grandchildren and great grandchildren will think most interesting about us is that we worked with Margaret Thatcher.' I believe that still and I am glad that I said it to her at that moment.

Lord Howe of Aberavon

CABINET MINISTER 1979–90

Geoffrey Howe was Margaret Thatcher's first Chancellor of the Exchequer (1979–83). He went on to become Foreign Secretary (1983–9) and Deputy Prime Minister (1989–90). His resignation in 1990 over European policy and his savage resignation speech in the House of Commons were key factors in Margaret Thatcher's eventual downfall.

1969

ARTHUR SELDON SOUGHT MY VIEW of Margaret Thatcher, as a possible target for the Institute of Economic Affairs. My response was cautiously encouraging: 'I am not at all sure about Margaret. Many of her economic prejudices are certainly sound. But she is inclined to be rather too dogmatic for my liking on sensitive issues like education and might actually retard the cause by over-simplification. We should certainly be able to hope for something better from her – but I suspect that she will need to be exposed to the humanising side of your character as much as to the pure welfare market-monger. There is much scope for her to be influenced between triumph and disaster.'

February 1975

Two days after her election as Leader of the Party, Margaret Thatcher came to address the regular Thursday meeting of the 1922 Committee. The room was packed. Unusually, Shadow Cabinet members were present as well. The new Leader, escorted by the chairman, Edward du Cann, entered the Committee room through the door opening onto the platform. She was flanked only by the all-male officers of the Committee. Suddenly she looked very beautiful – and very frail, as the half-dozen knights of the shires towered over her. It was a moving, almost feudal, occasion. Tears came to my eyes. The Conservative Party had elected its first woman Leader. And this overwhelmingly male gathering dedicated themselves enthusiastically to the service of this remarkable woman. By her almost reckless courage she had won their support, if not yet their hearts. A new bond of loyalty had been forged.

No! No! No!

June 1979, Tokyo

The real star of the Summit was Margaret Thatcher, making her first appearance on the world stage as Prime Minister. In those days it was still the custom for each head of government to make a separate closing statement to the final press conference – a fearful recipe for competitive tedium. As the newest member, Margaret was the last head to perform. The 'press corps' assembled at the new Otani Hotel contained a startlingly large clutch of Japanese women – some journalists, no doubt, but many more diplomatic and political wives, secretaries and the like, all fired with curiosity by this female phenomenon. Margaret did not disappoint them. Speaking without a note (but far from extempore) she sparkled alongside the soberly scripted statesmen who had gone before. For the first time I realised just how powerful an international champion Britain now had.

Spring 1982

One colleague had concluded that: 'the way in which Margaret operates, the way
her time is consumed, the lack of a methodical mode of working and of orderly
discussion and communication on key issues with other colleagues, mean that our
chance of implementing a carefully worked out strategy is very low indeed ...'
There never was any real improvement in Margaret's working methods of the
kind that he would have liked. Yet the important agenda items were being tackled,
albeit in a less systematic way than he or I might have wished. This was happening,
above all, as a result of Margaret's input, authority and, sometimes, judgment.
The difference from our more analytical approach was that her influence was
deployed much more opportunistically and instinctively than we should have
planned. But throughout Whitehall and Westminster her instinct, her thinking,
her authority, was almost always present, making itself felt pervasively, tenaciously
and effectively. It came gradually to feel, as the months went by, as though the
Prime Minister was present, unseen and unspeaking, at almost every meeting. The

questions were always being asked, even if unspoken: how will this play at Number 10? What's the best way of getting the Prime Minister on side for that? And so on.

May 1983: Williamsburg Summit
Ronald Reagan was a splendidly natural host, with a straightforward and engaging tenacity on points that mattered. There was a spontaneity about his mutually supportive attitude towards Margaret. She likewise blossomed with admiring, almost affectionate, directness towards him. It was for both of them a personally satisfying and politically supportive relationship.

September 1983: Foreign Policy Seminar at Chequers
I explained to Margaret that her own unique relationship with President Reagan, and her standing in Europe and elsewhere, could give Britain a voice in the Alliance which it badly needed at a time when the Soviet campaign against our deployment of intermediate range nuclear forces was obviously entering its peak period. 'One notable success,' said one official, 'had been to convince the PM that there was very little scope for destabilising the Soviet Union or Eastern Europe.' This important advance in understanding was probably to prove crucial to the successful outcome of Margaret's first encounter, still more than twelve months ahead, with Mikhail Gorbachev. The force with which Margaret later expounded this and argued the case for dialogue with Moscow was no less crucial in turning President Reagan away from the 'evil empire' rhetoric and encouraging him towards a similar relationship with Gorbachev. I sometimes think this may be seen by historians as her greatest achievement in foreign affairs.

February 1984
It was her unflattering perception of union loyalty that caused Len Murray and his colleagues such distress. For them the charge of disloyalty to the Crown, which Margaret implied was a consequence of union membership, was equivalent to a charge of treason. It was that insult, as they saw it, which made them angry. But this was a case where Margaret was at the end driven by her 'all or nothing' absolutist instinct. She could not find room in her thinking for acceptance of the parallel legitimacy of someone else's loyalty. It was probably the clearest example I had seen so far of one of Margaret's most tragic failings: an inability to appreciate, still less accommodate, somebody else's patriotism. A great patriot herself, with an enormous instinctive loyalty, she found it hard to respect or sympathise with the sense of loyalty of others, or even with the idea of a wider or different loyalty for herself. Even Welshness, I sometimes felt, she regarded as somehow beyond some unspoken pale – still more Irishness. A citizen, she seemed to feel, could never safely be allowed to carry more than one card in his or her pocket, and at GCHQ that could only be Her Majesty's card.

March 1985: Funeral of General Secretary Chernenko
The style of Margaret's second meeting with Mikhail Gorbachev, late evening at the Kremlin, was to the point and friendly. Scheduled for only fifteen minutes, we

'Margaret proclaimed that she had moved "only a tiny little bit".'
Lord Howe

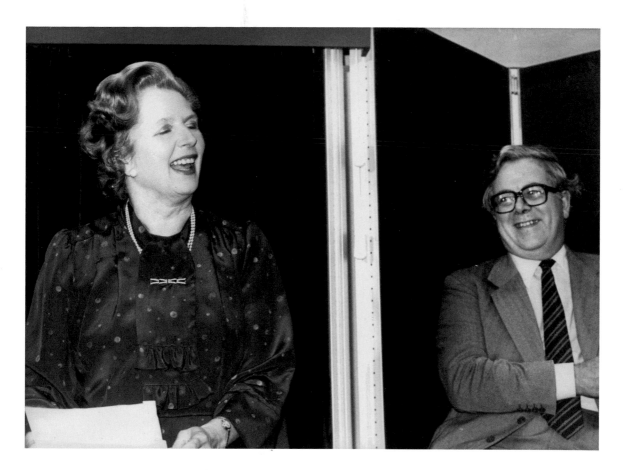

were there for almost an hour. Margaret enthused over Gorbachev's recent London visit ('one of the most successful ever'). 'We must,' replied Gorbachev, 'continue to meet and talk to one another.' 'People in Britain,' concluded Margaret, 'took great pleasure in Gorbachev's appointment and would be pleased to see Gromyko in London.' Gorbachev chuckled. 'Mr Gromyko,' he said, 'is waiting for the London fog to clear.' Certainly the two leaders were attracted to each other, relished each other's company. But neither Margaret nor Mikhail ever completely lowered their guard.

October 1985: Commonwealth Heads of Governments, Nassau
Before the world's television cameras, Margaret set out to present not the successful achievement of a concerted Commonwealth policy for change in South Africa but only the triumphant insignificance of the concessions she had had to make to achieve it. With forefinger and thumb only a few millimetres apart and contemptuously presented to the cameras, Margaret proclaimed that she had moved only 'a tiny little bit'. With four little words she had at one and the same time humiliated three dozen other heads of government, devalued the policy on which they had just agreed – and demeaned herself. She had certainly ensured that things would be a good deal less easy at any future such meeting. Even I could scarcely believe my eyes.

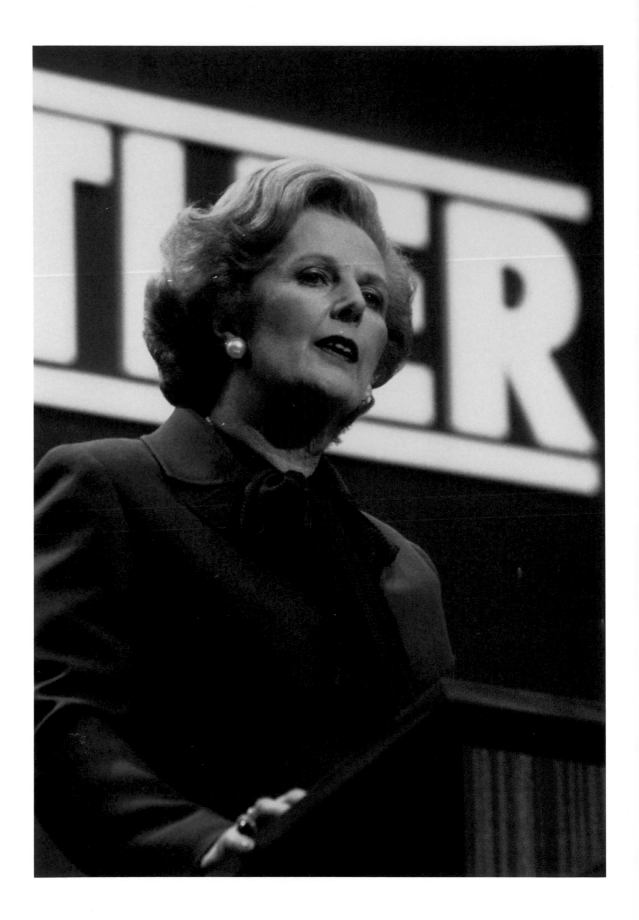

March 1987: Russia

It was marvellous to behold the impact which Margaret herself had on ordinary Russians whose path she happened to cross. The three Soviet television journalists, who interviewed her for the long, uncensored interview which they broadcast, had never encountered anything like the whirlwind that swept them aside. The nationwide television audience loved it. This was indeed reflected in the reaction of Russians in the streets of Moscow and, even more, of Georgians in the streets of Tbilisi. When Margaret decided, as she did on more than one occasion, to make an unconventional exit from her Zil limousine to greet passing pedestrians, she was instantly overwhelmed by enthusiastic recognition and acclaim. 'Her driving personality', said the *Mail on Sunday*, 'puts her head and shoulders above anyone else on the world stage.'

September 1988

I was driven finally to conclude that for Margaret the Bruges speech represented, subconsciously at least, her escape from the collective responsibility of her days in the Heath Cabinet – when European policy had arrived, as it were, with the rations. Margaret had waited almost fifteen years to display her own distaste for the policies which she had accepted as a member of that government. I began to see her – and I do so even more clearly now – as a natural member of the gallant but misguided back-bench group of Enoch Powells, Robin Turtons and Derek Walker-Smiths, who had fought so long and hard against the European Communities Bill in 1971. Yet her deeds from day to day generally continued to belie that analysis. For she went on acting, for the moment at least, as though she was indeed the Prime Minister of a Member State of the European Community. And we had to continue conducting business on that basis. It was, I imagined, a little like being married to a clergyman who had suddenly proclaimed his disbelief in God. I can see now that this was probably the moment at which there began to crystallise the conflict of loyalty, with which I was to 'struggle for perhaps too long'.

> *'Her driving personality', said the* Mail on Sunday, *'puts her head and shoulders above anyone else on the world stage.'*
>
> Lord Howe

Conclusion

And so came the years of triumph that ended in tragedy. Margaret Thatcher's eleven years as Prime Minister still stand as a period of remarkable achievement, albeit marred by decisive errors in her final term in office. She was beyond argument a great Prime Minister. Her tragedy is that she may be remembered less for the brilliance of her many achievements than for the recklessness with which she later sought to impose her own increasingly uncompromising views. For Margaret Thatcher in her final years, there was no distinction to be drawn between person, government, party and nation. They merged in her mind as one seamless whole. Her interests were axiomatically those of Britain. Any criticism of her was an unpatriotic act. The insistence on the undivided sovereignty of her own opinion dressed up as the nation's sovereignty was her own undoing.

At the 1980 Conservative Party Conference: 'You turn if you want to …'

Greg Knight

CONSERVATIVE MP

Greg Knight was MP for Derby North from 1987 to 1997 and was elected MP for East Yorkshire in 2001.

A flea in the ear

THERE ARE TWO INCIDENTS that I recall that perfectly sum up Margaret. In October 1984 I was having dinner with Ian Gow, who was then Housing Minister. He told me how he had earlier in the day got a 'flea in his ear' from the Prime Minister.

He had been visiting a new housing estate and whilst there he had given a live radio interview. He said he had told the interviewer that he held 'very high aspirations for increasing home ownership in Britain' and went on to say that he hoped that 'one day it might be possible for it to become as high as eighty per cent.'

He then left the housing site to open a factory, before returning to Westminster. Whilst at the factory, he was called to the site foreman's office to take a phone call and was astonished to find that it was the Prime Minister on the phone.

'Ian,' Margaret began, 'What is wrong with one hundred per cent?'

The second incident took place in the mid 1980s, on an extremely hot day in one of the reception rooms at 10 Downing Street. Most of the Parliamentary

It costs just as much to train a bad teacher as it does to train a good teacher.

Margaret Thatcher takes control in the cockpit of an historic Shorts Sunderland flying boat in 1980.

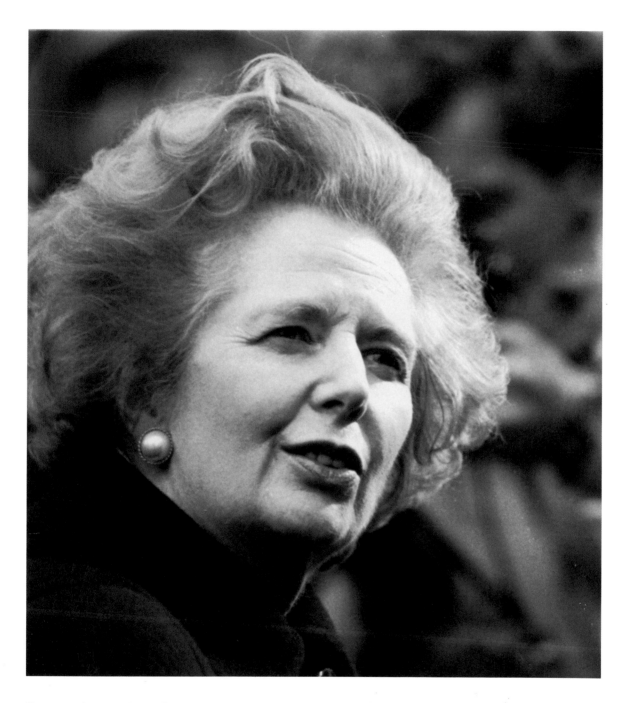

Party was in attendance. I was circulating around the guests and found myself joining some Conservative MPs, most of them 'Knights of the Shires', who were standing near to a closed window complaining about the oppressive heat. 'Can't you get a footman to open this bloody window, Greg?' one of them enquired. Before I could respond, Margaret appeared from behind the MP standing opposite to me, jumped on a chair and opened up the window herself. At this, one of the staff serving drinks leaned over my shoulder and said: 'She's bloody marvellous. She never asks anyone to do a job if she can do it quicker herself!'

Julia Langdon
POLITICAL JOURNALIST

Julia Langdon is a freelance political journalist and former Political Editor of the *Daily Mirror* and the *Sunday Telegraph*. She is the author of *Mo Mowlam: The Biography*.

On the road with Maggie

PERHAPS THE MOST CHILLING MOMENT of my relationship with Margaret Thatcher occurred at about 30,000 feet. We were in an RAF VC10 – as we so often were – en route on this occasion to Australia. I had looked with horror at the official itinerary when it had arrived shortly beforehand. It was long and characteristically busy and the worst thing was that we had one night in the air on the outward journey and then a row of one-night stopovers in a series of different Australian cities. I realised gloomily that we wouldn't be able to get any laundry done until we reached Bangkok, ten days or so into the journey. When the Prime Minister came back in the plane to rough it with the riff-raff on the first leg of the journey to somewhere in the Middle East, I politely asked her, by way of conversational small talk, what she had made of her programme. 'Well!' she said, clearly much exercised on the point, 'do you realise we won't even be able to get any laundry done until we reach Bangkok!'

It was, I have to report, quite alarming to discover that one's reaction in an unpredictable set of circumstances should be so completely identical to that of the Prime Minister. And not any old Prime Minister either.

We went around the world together several times, Mrs Thatcher and I. Entirely at her behest, of course. During her years as Prime Minister, I was Political Editor of this and that and instructed by my various employers always to accompany Her Nibs wherever she went. It was the most brilliant fun, although probably more particularly in retrospect because there were lots of endless days and sleepless nights. And when you did get into bed for the first time in what felt like weeks, somewhere on the other side of the world, you could always rely on the newsdesk to ring and say that a reader had rung in about some trivial fact they wished to challenge.

I was there when military bands turned out at midnight to play obscure national anthems at the other end of the interminable lengths of red carpet laid across some foreign airport tarmac. I have watched elderly despots dance attendance upon her and I have watched her dance. It isn't always quite as glamorous as it might sound. I have trailed her around building sites in the Middle East, a sewer works in Cairo, a mining operation in Namibia, a new mass transit system in Singapore. I have watched as she took tea in a trench with two African Presidents in a war zone on the Mozambique border and as she was unexpectedly presented with an Arab stallion in a Middle Eastern desert and didn't quite know how to explain that it wasn't quite her thing. I have winced in feminist sympathy as the light of the Jordanian sun cut through her dress and made it look as if she was stark naked as she inspected the honour guard lined up to salute her. I have watched strong men and women faint from heat in refugee camps in Israel and Zimbabwe and Jordan and Cambodia and wondered if she was going to make it

It will be years, and not in my lifetime before a woman will become Prime Minister.

HM The Queen greets Lady Thatcher at her seventieth birthday celebrations in October 1995.

– and, yes, whether I was too. Possibly not in that order. I was on her plane when we were shot at by guerrillas on the way to visit Malawi – not that I knew about it until her first volume of memoirs was published. 'Fortunately they missed,' she said, recounting the incident. Together we have attended the Bolshoi, a wedding in Tiblisi, a mass in Zagorsk, a riot in Melbourne, another one in the heat and dust of a Saharan harmattan as we watched a dhurbar in Kano.

It was always work. She didn't relax. There were very few opportunities for hanging around the swimming pool if there was one. She didn't like sightseeing and she wasn't really interested in culture. She didn't want anybody to think that she was pleasure-seeking, or enjoying herself – except, of course, in a political sense. She was once prevailed upon to show that she had an understanding of these things, however. We had whizzed around the wonders of Luxor in a couple of hours, typically at midday with the temperature at 120 degrees or so, simply because it suited her programme to do it at this insane time of day. Someone told her that really she ought to show she was interested in the wonders of ancient Egypt for its own sake. So when we took off she ordered the pilot to take the VC10 down to 3,000 feet so we could admire the temples of Abu Simbel in the Upper Nile. On the next trip we circled Ayers Rock in Australia.

There were many wonderful moments of our travels together and I cherish some in particular. There was, for example, the time at the Expo in Brisbane when she was touring the site and many eager Australians had packed the area for a glimpse of the great Maggie Thatcher. It was terribly crowded and the public were penned away from the celebrity tour of the exhibits. There was, however, a middle-ranking reptile enclosure which contained the press. Mrs Thatcher was about to move among us and, seeing some small children who were eager to catch a glimpse of this legend of their lifetime, I offered to take one small child off her mother and give her a better view. I was holding her up to see the great one pass and Mrs Thatcher stopped at the sight of the little girl's excited small face. There were no other children around because this was the press area and the public were so much further away. Mrs Thatcher didn't realise this, however, and with a politician's instinct homed in. The horror on her face when she realised that I was holding the child was a wonder to behold. 'Oh !' she said with complete disgust and incomprehension. 'It's you!'

I think my favourite moment, however, was in Moscow when Mrs Thatcher was due to meet the armed service chiefs of the USSR at their equivalent of the Ministry of Defence. I had arrived somewhat latterly, behind the rest of my press colleagues but very slightly before the Prime Minister. For the purposes of this anecdote it is necessary to recognise that to someone in the Soviet Union one middle-aged West European woman looks very much like another. Anyway, I whizzed into the lift to go to the appropriate floor where Mrs T was due to meet the top brass – literally – of the Soviet military machine and when the lift doors opened they thought she had arrived. There was music and an attendant group of military snapped to attention, saluted and clipped their heels. A man with a lot of scrambled egg on his shoulders stepped forward to greet me. 'I'm from the *Daily Mirror*,' I said, by way of explanation. 'Mrs Thatcher isn't here yet.'

With Sir Geoffrey Howe at the 1983 EEC Summit in Stuttgart.

Ann Widdecombe

CONSERVATIVE MP

Ann Widdecombe has been the MP for Maidstone since 1987. She served as a junior Minister in John Major's Government, and joined the Shadow Cabinet in 1998, where she served as Shadow Health and then Shadow Home Secretary. She is also a best-selling novelist.

Photo opportunity

IN THE 1980S WHEN THE ISSUE of CND was still a very live one, I helped Lady Olga Maitland set up an organisation known as Women and Families for Defence. My contribution to the group was to write a booklet entitled, 'A Layman's Guide to Defence'. The group, deciding that it would like a photo opportunity, asked to see the Prime Minister. Margaret Thatcher agreed to see us but in her usual way it was before breakfast on an extremely dark winter's morning. We trudged along to 10 Downing Street scarcely past dawn and were received by the Prime Minister looking as if she had just walked out of a beauty salon. She was very lively and interested in what we were doing.

After we had been there about ten minutes the door bell of Number 10 went and Edwina Currie arrived on the doorstep wearing a hat! She had never been active in the group and none of us was quite sure what she was doing there, and a very embarrassed Olga, who had had to turn several people away as the invitation limited the numbers very stringently, had the job of turning away this formidable lady from the doorstep of Number 10.

We had expected a five-minute audience but Mrs Thatcher gave us the best part of an hour.

Right: Margaret and Denis cast their votes in Chelsea on Polling Day, 3 May 1979.

Below left: Margaret Thatcher collects her prize at the Blue Ball raffle at the Hurlingham Club in 1983. Pictured left is Conservative MP Michael Grylls.

Sir Michael Spicer

CONSERVATIVE MP

Sir Michael Spicer has served as the Member for South Worcestershire from 1974 until 1997 and as the Member for West Worcestershire since 1997. He has held ministerial positions in the Department of Transport, Department of Energy and Department of the Environment. He is currently Chairman of the 1922 Committee.

A heroine of Elizabethan proportions

FOR A BRIEF PERIOD during the 1983 General Election I acted as Parliamentary Private Secretary to Margaret Thatcher. I was already Deputy Chairman of the Party. As I had coordinated most of the detailed planning for the election, it was decided that I was sufficiently under the skin of what was going on to stand in as the Prime Minister's bag carrier in place of Ian Gow, who somewhat understandably felt he needed to spend a little more time in his constituency of Eastbourne.

For me personally this was an exciting time. Margaret Thatcher was at the height of her prowess and Conservative policies were rampant. It was also for me a dangerous time. Margaret was always wary of those who had seen her at very close quarters in moments of high intensity. A few events may help to explain why my career went into something of a tail-spin after my spell as PPS to the PM.

In the run-up to the election I went on a practice tour with the PM around East Anglia. The trip took us to the privatised Felixstowe docks. When we were shown the highest crane in Europe, Margaret Thatcher expressed a desire to climb it. Not a single voter waited for us at the top, but the world's press stood slobbering with expectancy at the bottom; this was partly because she was dressed in a tight black skirt in which she intended to climb hundreds of feet of vertical iron laddering.

My job was to climb up so closely behind her that they never got the photo they were hoping for. Going up was a piece of cake. Coming down required me to guide the Prime Ministerial feet from rung to rung. The inevitably embarrassing (for me) picture did make the national press.

Then there was the occasion during the election itself when we were landing at Edinburgh Airport. I was chatting to Denis Thatcher in the seat behind me. Next to me was David Wolfson; beside him was the PM. Suddenly there came what were for me fatal words, 'See what Michael thinks of the last sentence of the speech.' I looked at it and said something banal like 'could do with some tightening up'. The PM exploded – she was hyping herself up for a mass rally of supporters waiting for her in the Scottish capital. 'Why am I always surrounded by so much negative unhelpfulness?'

When we landed I was put in a car with the Secretary of State for Scotland and his Deputy and told to come up with a 'last sentence' before we reached the city centre. I was still fairly relaxed and told the others that this was normal before a big speech. We came up quite easily with not one, but three 'last sentences' – each to be tossed back at us with contempt when through screaming crowds we finally reached the ante-room to the conference hall. The Press Secretary was going

I have never knowingly made a non-controversial speech in my life.

frantic. 'We've got to give something to the press.' It was Denis who found the answer. 'Don't have a last sentence,' he said, and the PM went on to make one of her best speeches of the campaign. I don't think I was ever forgiven.

Then there was the time when, returning from a BBC programme chaired by Sue Lawley, on which someone called in to be rude to the PM about the sinking of the *Belgrano*, I was asked to enquire of the Chairman of the Party (my old friend Cecil Parkinson) whether we could abolish the BBC after we had won the election. The PM was a few yards from me when I made the appropriate telephone call from her flat in Number 10. She could therefore clearly hear the Chairman's expletives, and laughingly turned to Denis with the words, 'I don't think the Chairman likes our little idea.' It was a good joke.

Winning that election was never much in doubt, so much so that I was asked to leave the Prime Minister's aeroplane in the last week of the campaign while it waited for me on the tarmac. I found the nearest payphone in the airport terminal. My instructions were to ask Tim Bell to 'pull' a three-page advertisement from all national newspapers attacking our rivals; the last page of this was a complete blank and was meant to represent the Liberal manifesto. 'People will think that a total waste of paper,' the Prime Minister had pronounced, 'especially as we are going to win.' She was right. The 1983 election was the high water mark of Conservative fortunes in the second half of the twentieth century.

She was the victor, a heroine of Elizabethan proportions. As at the court of the Fairy Queen, it was best to be a pace or two apart. No politician progressed very far after working intimately at her court.

Admiral Sir John Woodward
COMMANDER IN CHIEF, NAVAL HOME COMMAND 1987–9

Admiral Sir John Woodward, known as Sandy, has had a long and distinguished career in the Royal Navy which he joined at the age of fourteen. He has served on numerous ships and in numerous positions at the MOD, eventually rising to the rank of Admiral and the position of Commander in Chief of Naval Home Command. He led the 1982 Task Force in its mission to recover the Falklands.

Interrupting the Prime Minister

IN 1985–6, I WAS JUST SUFFICIENTLY SENIOR in the Defence Ministry to stand in for the Chief of the Defence Staff as professional military adviser to the Secretary of State for Defence once or twice at a Cabinet meeting. The day after one such occasion, I was having lunch with one of Mrs Thatcher's Civil Service secretaries who said, more or less out of the blue, 'You were very lucky yesterday.'

Being unaware of having had any particular stroke of good fortune recently, I asked him what he was talking about. He replied: 'You interrupted the Chairman'.

'Chairman?' I said, 'Chairman? What chairman?'

'The Prime Minister – Mrs Thatcher – you interrupted her in mid-flow.'

'Oh, that Chairman – well, what's wrong with that? She was giving her views on a professional military matter – and she was getting it wrong. Someone had to tell her.'

'Nothing's wrong with that as such, only…'

'But surely, if the Prime Minister is about to do something fairly crass as a result of less than full knowledge of the subject, someone has to interrupt, give her the additional facts, and let her make her political decision on the basis of a full and proper professional brief. And anyway, she stopped, let me say what needed to be said to keep her straight on military facts, took it in, and went on to arrive at a sensible course of action. What on earth is wrong with that? Where does the luck come in? Is this how business is ordinarily conducted, how it should be conducted?'

'Well, yes and no', he replied, 'the last junior minister to interrupt her like that was fired.'

'Serve him right,' I said. 'He can only have been giving her "professional military advice" from a profound ignorance of the subject, or political advice which, after eight years as Prime Minister, she had already heard two or three times before. Hardly a valuable interruption, indeed a complete waste of her time most likely. He should have known better.'

My conclusion from this rather odd conversation was that we still had an excellent Chief Executive – provided only that she retained a few advisers who were prepared to say 'No, Prime Minister' from time to time. Luck didn't enter it.

I have to admit that the conversation is slightly embellished, mainly to make better sense. It is intended to bring out the point that in 1986 at least, she was still a good, if rather intimidating listener to sensible advice. I suspect that the cause of her later downfall was as much to do with running out of such advisers, as anything else.

Just rejoice at the news and congratulate our armed forces and the marines. Rejoice!

Margaret Thatcher almost gets carried away at the 1979 Boat Show at London's Earls Court.

Overleaf: Demonstrating the need for regenerating wasteland on Teeside, 1987.

Lord Denham

CONSERVATIVE MP

Lord Denham served under Margaret Thatcher as Chief Whip in the House of Lords throughout her time as Prime Minister. He is also a successful novelist.

Winning in the Lords

LIKE MOST MEMBERS of the House of Commons, Margaret Thatcher was never quite able to understand what the House of Lords was all about. Until she reached it herself, that is. But throughout her twelve years as Prime Minister, it fell to me, as her Chief Whip, to try and put this right.

'Why is it,' she asked me once, 'that you are always being defeated in the House of Lords, whereas we never are in the Commons?' The short answer was that, the House of Lords being a revising Chamber, without regular defeats of a Government of whatever party, the system simply wouldn't work. But I gave the more practical one. 'Because, Prime Minister, you have an overall majority of over 140 in your House, whereas in ours we haven't got an overall majority at all.' It was absolutely true, both on paper and in practice. Even at that time, if both the official Opposition and the Liberals voted against us, we still needed the support of a majority of Cross Bench Peers if we were ever to win a division. But Margaret somehow couldn't be persuaded of that at all.

'Why,' she asked me on another occasion, 'don't your revise the procedures of the House of Lords so that you can get our business through more smoothly?'

'I can't do that, Prime Minister.'

'Why not?' 'Because next time there's a Labour Government,' I said, 'we're going to need those very procedures to prevent whatever enormities they try and inflict on us.'

There was an awful silence, at the end of which I couldn't help feeling that I was lucky not to have been taken out and shot as a traitor for the very suggestion that there could be a Labour Government again.

One of Margaret's great charms, however, was that she had the most beautiful manners. There was an awful occasion when a Housing Bill was going through the Lords and a Memorial Service for Lord Dilhorne, a highly popular former Conservative Lord Chancellor, had been scheduled for that same afternoon. It was attended by almost every back-bench Tory peer. The Opposition had divided the House on one of their early amendments and, much to their surprise, had inflicted a crashing defeat on the Government. Highly delighted, they thereupon called division after division and won three more amendments in quick succession, before enough Government peers to stop the rot had managed to filter back in.

It so happened that the Prime Minister was holding one of her periodic parties for the hired help in Downing Street that evening, and I reached the top of the stairs at Number Ten just as she had been informed of the fourth defeat. I was her guest and she gallantly contrived to make a joke of it … but any one could see that in reality she didn't think it funny at all. My only consolation was that Reggie Dilhorne himself would have enjoyed the whole thing quite enormously.

It is not the job of politicians to please everyone.

Margaret Thatcher visits Moscow in April 1987.

Robert Key
MP FOR SALISBURY

Robert Key has been the MP for Salisbury since 1983. He served under Margaret Thatcher and John Major in a number of ministerial posts.

Matron?

I FIRST CAME ACROSS MARGARET THATCHER when I was a master at Harrow School and her son Mark was a pupil. She was one of a galaxy of Conservative politicians whose children were entrusted to Winston Churchill's old school. In the 1970s, in addition to the Thatchers, Harrow pupils included young men bearing the names Macmillan, Heseltine, Maudling, Churchill, Onslow, Oppenheim and others. The former MP Bobby Allen (whose son served for many years in the Private Office at Number 10) was a Governor of the school, as was Mary Soames. To varying degrees they all encouraged and assisted the development of my political leanings.

As a House Tutor at Harrow, I had a lot of contact particularly with the senior boys and with their parents. Margaret Thatcher's son, Mark, was in Bradbys and his House Tutor, Alan Sankey, was charming, assiduous and courteous. After lunch one day he walked into the entrance hall at the house to find a woman waiting to see the House Master. He enquired whether she had come about the job of house matron. What a pity he did not recognise the Secretary of State for Education! This tale does say something about that generation of politicians who placed huge faith in the schools they chose and their teachers – and who expected no special favours.

I was accepted onto the Candidates List in 1975 and I fought Frank Dobson in Holborn and St Pancras South in 1979. Our long suffering daughter Helen was born just before the General Election that year and her second name is Margaret. Helen met Margaret for the first time on the day before polling day in the 1983 General Election. The Liberals had declared Salisbury in their top ten target seats (as they always do!) and since I was a new candidate in my home town the powers that be at Central Office ordained that the Prime Minister should pay a flying visit to Salisbury. She landed at Old Sarum Airfield by helicopter and came by coach into the Guildhall Square where over 10,000 people were waiting for her. In the middle of the square was a Land Rover provided by my farming friend Richard Crook. On it waited the Key family including four-year-old Helen. Margaret made magnificent progress through the throng and as she climbed aboard a friend asked Helen what was special about today. 'After this, I'm going swimming,' she piped. We won the seat with a healthy majority.

In the autumn of 1984 I received a mysterious message on the Members' Letterboard in the House to contact the Chief Whip urgently. What had I done? He explained that in the Tory Party there was a long tradition of an honorary PPS being provided for former Prime Ministers. Would I look after Ted? I knew the dangers of acceptance.

I took the risk. It would not be true to say I never regretted it – it was misconstrued by some of the press and it was certainly misconstrued by quite a

If you wash your hands of Northern Ireland, you wash them in blood.

Margaret and Denis at Chequers.

lot of people in Salisbury! However, I learnt a huge amount not only about Ted Heath and his beliefs and vision – but also about Margaret Thatcher. One of my duties was to act as go-between. On one occasion there was a confidence motion put down by Labour. Ted was in Israel, adding to the political round by conducting a major symphony orchestra in Jerusalem. The message came from the Chief Whip that I must tell Ted to return to London. The Whips could not contact him.

I did! He was out in the desert and somehow I managed to speak to him. He said he would not come back. I asked if I could tell Number 10 that if he had been able to come back he would have supported the Government in the no-confidence motion.

He agreed and he also let me put out an appropriate press notice. I telephoned Number 10 and spoke to Margaret's PPS. We agreed there was no alternative.

Margaret was always approachable. She would always listen to a good argument with terrifying attention and total concentration as she fixed you with her laser-beam eyes. She would listen and if she decided you were right she would back you. She did this twice for me.

On the first occasion, a group of us were absolutely convinced of the basic injustice of no financial provision to help haemophiliacs who had been infected with the HIV virus from contaminated NHS blood transfusions. A distraught mother in Salisbury came to me to tell me that her little boy at primary school had become infected this way. Other parents had found out – and they would not allow their children to attend the same school. The Head was forced to tell the mother her child must leave the school. It was absolutely terrible. I joined with a small band of Conservative MPs and we went from Junior Health Minister to Secretary of State for Health – all to no avail. John Hannam persuaded us that we must go to the top. We did. Margaret met us in her small upstairs study at Number 10. She clipped her famous handbag shut, put it on the floor, and gave us her total concentration as we put the case. In spite of all the briefing from the Number 10 Policy Unit and the Department of Health, she had never seen it or thought about it in our terms. She knew we were right. The next day there was a statement in the House announcing a substantial ex-gratia payment to establish a trust fund to be administered by the Haemophilia Society. Many of us know that at heart Margaret is a compassionate woman.

On the second occasion, in the never-ending saga of what to do with Stonehenge (in my constituency) – a problem that has defeated Margaret Thatcher, John Major and Tony Blair – I was convinced that she had been given faulty briefing by the Ministry of Defence who are big landowners near the site. The location of the current English Heritage favourite for a new visitors' centre was unacceptable to local people and I had battled through the Whitehall machine and the PM had agreed to see me. We met in her room at the Commons. I came equipped with maps – and she was soon on her hands and knees on the carpet as I explained the problem. She agreed with me. The site was dropped.

That degree of access, concentration on detail and compassion was all part of the magic that made Margaret great. That was at the height of her power. Towards the end of her term she became less accessible and I am sure that led to

'Margaret was always approachable. She would always listen to a good argument with terrifying attention and total concentration as she fixed you with her laser-beam eyes.'
Robert Key

disenchantment with her style. She had set impossibly high standards to maintain for as long as ten years. Incidentally, that degree of accessibility was never matched by her successor, John Major.

Having served Ted Heath as unofficial PPS, then Alick Buchanan-Smith and subsequently Chris Patten as PPS for four years, my moment came. In 1990 I was the lay member of the Medical Research Council. In spite of my duties to Chris Patten (who was Secretary of State for the Environment) I really had to attend a Medical Research Council meeting in London even though it was the middle of the Party Conference in Bournemouth. I had caught the train up to London and arrived at the MRC in Park Crescent to be told by the receptionist to phone Chris Patten's Private Secretary immediately. He was already on the way to collect me in a Government car. When he arrived, the Private Secretary bundled me straight into the car and took me to Waterloo where I caught a train back to Bournemouth. I would be met by the Chief Constable who would take me straight to the Prime Minister. The Chief Constable took me in his Jag to the Highcliffe Hotel. There I was ushered up to Margaret Thatcher's modest suite where she asked me if I would be prepared to join her Government. What can a man say? 'Yes, Prime Minister. Thank you very much. I will not let you down.' Nor did I. Within a couple of months she had been challenged for the leadership of the Party – and of course I voted for Margaret.

By the time I got downstairs in the hotel, slightly numb at the thought that I was now a Minister of the Crown, however humble, the world had already been informed of the appointment and I was surrounded by the press. Suddenly the sea of cameras parted and there was Ted Heath. He walked up to me, grinned broadly said, 'Congratulations – you poor sod!' and stumped off.

Margaret and Denis with the 1987 General Election campaign battlebus.

Lord Steel of Aikwood

LEADER OF THE LIBERAL PARTY 1976–87

David Steel was Leader of the Liberal Party for almost all of Margaret Thatcher's period as Prime Minister. He led the Party into an Alliance and later a merger with the SDP, becoming a founding father of the Liberal Democrat Party. Sir David Steel was the first Presiding Officer of the Scottish Parliament.

Contradictory memories

I HAVE TWO CONTRADICTORY MEMORIES of Margaret Thatcher. The first is the public one – her strident uncompromising battling at House of Commons Question Time, especially her memorable (but rather flattering) put-downs of me: 'Let me tell this young man …'

The second is a private one. On one of the many occasions when she felt obliged to invite me as Leader of the Liberal Party to dinner at Number 10 for a distinguished foreign guest (we always parade our multi-party democracy on such occasions), my wife was struck down with 'flu and could not travel from Scotland. She greeted me: 'So sorry to hear Judy is ill. I didn't want you to be alone so I've arranged for Carol to join us and partner you into dinner.' A genuinely thoughtful and kind touch.

Right: Margaret Thatcher flying the flag following an Election Campaign speech in May 1987.

Harvey Thomas

INTERNATIONAL PUBLIC RELATIONS CONSULTANT

Harvey Thomas was the Director of Press and Communications at Conservative Central Office from 1985 until 1987. He continued to serve as Director of Presentation to the Conservative Party until 1991.

Selling Maggie

I SUPPOSE I AM ONE OF THE ORIGINAL PEOPLE accused of being a 'spin doctor'. It amazes me now how little 'spin' we needed to do with Mrs T compared with today's requirement for constant spin on everything and everybody in politics, in an apparent desperate attempt to make it look as though they know where they are going.

Agree with her or not, Maggie knew where she was going, and for the most part the media was so busy keeping up that 'news management' was pretty straight forward.

But that never really included too much on the personal side. Behind the unavoidable 'public personae', Denis and Margaret Thatcher were, and are, pleasantly private people. So, perhaps the memories that are most appropriate for me are those that illustrate her personal touch – and her concern for, and loyalty to, friends.

The phrase that I recall hearing more than others, was 'Because it's right'. People would suggest political direction or action and Mrs T would say time and again, 'No, we've got to do it this way, because it's right!'

In many ways, her thinking was quite simplistic – even though she has considerable capacity to master detail as well. But 'because it's right' has always been the driving motive in her private as well as her public life.

In 1985 I had gone to New York to prepare for her speech to the United Nations 40th Anniversary Celebration.

She had been out of the country for more than two weeks – I believe at the Commonwealth Heads of Government Meeting in the Bahamas. While she had been away, a number of critical comments about me had appeared in *The Times* Diary, the Peterborough column in the *Telegraph*, and one or two other political gossip columns. Nothing in the mainstream news passed on to the Prime Minister in the Bahamas – but enough to be personally hurtful.

When the Prime Minister arrived at the hotel in New York, she came full steam into the suite, and the first thing she said was, 'I hear there have been some nasty comments in the papers, Harvey – don't worry about it. I know where they are coming from and I'll make sure they stop.' I would never have brought it up – and I have no idea who did – but she certainly made my day!

And in private, she has a dry sense of humour. Four of us were sitting with her having a sandwich lunch in the Finchley Constituency Office during the 1987 election. It had been a frantic morning and we had afternoon and evening visits ahead of us.

After two weeks of campaigning, we were all struggling to keep going, and as we shovelled the sandwiches down I said, 'Boy, I am ready for a siesta now.'

Northern Ireland is as British as Finchley.

Margaret Thatcher leans out of the window of Conservative Central Office, acknowledging the cheers of supporters on election night, June 1987.

The other three nodded and agreed and I looked at Mrs Thatcher at the other end of the table and said, not very hopefully, 'Well that makes it almost unanimous.'

'It's certainly not unanimous,' she said, 'it's a majority of one against!'

I'm not sure that Maggie ever really understood that it was simplicity and integrity that gained her so much support, especially inside the Conservative Party.

The media consistently speculated on whether we deliberately kept applause going at the big rallies in the eighties. And if so, how we did it! We did, and it wasn't hard. I would zoom the cameras projecting her picture onto the giant screens, into a tight close-up shot of her face.

I first used this approach with Billy Graham fifteen years earlier. When the audience sees a speaker's face occupying a whole twenty-feet screen, the eyes are about two feet wide – and they give away all the speaker's emotional feelings.

Integrity shines through, and, perhaps surprising to some, Mrs T's eyes at the end of a speech always had the message, 'Wow, you're all being a bit overgenerous with the applause – but thank you!'

It was as though those words were printed across the screen – and as long as we kept the cameras close-up, the applause would continue – once in a while helped by a six inch tear appearing out of the corner of an eye!

For her, she was simply 'telling it like it is' and for all of us who saw our role as 'a ministry of helps', that just made it easy for people to get the 'Maggie Message'.

Adam Boulton
POLITICAL JOURNALIST

Adam Boulton is the Political Editor of Sky News and was formerly the political editor of TV-am. He has been a Lobby Correspondent since 1983.

Maggie and me

I DOUBT EVEN BILL CLINTON has had a British Prime Minister on hands and knees before him but it's happened to me, and it was the mighty Iron Lady as well. We were in her constituency office in Finchley preparing for an interview. When the crew moved a desk they exposed the generations of fluff and paper-clips gathered in a pit in the carpet pile. It was too much for the grocer's daughter; the Housewife Prime Minister was kneeling in a split second to tidy things up. Whatever you think of her, that's vintage Margaret Thatcher: she lived in her own world and honoured her own values with never a thought for the concerns or pomposities of others. At times her personal cocoon may have made her insensitive, but if you got to deal with her face-to-face it also meant she was unprejudiced without airs and graces.

For the most part though, I had only a passing acquaintance with 'Prime Minister Thatcher', passing me on a thousand doorsteps, in planes, in corridors, always on the way to something more important.

Or was it really something more important? Certainly Margaret Thatcher always gave full value on the doorstep. The impression at least was that she would stop, think and voice a spontaneous reaction to the questions unceremoniously shouted at her by the hack-pack. It's a marked contrast to Tony Blair. 'The Prime Minister doesn't do doorsteps!' is one of Alastair Campbell's proudest boasts – by which he means that even if you asked Mr Blair what he thought about the Second Coming now underway, he'd still walk past your cries, consult with his advisers and, maybe, come back out with a carefully crafted soundbite on his lips.

Maggie wasn't like that. Indeed the best bit of advice I ever got about her was the first I ever received, from Andy Webb, then my boss and Political Editor of TV-am. 'She takes everything at face value,' he said, 'so think before you speak. If you say "good morning", she's quite likely to reply "is it?" and go into a full appraisal of current meteorological conditions.' This, of course, made her fantastic television for reporters like me. She could always take you aback, for example likening the 'ANC to IRA killers' even as the one-day South African President Thabo Mbeki was being feted under the same roof at the 1987 Vancouver Commonwealth Conference.

At work and study in the USA from 1980–82, I missed out on the rise of Thatcherism at home. I sat out the Falklands in Washington: my most vivid memory of her then is of an over-stimulated Secretary of State Alexander Haig speculating luridly with the White House Corps about the precise intimate nature of the relationship between Thatcher and Reagan given their frequent one-on-one meetings. So I suppose I didn't know any better and was fair game to be sent into the Iron Lady's den as a Lobby Correspondent shortly after joining TV-am in 1983.

Thatcher's other-worldliness, or at least her determination to live in her own

Consensus is something you reach when you cannot agree.

Margaret Thatcher convincing the party faithful.

world, worked in my favour. She didn't read the newspapers and her ability to discriminate between TV networks depended entirely on who she recognised with her basilisk eyes.

Indeed, when she remembered it, she tended to get my name right. Perhaps because 'Mr Boulton' gave her the chance to exercise her elocution on the long 'o'. My more illustrious rivals John Cole and Michael Brunson usually had to settle for the not-quite-right 'Mr Brunston' and 'Mr Coles'.

Mind you, you were never quite sure she knew who you were. Sometimes she didn't seem to distinguish between journalists and her hard-pressed handbag carriers. Working on a David Frost interview during the 1987 election, I was a little bemused to find the Prime Minister's finger poking into my chest in the Green Room, telling me 'the message you've got to get out'.

I have no doubt that she was an instinctive 'gut' politician, what in politer circles is called 'a conviction politician'. But I still don't know what to make of one incident. In the 1987 General Election Campaign Labour had made much of the case of Mark Burgess, a 10-year-old-boy awaiting an NHS operation for a hole-in-the-heart. Several years later, long after Margaret Thatcher's third election victory, Mark, very sadly, died.

This coincided with the end of a European Council in Denmark, when Mrs Thatcher was due to give a series of television interviews. You would not be allowed to eavesdrop today, but in those days, with the latest deadline, I was allowed to wait my turn in the interview room itself. And so I heard four separate uneasy interviewers ask the same final question: 'I know it's got nothing to do with the summit, but my newsdesk insist … your reaction to Mark's death'. And I saw the same emotional reaction repeated four times: the hand to the heart, the catch in the throat … the 'as a mother I know how terrible this must be'.

True or bluff? I still don't know.

I do know how sensitive she is about her family. Even after her enforced retirement, the affairs of her son Mark remained the only subject absolutely off-limits in interviews tied to her memoirs. By contrast, her husband Denis was no buffoon; brief encounters left no doubt how sharp he was, and how fiercely right-wing.

Chris Moncrieff of the Press Association is rightly the reporter most associated with the Thatcher years. One day I hope he delivers on his promise to publish his memoirs. His working title is 'Maggie Thatcher's Flying Circus'. It's a good one because we used to get closest to her on her numerous foreign trips. There were drawbacks because where her successors have favoured commercial charters, Mrs Thatcher insisted on using the ageing VC 10s in the Queen's Flight. The acoustics were so poor that only the person bold enough to sit in the seat next to her ever heard the briefings which she gave in the soft voice reserved for social occasions.

Bernard Ingham would always ensure that the print journalists had plenty of time for sightseeing, shopping and golf, with a briefing conveniently timed for deadlines. But for those of us who had to record the visit on tape, the pace was more hectic. The day usually started with a dawn call for a wreath laying. I've visited practically every British War Cemetery in the world with Maggie; including

'I have no doubt that she was an instinctive "gut" politician, what in politer circles is called "a conviction politician".'

Adam Boulton

With Saudi politicians during the visit of the late King Fahd of Saudi Arabia to the UK in 1982.

in Turkey the graves from the Crimean War (the more recent Gallipoli battlefield was held back for a visit of its own the next year). Turkey was also a first for the one-and-only recorded cultural stop on a Thatcher tour. I had expected the visit to the British-made Istanbul sewage works, and the gas plant where the gasometers were painted with giant portraits of PMs Ozal and Thatcher. Even the courtesy call on the general widely whispered to be the government's 'head of torture' was not a surprise. But I never thought I'd accompany Mrs Thatcher on a canter through St Sofia and the Okapi Palace. A British Embassy Official explained: 'She struck it out of the programme but we told her there would be an international diplomatic incident if she didn't come.'

There was a real crusading spirit about those foreign trips. Downing Street did not boast a White House-style advance team, and no one seemed quite certain what was going to happen. Suspense was at its highest in her ground-breaking forays behind the Iron Curtain. Here again she not only bolstered politicians like Lech Walesa and Mikhail Gorbachev, she also sought out dissidents in their freezing flats. Margaret Thatcher, clad in her new Aquascutum wardrobe, careering round the outer-Moscow tenement blocks is still the most impressive exercise in political canvassing I've seen. Thatcher certainly worked hard on her foreign policy. The most shaken I ever saw her was in Brussels – ashen and near tears when the new President Bush made clear Helmut Kohl was his preferred special relation in Europe. A couple of years later, of course, she'd won Bush back, as he took up her strong line against Saddam Hussein.

With hindsight, we in the Westminster press corps were as well placed as anyone to see the end coming. Cabinet Ministers complained she stopped listening. With us she stopped engaging. The gleam faded in her eyes and the fresh response to questions was replaced by a rambling monologue. 'On and on and on' was too long as she began to believe her own publicity. In the way that generals tend to fight the last war, I'm sure Tony Blair has learnt this lesson.

It was a splendid exit: 'We fight on, we fight to win' on the doorstep of Downing Street; the tears in the car. Transitions of power are difficult for impartial reporters to cover: it's about people you know, you can feel the elation of the victors and the desolation of the vanquished.

Finally I'd like to confess that I've returned the compliment and been on my hands and knees before Margaret Thatcher – crawling quite literally under a live camera before an interview. Ever frank she cried, 'You look like a giant mouse.'

Last year a *Guardian* reporter rang to ask me to nominate an icon of the twentieth century. There was an intake of breath on the line when I said, 'I assume you've already got the obvious ones like Thatcher.' I chose her anyway.

Lord Young of Graffham

CABINET MINISTER 1984–9

David Young served in Margaret Thatcher's Cabinet as Minister without Portfolio, then as Secretary of State for Employment and finally as Secretary of State for Trade and Industry before retiring from the Cabinet in 1989.

Persuading the PM

I FIRST MET MARGARET THATCHER when she spoke at a lunch I chaired in the late seventies. Many of the guests came up to me afterwards and said 'If only…' None thought that she had any real chance of winning the next election.

At that time I was already working for Keith Joseph but I did not meet her again until some time after the '79 election when, as Special Adviser to the Department of Industry, I would accompany Keith to occasional meetings at Number 10. However, observing Margaret at work from the far end of the table was one thing, dealing directly with her when she felt strongly about something was quite another.

Keith left Industry for the Department of Education and some time later I went to the Manpower Services Commission. Eventually in the autumn of 1984 she invited me into Cabinet as Minister without Portfolio with responsibilities for employment.

I chaired a number of sub-committees, one of which was engaged in developing a two-year YTS and in due course we agreed the terms of a new scheme. One of the issues was the benefit of £16 per week payable to unemployed

I am the Cabinet rebel.

At the Thatcher residence in Dulwich, South London, in 1990.

school leavers and many of my colleagues, myself included, thought that this early indoctrination into the welfare state was quite wrong. I persuaded my committee that we should abolish this benefit but give the YTS entrants £25 per week, which they would be expected to earn.

Our White Paper was due to be published just before the Easter recess. When the Prime Minister was in Beijing the previous December to sign the Accord on Hong Kong she announced that I was to bring a trade delegation of some of the biggest UK companies at the beginning of March.

I was busy selecting and inviting my delegation when the bombshell dropped. I received an invitation to call on the Chief Secretary who gave me a simple message. Since the Treasury thought that many more young people would be attracted into our new scheme than collect benefit, it would cost £200m more of public expenditure, and where was the additional money coming from? Now, I had no department, thus no budget to cut, so I was told that if I wanted this scheme, I must persuade my colleagues to find the amount for me. No one volunteered, so I went back to my committee and persuaded them to restore unemployment pay provisions once again.

Then the day came when I had to obtain the Prime Minister's agreement to our Paper. As soon as the meeting started I knew that I was in trouble. She was adamant that we should stop paying school leavers benefit if they wouldn't enter the scheme, and nothing I could say would change her mind. The scheme in full, or nothing.

The following day was my last before I left for China. I asked for a meeting to raise the matter again and she met me in the morning with a small number of colleagues. Again nothing I could say would change her attitude. Paying benefit to school leavers was wrong, when they had the chance to earn more by entering YTS and that was that. I had rarely known her so adamant.

My White Paper, my first, was in ruins. I asked to see her, one to one, and she saw me in the middle of the afternoon. No matter what argument I used she would not budge. The terrible thing was that I knew that she was right, but I also knew that without my White Paper, the chance for a two-year scheme was gone, probably for good.

I had to take the Committee stage of a Bill in the Lords that evening and I went through the motions in the House in a deep depression. At about eight o'clock I slipped a note to my Private Secretary to see if the PM would see me later that evening. She would, and at eleven o'clock after the business in the House I went over to Number 10.

The discussion ranged back and forth for about an hour and I did not appear to be making any progress. The clock struck and I told the Prime Minister that it was now my birthday. Suddenly she changed and reluctantly, but with good grace, agreed to the amended scheme. I left as quickly as I could before she could change her mind. I still had my boxes to do, I still had to pack and we were leaving at the crack of dawn but I was happy.

We introduced two-year YTS and the year after we were able to abolish benefit for school leavers.

'As soon as the meeting started I knew that I was in trouble. She was adamant that we should stop paying school leavers benefit.'

Lord Young

Mrs Thatcher sits beneath her portrait by Helmut Norton at the National Portrait Gallery, London.

Michael Cockerell
DOCUMENTARY FILM MAKER AND AUTHOR

The award-winning documentary film maker Michael Cockerell has been involved in the production of political television for over twenty-five years, most famously as the BBC *Panorama's* chief political reporter. His acclaimed study of prime ministers and television, *Live From Number 10*, was published in 1988.

Maggie's prime time

MY RELATIONSHIP WITH MARGARET THATCHER did not always run smooth. Some years after she had left office I filmed Lady Thatcher and Lord (Bill) Deedes at a Foyles Literary Lunch for a BBC TV profile I was making of Deedes. 'You know Michael Cockerell,' he said to her mischievously, 'was he always kind to you when you were Prime Minister?' 'No', she replied, with her special brand of emphasis, 'no he was not.'

Perhaps she had in mind a *Panorama* I had made in 1982 after the Falklands crisis broke, but before our troops were in action. On the programme, some Tory MPs had expressed their hopes that war might be avoided and an honourable settlement negotiated. It was not a popular view and in the Commons the next day, the Conservative Mrs Sally Oppenheim, asked Mrs Thatcher at Question Time: 'Will the Prime Minister take time off in the course of her busy day to watch a recording of last night's *Panorama* in which Michael Cockerell dishonoured the right of freedom of speech in this country?' I had not, until that moment, realised that the programme was quite as good as that.

But the PM rather agreed with the sentiments of her questioner, saying: 'There are some people in this country who do not understand their duty in a democracy to stand up for our boys.' That response marked a low point in our relationship – but she was magnanimous in her Falklands victory and agreed – after a break – to give me further prime ministerial interviews.

I suppose the high point in our encounters had come three years earlier during the 1979 General Election. I was making a film for the BBC about her campaign and the Iron Lady was determined to counter Labour's charges that she was harsh and uncaring. In an interview with me, she assumed a kittenish persona.

I put it to her that there sometimes seemed to be two Mrs Thatchers: one toured supermarkets and factory floors, exhibiting endless fascination about the minutiae of people's lives and jobs; the other was the platform politician – full of zealous conviction.

'How many Mrs Thatchers are there?' I asked.

'Oh, three at least,' she responded in a low, confiding voice: 'There is the intellectual one, the intuitive one and the one at home.' Her manner was so intimate – even coquettish – that the late Sir Robin Day, watching in the studio when the filmed interview went out, joked: 'The untold story of the election campaign: Margaret Thatcher is having an affair with Michael Cockerell'.

The last time I interviewed her as Prime Minister was for a portrait I was making of Willie Whitelaw for the BBC. It was May 1989 and Mrs T had just celebrated her tenth anniversary in office – but ringing in her ears was her deputy

I hope to go on and on and on.

Chief Whip Tristan Garel Jones' warning: 'The assassins are lurking in the bushes waiting to get you.'

I had asked Lord Whitelaw how long he felt Mrs Thatcher would continue in office: 'Oh, she is very fit, very strong. I hope she'll go on for a very long time,' he replied.

'But she is not immortal,' I ventured to suggest.

'No she is not immortal,' responded Willie, then added, 'but perhaps she is.'

In Number 10, I recounted this exchange on camera to Mrs T. Reviewing the tape today is revealing.

On freezing the frame at exactly the moment she hears my intimation of her mortality, a remarkable look comes over her face for an instant: an apparent mix of panic and blinding revelation. Within a few frames it is gone and she recovers her composure on hearing me recount Whitelaw's response. 'What a sweet thing of Willie to say – no, I am not immortal and I don't know how long I will go on – and no one does.'

Within months she was gone. And like every TV journalist I missed her. Once you had Margaret Thatcher in your viewfinder she never failed to produce riveting images and powerful quotes. A medium which in any case tends to magnify personalities had for the fifteen years of her Tory leadership been faced with a giant-sized one. Disraeli, Lloyd George and Winston Churchill became Prime Ministers before the age of television.

Happily Mrs T did not.

Margaret Thatcher sharing her joy with supporters outside Number 10 Downing Street after the Falklands victory.

Lord Crickhowell

SECRETARY OF STATE FOR WALES 1979–87

Lord Crickhowell, then Nicholas Edwards, served in Margaret Thatcher's Cabinet as Secretary of State for Wales from 1979 until 1987 when he was raised to the Peerage. He became Chairman of the National Rivers Authority in 1989, a position he held until 1996.

She loved an argument

MEETING IN THE PRIME MINISTER'S ROOM in the House of Commons, we were discussing education policy. Keith Joseph, who she liked and admired and to whom she owed an immense debt of gratitude, but who she sometimes treated badly, was interrupted with increasing frequency as he attempted to present his case. At first these astringent interjections came every few sentences and then with the staccato bark of an automatic weapon they ripped every sentence into increasingly minute fragments. Most of us examined our papers in silence with increasing irritation and embarrassment; but Nigel Lawson, deciding that enough was enough, suddenly leant across the table and snapped, 'Shut up, Prime Minister, just occasionally let someone get a word in edgeways.' There was a stunned silence: we all looked up waiting to see what would happen. For the first and last time I saw Margaret Thatcher blush and then for twenty minutes she was silent, and during this extraordinary lull Keith presented his Paper and we went on to have one of the most constructive discussions that I ever remember in a Cabinet Committee chaired by the Prime Minister. I don't remember any other occasion when a Cabinet colleague was quite so blunt; but it is nonetheless a myth that we were all always supine and subservient. The techniques for standing up to the Prime Minister's extremely combative conduct of business varied; but they were more effective than has been generally acknowledged. In reality she seldom behaved quite so badly as on that occasion with Keith Joseph and there is much to be said for the technique of testing the strength of a case by vigorous argument, though there were a few members of the Cabinet who found it unendurable.

Margaret Thatcher loved an argument and respected those who stood up to her when they had command of their subject. She invited contributions from around the table, sometimes from those of us who would have preferred at that particular moment to stay silent. The system of testing a case to destruction had the great advantage that it frequently exposed a flaw and prevented a disaster; but the drawback was that it sometimes destroyed perfectly good policy and prevented it being pressed further. As time went on, the runners in the race also found that the challenge had been made more severe by the simple manoeuvre of packing the committees with hostile critics. After the Industry Committee had produced a series of decisions and recommendations with which the Prime Minister disagreed, she regained control by assuming the chair herself. Committees that were not considered sufficiently robust found that the membership was changed, or decisions were taken by ad hoc groups of Ministers, frequently without the circulation of papers or adequate interdepartmental consultation. There was nothing very new in this but the Prime Minister carried the process further than

In a socialist society, parents should be seen and not heard.

Talking to a resident of Lockerbie after the 1988 air disaster, surrounded by the media throng.

most of her predecessors. Despite these manoeuvres there were frequent occasions when the Prime Minister did not get her way and when she accepted, sometimes with visible irritation, the majority decision.

She always came to the table impeccably well briefed. The Treasury commentary would be to hand; she would have underlined key passages in the papers before her with a yellow marking pen; her extraordinary memory provided a further challenge. On occasions she positively overwhelmed the opposition. This was always relatively easy if the unfortunate Minister's colleagues simply did not believe that this was a policy for which they were prepared to fight and risk injury or worse. For most Ministers the injury they feared most was the loss of some treasured policy of their own: if your own paper was next on the agenda, you would not prejudice its progress by stirring up advance hostility. Having said that, it is also true that in the great majority of cases when the Minister sought approval for a policy he considered important and was prepared to fight, he would get his way, although sometimes it did not feel like it at the time.

An account that concentrates on arguments round the Cabinet table inevitably gives a partial and distorted picture of the Prime Minister's character and conduct. The aggressive and dominating characteristics which she used to such effect in Cabinet discussions were frequently matched by acts of great personal kindness. She always seemed to know a great deal about her colleagues and their troubles, and a Member of Parliament would be surprised to be stopped in a corridor with an inquiry about a recent sickness or a family problem. It was because of actions of that kind that she was so much loved by her staff at Chequers and Number 10, and by all those who worked closely with her.

She paid numerous visits to Wales and for nearly eight years gave me all the support I could have wished, even though my instruments were government agencies and regional policies that she did not much favour. As in so many other cases, she was more pragmatic and flexible in achieving her objectives than many of her critics have understood or acknowledged. She seemed most at home with the people of Wales in the period before tight security restricted her movements and cut her off from contact with ordinary people. On the last Christmas in Opposition before she became Prime Minister, we arrived in Wrexham late one evening when the streets were packed with shoppers. She went from stall to stall in the market buying groceries and talking to stallholders and customers and then we emerged into the main street just at the moment that a huge float bearing Father Christmas appeared round the corner. The crowd surged forward and in a moment of inspiration, and perhaps because there was almost nowhere else to go, we pulled her up onto the float beside Father Christmas and there through the packed crowd they travelled together to a surging, warm, enthusiastic welcome that was unique in all my experience of political life. During the last Election Campaign in which I took part in the summer of 1987, things were very different – every move was carefully scheduled. Security was tight, contact with crowds was minimal. I took her down to Cardiff Bay, and as we drove away, a small but noisy group booed and one man raised his fingers in an obscene gesture. The Prime Minister visibly froze, obviously offended, and turned to me saying, 'Oh what dreadful people, we are really wasting our time – what is the point of all your efforts if they appreciate them so little.' One felt that she was not at her best and this was alien territory, far from the England that she knew and understood. In a way it was the Scottish story all over again. Her efforts to help were not rewarded; the support that she gave for her Secretaries of State was not appreciated; there was a barrier that somehow she was not able to surmount.

My formal responsibilities as Secretary of State finally came to an end on Election Day and that weekend, as I sat in my Welsh home with Ann, I was surprised to receive a telephone call from Number 10.

'The Prime Minister would like to speak to you.' There were a few words said

Oh what dreadful people, we are really wasting our time – what is the point of all your efforts if they appreciate them so little.

about the way that the election had gone, sadness at seats that had been lost, and then she said, 'I have decided to appoint a very senior member of my Cabinet as Secretary of State for Wales.' 'Oh, yes, Prime Minister,' I said, 'And who is that?'

'Oh, I can't tell you', she replied, 'because I have not yet told him.'

'In that case I cannot really comment,' I responded.

By this time Ann was in a fever of excitement, all agog to know who it was to be – we had been speculating long and hard. 'Well, I will tell you if you promise not to tell anyone,' she said.

'Of course,' I replied.

'I have decided to ask Peter Walker to take on the job,' she told me.

'Peter Walker,' I repeated clearly, at least in part for Ann's benefit, 'I am sure he will do it excellently, what a brilliant idea.'

After she had rung off, I wondered why she had telephoned. It cannot be that if my reaction had been hostile she would have changed her mind. In any event I was rather touched and I appreciated the fact that she had taken the trouble to tell me, particularly as Peter Walker was apparently still totally ignorant of his fate.

'Will he accept it?' said Ann doubtfully. 'Oh, yes, I am sure he will,' I said. 'After all, he knows the difference between being in and out, and in the circumstances he will have an almost free hand to do anything he likes.'

Margaret Thatcher graphically demonstrates the effects of inflation on a housewife's daily shopping during the 1979 Election Campaign.

Edwina Currie

NOVELIST, BROADCASTER AND FORMER MP

Edwina Currie was the MP for Derbyshire South from 1983 until 1997 and served as a junior Minister at the Department of Health. She currently works as a bestselling novelist and broadcaster.

A magical experience

I FIRST SAW MARGARET THATCHER in 1975 at the Party Conference, her first after she had defeated Ted Heath. She was our new Party Leader, a pretty young (forty-nine) married woman with young children, a scientist, a brain. I was a recently elected Birmingham City Councillor. I put in slip after slip to speak and was turned down. Eventually I was told, 'You're not important enough.' I went away, determined to return when I was.

Yet our paths were very similar. Some were coincidences I exploited to the full – for example, that we had the same birthday. Others were not chance. We both came from the provinces, had fathers with small businesses who loved talking politics, mothers who were quiet homemakers: our fathers were the models. We both went to state grammar schools, and on to Oxford to read chemistry. The old universities were looking for provincial girl state school scientists. It was much easier for an ambitious girl to win a place in science than in anything else.

So it meant I knew about her, and that it was possible to leap over all the barriers and become an MP like that. We were both outsiders. It also meant that I worshipped her, as did all the young Turks of the day.

I first came across her face to face at a new MPs' tea party in her room at the Commons in the summer of 1983. My colleague Robert Jackson was at that time still an MEP, and rapporteur of the budget committee in Brussels. Margaret turned to him sweetly. 'When will we get our rebate back, Robert?' she asked. 'Oh, Prime Minister, it's not our money …' the unfortunate man began to explain. 'Not OUR money?' she squawked, and proceeded to demolish him, until nothing but a smoking heap of ash was left in his seat.

She turned to me. 'How are you getting on, dear?'

I decided to choose an anodyne subject. 'Fine – except with 158 new Members, accommodation is a bit of a problem,' I began (we didn't have the spanking new parliamentary building then).

'Really?' the eyebrows shot up, 'Do you have a desk?'

'Yes, I found my predecessor's.'

'Good. And a secretary?'

'Yes, I brought one from Derbyshire.'

'And a phone?'

'Yes, we …' my voice began to falter.

'And a filing cabinet?'

'Yes, Prime Minister, I have two …'

She sat back, 'Well, you've only been here six weeks, I should say you're doing rather well. When I arrived in 1959 it was six months before I had anywhere to sit …'

> *'Our paths were very similar.'*
>
> Edwina Currie

Margaret Thatcher emulates her political hero Winston Churchill and makes a V for Victory sign, November 1976.

An important early event in that Parliament was the defeat of the unions, and of Arthur Scargill's miners in particular. With a mining seat (it used to be George Brown's) I was at the coal face on this. It was a meticulously planned operation. Scargill had piqued the Government by threatening strike action in 1981, before Ministers were ready for him. Nick Ridley was put to the task. Soon, mountains of coal were piling up at the power stations – as we could observe daily, since five coal-fired power stations were visible from my own home. After the 1983 election, Scargill was finessed all through the winter, and bounced into calling the strike as spring started. That meant he would have to stay out at least six months to have any effect.

My miner constituents took a postal ballot. Over 90 per cent voted, with 85 per cent voting to continue working. The UDM was born. What they hated most was the use of the strike weapon to try and bring down a government – as it had Jim Callaghan's in 1979 – just after another election. It seemed anti-democratic to them, an impression reinforced by Scargill's refusal to ballot his own members, as the rule-book required. 'What's this about rolling back the tides of Thatcherism, Edwina?' one miner said to me. 'We voted for the tides of Thatcherism. That's why you're here.' The tide had turned, and washed Mr Scargill and all the strikers away with it.

It was a famous victory – more so, and more enduring, than the Falklands. With it went any hope of a union bringing this country to its knees again. The effect on our reputation abroad was dramatic and beneficial. When Toyota wanted to come to Europe in 1989, there was no question: it had to be strike-free Britain. And it was no accident that they chose a spot away from existing car factories and in the middle of a strike-free country – again, within view of my house in South Derbyshire.

The story of Margaret Thatcher's later years included both remarkable success such as the ending of the Cold War and her friendship with Gorbachev, and ignominy and failure. I voted against her in 1990, knowing full well that had she continued as Party Leader we would have lost my marginal seat and many others with it. By then, voters other than committed Tories had had enough.

But serving with her was a magical experience, one which could never be bettered. We are a stronger, finer country for the standards she set, and the leadership she gave.

'If you have a good Thatcher, you keep your home water and windproof.'

Edwina Currie

Quentin Davies

CONSERVATIVE MP

Quentin Davies was the MP for Stamford and Spalding from 1987 until 1997 when he became the MP for Margaret Thatcher's home constituency of Grantham and Stamford.

Plunging in

I AM NOT WIDELY THOUGHT OF AS A THATCHERITE, but I would certainly have described myself as that when I was first elected to Parliament in 1987. I regarded – and still regard – Margaret Thatcher's first two terms of Government as a period of heroic achievement – the economic successes, the end of the 'British Disease', the privatisations, the Right to Buy, Personal Pensions, the creation of a property-owning democracy, standing up to bullying from any quarter, and historic victories against trade union power, Argentinian invasion and the Cold War. Until the Bruges speech I never found myself in anything other than enthusiastic agreement with her. Her personal attitude to politics – conviction, consistency, unstinting and tireless conscientiousness, setting the highest standards for herself and her Ministers, absolute integrity – I still regard as a model for any age. And her period of office transformed, at least temporarily, the attitude of the British electorate to politics itself. In retrospect it was a shining oasis between the Wilsonian cynicism and national decline that preceded her, and the drift and scandals that followed. One of my proudest moments was when I was made a PPS at the end of my first year – sadly for me on the eve of the shattering Bruges speech!

Two recollections – which illustrate both one of her weaknesses and one of her outstanding strengths. Six months after my election I was invited to her room in the Commons with a dozen other new arrivals. We sat around the table. She made a few introductory remarks and then asked for our comments on how things were going. Everyone said 'wonderful, Prime Minister' or words to that effect – indeed she was at her apogee and there was little enough to criticise. 'Well, come on,' she said, 'something must be less than perfect.' I thought that an admirable approach. So I plunged in. I said that I thought we ought not to fight the next election without being able to point to something we had done for the old age pensioner – it had been the one serious difficulty during the 1987 election.

I didn't make it into a second sentence. She flew at me with a string of well remembered statistics. Didn't I know that average pensioner household incomes had increased by 50 per cent since 1979, that now two thirds instead of one third of those retiring had some income other than the National Insurance pension etc, etc.? (As it happened I knew most of this almost as pat as she did – but it didn't really meet my point.) The monologue lasted perhaps twenty minutes and began to cover the whole issue of Treasury controls and how essential they were. My colleagues sat motionless, as if paralysed, as the diatribe gathered in intensity. Some surreptitiously moved their eyes towards me though without daring to move their heads – glances of horror or fascinated anticipation rather than of sympathy. Clearly I had committed lèse-majesté, and now fully deserved to be thrown to the lions. Then finally the energy of the volcano seemed spent. There was neither

A quick cure is a quack cure.

Overleaf: Mrs Thatcher at her desk in the study of Number 10 Downing Street, October 1989.

time, nor inclination, nor I suspect breath left to discuss anything else. We filed out in silence – I, and to a lesser extent I suspect all of us, feeling a little giddy.

Of course I had misjudged the invitation to express dissent – however respectfully or tentatively I had endeavoured to do so. I had fallen into the trap set by Mao Tse Tung when he launched his Hundred Flowers Campaign and begged loyal Party members to speak up with any complaints or criticisms they had. The difference was that Mao's victims were rapidly physically liquidated. Margaret remained utterly friendly in the lobbies – and clearly did not veto my promotion to PPS. Nor was that the last occasion when I ventured some comment or suggestion. But the response was always of a predictably binary kind – either she had already thought of the point herself, or it was a very silly idea. Perhaps it often was. But for all my great respect and admiration for Margaret I began to pity her Cabinet colleagues. And I started to fear that with Margaret bearing such an immense burden of work, and taking alone such a vast range of short-term and long-term decisions, some terrible mistake might one day be made.

My second recollection comes from the end. It was well known in the Party that I was supporting Michael Heseltine in his bid for the leadership. I had never disguised my views from Peter Morrison, Margaret's Private Secretary, from the Whips or from anyone else in the House. But I felt it cowardly to leave it there, especially as I genuinely admired so much that she stood for, and was conscious of the historical greatness of the personage, and the somewhat awesome gravity of the decision we were about to take. So I wrote her a personal letter. I expressed the sincerest admiration but I explained why I had found it necessary to vote and campaign against her. I said I thought her European policy had split the Party irredeemably, was inconsistent with her own Single European Act, and while we remained in the European Community (as it was then called) inhibited us from exercising any real influence within it, thus inevitably preventing us from optimising the national interest. I might have added that we had lost a historic opportunity to take the lead in Europe.

Of course I never expected any reply. Under the emotional stress and trauma of the moment any other political leader I feel sure would simply have flung the letter into the nearest waste-paper basket – I do not doubt I would have done so myself. But two days after the second round, when there was no conceivable political or ulterior motive in conciliating me, I received a courteous hand-written response. I recall the surprise I felt as I opened it. My conflicting emotions were I think, once again, though for rather different reasons, almost giddying. But this time, as I thought of Margaret Thatcher, the human being beneath her public greatness, I could only marvel.

'As I thought of Margaret Thatcher, the human being beneath her public greatness, I could only marvel.'

Quentin Davies

A portrait for *Chat* magazine in March 1989.

David Davis
CONSERVATIVE MP

David Davis was first elected to Parliament in 1987 as MP for Goole. He has served in the Whips' office, as a junior Minister in the Cabinet Office and then as Minister for Europe. He was chairman of the Public Accounts Committee from 1997–2001.

Building Rome

SOON AFTER MY ELECTION TO PARLIAMENT in 1987 I happened to be walking through the Members' Lobby when I suddenly observed an old friend, Michael Forsyth, a well-known Thatcherite and later to become a leading light in the No Turning Back Group.

Michael had been elected in 1983 and by now had become a junior minister. He was running, literally running. His hair was dishevelled and he was carrying not only his box, but somehow balancing a full tray of papers on his arm.

'Slow down,' I called out. 'Rome wasn't built in a day,' I added as an afterthought.

'Yes,' cried Forsyth over his shoulder, as he swept passed me. 'But Margaret wasn't the foreman on that job.'

Margaret Thatcher formally opens the M25 London orbital ringroad in 1986.

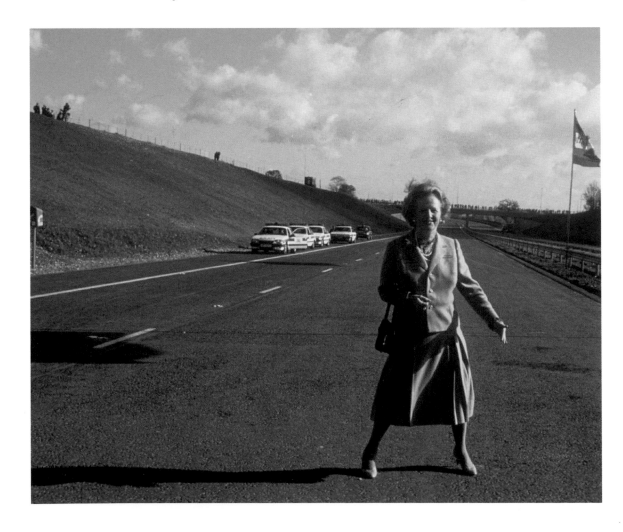

Michael Dobbs

NOVELIST AND BROADCASTER

A former Chief of Staff and Deputy Chairman of the Conservative Party, Michael Dobbs is most famous as the author of the *House of Cards* trilogy of political novels. His latest novel is *Churchill's Hour*.

The fall and rise of the house of cards

THEY SOW THE SEEDS OF THEIR OWN DESTRUCTION, even the greatest. And so it was with Margaret.

The date was 4 June 1987, exactly one week before the election triumph that returned her to Downing Street for a record third time. Her victory was unprecedented, and it was to be her last.

I was Chief of Staff of the Conservative Party and on that fateful day was sitting in my claustrophobic room in Conservative Central Office. When I had been appointed to the position I had been told by Norman Tebbit, the Chairman of the Party, what to expect. 'There comes a point in every war when the generals require that someone be taken out into a courtyard, put up against a wall and shot. Your job is to find the body. Or to be the body.' I had thought he was joking.

A Gallup poll the night before had shown an alarming reduction in the size of the Tory lead. On the basis of the poll we were headed for trouble, but every other piece of information suggested we were going to win, and win big.

It was a rogue poll.

It didn't, however, stop the panic. Margaret was holding a morning summit in the room next door to mine with Norman, David Young, Willie Whitelaw and Stephen Sherbourne. Suddenly John Wakeham burst into my room and asked for the press advertising that was proposed for the following day. I was not responsible for the advertising but it had been left in my room for security. I handed the layouts to John, but he shook his head. 'I'm not going back into that room without you.'

So I took the layouts and walked into the room. If John had been kind he would have offered me a blindfold. It was time to be stood up against the wall.

The next few minutes of what became known as 'Wobbly Thursday' remain distinct in my mind, but I won't report the gory and distasteful details here, except to say that although the confrontation that took place was ostensibly about advertising, it had far more to do with power, access and intrigue. For the Court of Queen Margaret had turned into a Byzantine maze of crossed wires and conniving acolytes. Margaret was at the height of her powers, and it seemed that everyone wanted their own individual piece of it.

And that is the point of this story. She was at the height of her powers. She could rant and rage to the point of incoherence (and did during those minutes); I felt as though the handbag had been buried deep in the back of my skull. Willie Whitelaw rolled his oyster eyes at me in sympathy, but only Norman Tebbit tried to stand up to her, to restrain her, to direct her onto safer ground. It was to no purpose. In more than a decade of working for her I had seen her in pain, in tears, in triumph, but never had I seen her in such a condition.

She was the Leader, one of the greatest leaders of the century, and about to

If your only opportunity is to be equal then it is not opportunity.

score another historic victory. Except she seemed to doubt that herself.

As we left the meeting we were all shaking. I walked next to Willie Whitelaw, that wise and often underrated old bird, who said something that was to change my life. 'That is a woman who will never fight another election,' he muttered.

It seemed a preposterous suggestion. She bestrode the world. Yet three weeks later, as I sat beside a swimming pool in Gozo, the thought was still bothering me. I worked it over. They never know when to go, the great leaders. They all have to be pushed, shoved, hacked from office. Lloyd George. Churchill. And Thatcher, too. I realised that Willie was right.

She had lost the sensitivity and patience that had guided her so successfully through the difficult years when she had rebuilt a party in tatters and set it upon a course that transformed the country. It wasn't so much a matter of principle or policy but of personal style that, in the end, forced away from her even many of her closest allies. She became a political Chernobyl from whom so many were to distance themselves.

That realisation transformed my life. I sat down beside the swimming pool and began work on a novel about the destruction of a Prime Minister. It was called *House of Cards*.

Like so many of the ancient gods, she could not be brought down by mere mortals. She could only be brought down by herself. Oh, but while it was good, wasn't she magnificent!

Lord Lamont of Lerwick

CHANCELLOR OF THE EXCHEQUER 1990–93

The MP for Kingston-upon-Thames from 1972 until 1997, Norman Lamont served as a junior Minister in the Department of Energy, the Department of Trade and Industry, the Ministry of Defence and the Treasury between 1979 and 1989. In 1989 he became Chief Secretary to the Treasury in Margaret Thatcher's Cabinet and in 1990 he became Chancellor of the Exchequer, a position he held until 1993. He was raised to the Peerage as Lord Lamont of Lerwick in 1997.

Winning an argument

MARGARET THATCHER was one of the greatest ever peacetime Prime Ministers. I was very happy to be in her Government for all eleven years. But Margaret Thatcher was generally thought to be a somewhat fearsome colleague and demanding Prime Minister. However, she liked people to stand up to her and whatever her manner she respected those who put a good case against her. It was important also not to take everything she said literally.

I only once got the better of Mrs Thatcher in an argument. She had returned from a visit to the United States and had been sitting on the airplane next to a well-known American movie mogul. This person had somehow convinced Mrs Thatcher that Britain ought to create its own Hollywood and ought to use Government money to create a whole lot of new film studios. Mrs Thatcher, in an informal meeting, announced this to me and a group of astounded Ministers. She solemnly proposed that Government money should be used to subsidise these film studios which would be situated in Rainham Marshes in Essex.

I and other Ministers vainly pointed out that the whole thrust of her Government had been to remove subsidies from industry. There was no case for subsidising employment in Essex where there was little unemployment. Furthermore, the film industry was a curious one to subsidise. And lastly, Rainham Marshes was a strange site which would require massive investment in infrastructure to make the project practicable.

I remember vividly Mrs Thatcher turned on me, in front of colleagues, when I voiced my objections and said very sharply: 'You are hopeless. You are thoroughly negative. All you know is how to say "no". You do not have any imagination or any constructive ideas. If you had been in my Government since 1979 I would have achieved nothing!'

I was a little taken aback by this but managed to pull myself together and to reply: 'Well, Prime Minister you are invariably right on most matters, but there is one point on which you are wrong. I have been in your Government ever since 1979.'

Mrs Thatcher momentarily looked a little abashed but stuck to her argument. We ended the meeting by saying that if this was what she wanted to do of course we would put it into practice, although we all disagreed.

Forty-eight hours later I received a telephone call from her private office saying that she had changed her mind and that we should not proceed with the idea. It was often the case that if one put objections to her they might be overruled at the

> *You can't buck the market.*

time but nonetheless they were absorbed. Contrary to what critics said she both listened and was flexible.

Another characteristic of Margaret Thatcher was that she was always extremely thoughtful about all those who worked for her. She really did mind about them and their families. I was once told by the manager of Smythson, the Stationers in Bond Street, that their largest buyer of notelets was Mrs Thatcher. Certainly she was very adept at sending little handwritten notes commiserating with people or congratulating them on this or that. I have several such notes from her. I am quite sure that Mrs Thatcher has carried out many private acts of kindness that are unknown to the wider world because she simply has not told anyone about them and only the individuals know.

Mrs Thatcher had a very strong sense of the need to honour one's obligations. One year my Conservative Association in Kingston decided to ask the Prime Minister's husband, Denis, to speak at a function which was being held in the Banqueting Suite at Twickenham Rugby Ground. On the Saturday afternoon I was sitting at home reading a newspaper in an armchair when the telephone rang and a voice said, 'The Prime Minister for you.' Mrs Thatcher then came on the line and said, 'Denis has strained his back and can't be with you tonight at Kingston.'

I replied, 'Well, Prime Minister thank you very much for ringing, it is very good of you to tell me and I know everybody will understand.'

The PM went on, 'No no, you don't understand what I'm saying. I'm coming instead.'

I replied, 'Prime Minister that is extremely kind of you but it isn't really necessary because everybody will understand that Denis is not at all well.' I was rather worried as I didn't think it was a grand enough occasion for a Prime Minister. Some people would be annoyed they didn't know she was coming. I was also concerned about the short time available to lay on the necessary security and all the other complications that would follow from a unexpected visit by the PM. But Margaret was insistent. 'We always keep our promises, and I am coming,' she said. She did. She stood in for Denis at the dinner, and of course the evening was a huge success.

Speaking to the press outside Number 10 Downing Street.

Lord Owen

LEADER OF THE SDP 1983–92

Dr David Owen served as Foreign Secretary under James Callaghan from 1977 until 1979. In 1981 he resigned from the Labour Party to form the Social Democratic Party with Roy Jenkins, Bill Rodgers and Shirley Williams. He became Leader of the SDP after the 1983 election, resigning in 1987 over the merger with the Liberal Party. He was re-elected Leader of the SDP in 1988 and remained in that position until 1992 when he became Chairman of the International Conference on former Yugoslavia. Lord Owen now sits as a cross-bencher in the House of Lords.

Expensive scent and alcohol

MY FIRST PERSONAL MEMORY of Margaret Thatcher was as Secretary of State for Education in the early 1970s. A medical friend had come to dinner with her in the House of Commons to discuss a young patient and when she bumped into me in the division lobby she asked if I would go and have a drink with them. It was a revealing occasion, for as the conversation developed Margaret Thatcher's best and worst qualities were on display: consideration for a young constituent and the wish to get to the bottom of a problem coupled with a total inability to comprehend how any seventeen-year-old could be depressed.

As Foreign Secretary we met at many official functions. In April 1979 I was interviewed in the *Daily Mirror* and said, 'I saw her the other evening the House of Commons and for the first time she looked really rather attractive. She'd had a couple of whiskies and was quite glowing, in the nicest possible way. She came over, smiling that special smile of hers, and wafted a combination of expensive scent and alcohol over me.'

This was described by an angry Conservative Party as the first dirty trick of the forthcoming Election Campaign. It was mild compared to President Mitterrand's remark later that 'she has the lips of Marilyn Monroe and the smile of Caligula'. But John Junor, the editor of the *Sunday Express*, who had lunch with her next day, found her relaxed, even flattered. It was at about this time that I had realised that we faced in her a far more formidable opponent than it was fashionable for most Labour politicians to admit.

In addressing Margaret Thatcher's leadership I believe the 1984 miners' dispute showed her at her best. She had cut her losses and settled when challenged by Joe Gormley in 1981 and had then planned ahead for the inevitable confrontation with Arthur Scargill. When the pit deputies union, NACODS, threatened sympathetic strike action at the end of October 1984, I was extremely worried that any concession to them could be used by Scargill as a face-saver. I took the opportunity of being in the same room as Margaret Thatcher to have a private talk with her. She seemed genuinely pleased to find that my worries about letting Arthur Scargill off the hook were exactly the same as hers. She made no attempt to conceal the fact that some of her colleagues wanted to settle but that she was adamantly against it. She was clear-sighted about the danger of Scargill being able to claim a spurious victory. When the end came in March 1985, fifty-one weeks after the strike had started, it was the miners who disowned their leaders

> '*She'd had a couple of whiskies and was quite glowing, in the nicest possible way.*'
>
> Lord Owen

Margaret Thatcher about to cast her vote in the 1975 EEC referendum at her local polling station in the King's Road, Chelsea.

by streaming back to work with their funds running low and good men with their self-respect in tatters. But for the country as a whole it was essential for our self-confidence that intimidation and violence could be resisted without tear gas or mobilising the armed services. The police, with a few exceptions, did extremely well.

Meeting with the Prime Minister at Number 10 in 1983 I raised the question of SDP representation at the Cenotaph. I was barely halfway through my case than she intervened to reject it, declaring that she was adamantly opposed to widening representation. Suddenly the atmosphere was heated. I told her bluntly that I could see absolutely no reason why a party that had attracted three and a half million voters should not be entitled to lay a wreath at the Cenotaph. Eventually I rose to go and said that I hoped that, since the decision was formally the Home Secretary's, she would give the matter renewed thought, otherwise I would have to take my case before the bar of public opinion. She became incandescent, alternating between a prim 'How could you?' to a furious 'How dare you?' *The Daily Telegraph* reported that the issue sharply divided Ministers, that many senior members of the Government were unhappy and that one of the service chiefs had actually objected to our exclusion. Newspapers up and down the country took our side. It was a good example of the basic fairness and decency of the British people asserting itself. Eventually Whitehall produced a formula to save the Prime Minister's face. What the whole episode showed was that though she was still totally dominant, she did not have an absolute hold on public opinion or newspaper editors and was politically deeply partisan as she showed by taking the salute at the Falklands Victory parade instead of the Queen.

Some socialists seem to believe that people should be numbers in a state computer. We believe they should be individuals.

On the morning of 15 April 1986, Britain woke up to find that during the night the Americans had bombed terrorist targets in Libya using F-111 aircraft from bases in Britain. The Prime Minister was under immediate attack for authorising their use. Opposition leaders, like me, opposed the action as illegal. In government, however, decisions have to be made and the choice is often between two evils. The lesser evil in this case was to support President Reagan's request and try to pretend, as Margaret Thatcher did, that it was covered under Article 51 of the UN Charter and was an act of self-defence, whereas it was really retaliation forbidden under the UN Charter. Having been given crucial military support by President Reagan during the Falklands war, Margaret Thatcher knew that she owed him similar support. Given her personality, she would have found it impossible to refuse, and it is to her credit, in such trying circumstances, that she gave permission.

When history assesses whether Margaret Thatcher was a great Prime Minister, this decision deserves to be weighed in the balance. Her refusal would have done immense damage to our relations with the Reagan Administration. She showed courage and loyalty but she also demonstrated one of the distinguishing features of great leadership, the ability to turn a blind eye to instructions or to legal niceties and just to follow one's instincts.

After her 1987 election victory it was Margaret Thatcher in Number 10 on 7 July 1988 who proposed quite directly to me that I should join the Conservatives.

She had given a dinner for Lord Carrington to mark his retirement from the post of NATO Secretary General and had quite deliberately taken both Debbie, my wife, and me aside as we were leaving. In her blunt way she said to Debbie, 'Your husband has a big choice to make and it can no longer be avoided. There are only two serious parties in British politics and we women understand these things; it is time he made up his mind.' Debbie bridled and I politely refused to join the Conservative Party then, as I had refused all others who had raised the issue with me.

Margaret Thatcher's downfall began on Tuesday 30 October 1990 when she came to the House of Commons to make a statement on the Rome Summit. I helped wind her up by my question supporting the use of the veto. It was already clear from her earlier press conference, when she came out with her series of 'No, no, no' statements that she was on an emotional high and the adrenalin was pumping around her system as she handbagged every federalist proposal. She was taking her stand against the single currency and even beginning to backtrack from the agreed Government position over the hard ecu. I watched Geoffrey Howe's face as she answered these questions; he looked miserable and unhappy. Truly, I thought, a dead sheep. How wrong I proved to be. On 1 November Howe resigned and his forthright resignation speech gave Michael Heseltine the opening he longed for to challenge her leadership. She had been brought down by hubris over the European Community, not the Poll Tax. Her excessive self-confidence was by then being flaunted day by day in the face of friend or foe alike. She had pitted herself against her own source of power, the Conservative MPs. She had reached a stage where she was not only not listening to her parliamentary colleagues but was contemptuous of their views. The Cabinet had been reduced in stature and in quality. Majority opinion was frequently flouted or manipulated. People of substance, who well knew that Cabinet Government was a great constitutional safeguard, had allowed this to develop over the years to the detriment of us all. It was not just because she was a woman that the Cabinet had been so supine but it was a material factor. With the Cabinet too weak to act, the Conservative MPs had shown their power.

As Leader of the SDP I identified with those parts of her modernising counter-revolution which would help reverse Britain's economic decline. In the late 1990s Tony Blair, as Leader of New Labour, continued courageously with much the same modernising programme as, in fairness, did John Major before him. In a real sense this is a middle-class counter-revolution. It has by the start of the twenty-first century not yet achieved all its objectives, and its gains are not yet permanent. But it has made much needed changes in Britain. Its driving force and its chief architect was Margaret Thatcher, but it has not solely been her revolution, nor that of the Conservative Party. Indeed, in terms of monetary discipline the revolution began with Denis Healey and James Callaghan in 1976. Many people in the country have supported this counter-revolution who do not consider themselves party political. Essentially it has sought to reassert a national self-confidence, to rediscover the commercial market-orientated prosperity of the Victorian era which had not just been the product of our Empire but owed much

Your husband has a big choice to make and it can no longer be avoided.

to British invention, design, entrepreneurship, and industrial skill. It has also been a movement to reassert the role of the individual and to roll back the frontiers of an intrusive state. Sadly, Margaret Thatcher did not draw sufficiently on those other middle-class aspirations to serve the common good, to contribute to society as a whole, and indeed at times, as over the NHS, she quite unnecessarily upset those who held those values.

For centuries the middle-class had been patronised by those with hereditary wealth, but they had found they could escape from their backgrounds and by their own efforts create wealth. The crippling levels of personal taxation in the 1960s and 1970s, however, began to make it virtually impossible for the law-abiding, tax-paying, middle-class citizen to accumulate wealth. All that has changed. Now the middle-class are the wealth creators. Britain has become the fourth wealthiest country and we ought now to be able to progressively alleviate poverty and improve our health and education services.

Margaret Thatcher was one of the four radical Prime Ministers last century. As you walk through the door into the Members' Lobby in the House of Commons, you face statues of Winston Churchill and Lloyd George, guarding the entrance to the Chamber of the House of Commons. On the right of the door is a statue of Clement Attlee and on the left a place left empty for another statue. There is no doubt that eventually, as the first woman Prime Minister, she will occupy that position and deservedly so.

Oliver Letwin

CONSERVATIVE MP

Oliver Letwin became the MP for West Dorset in 1997. He was a special adviser to Sir Keith Joseph from 1982 until he became a special adviser to the Prime Minister's Policy Unit in 1983, staying there until 1986.

A little bit in love…

THE PRIME MINISTER WILL SEE YOU NOW – terrifying words for a young man, especially one about to be subjected to a job interview by the Iron Lady. And there she was, the victor of the Falklands, sitting in a wing-chair in her study. The 'interview' lasted a few seconds: 'I gather you are joining us.' It was welcome news to my ears – and, as I subsequently discovered, typical of her approach to the mechanics of administration: clear, decisive, no precious time wasted.

Once on the staff, you were a member of the family – and there was pretty much the same plain-speaking as in a family. When coming to discuss a speech I had drafted on science, it was not immediately encouraging to be greeted in the drawing-room at Chequers by the PM standing by the fireplace, and saying to the Chief Scientific Adviser in that inimitable but much imitated voice, 'Yes, that speech was as much of a dead loss as this one.'

You had to know what you were talking about, and you had to stand your ground. We quickly discovered that when she was interrogating and criticising and opining, seemingly without taking the slightest account of what you were saying, she was in fact at her most attentive – ceaselessly testing, often enough to destruction, the weak points in the argument, the facts that contradicted the assertions, the claims that could not be substantiated. And when, in a certain domain, you had established that you knew, and that you could defend a position, her trust was almost frightening. The memoranda – always to be short and clear – came back, with signal points doubly and triply underlined. In Cabinet committees, a note passed to her would be read out, 'I have a note …' as if the truth had been delivered, not always to the pleasure of her colleagues.

In the end, as in any family, the strongest bonds were those of affection. We loved her – perhaps we were a little bit in love with her, not least because of the tremendous compliment she continuously paid of knowing and knowing that she knew – great as she was, and small as we were – who and what we were. In disaster, there would be flowers sent. In error, there would be support and acceptance. The worst case I can recall arose from the Local Government expenditure round. I had a little computer, and felt terribly proud to have installed a little programme of my own invention to determine the fiscal effects of certain decisions that fell to be made. Alas, in committee, the conversation took an unexpected turn, and it was only the next morning that I discovered my programme failed to work when a negative replaced a positive. Down to the study, to admit the error. Not a single word of reproach from the Lady: she was, despite all the appearances to the contrary, wholly able to absorb the idea that her staff were imperfect human beings.

They were turbulent times. It was something of a shock to be sent home one

Advisers advise, Ministers decide.

weekend, when the miners were out, and the dockers had just come out, to read the histories of the General Strike. But they were also times of seemingly boundless possibility. The impossible was being done – the rolling back of the socialist state – and she was hungry for more ideas. They might be devoured with delight or spat out in disgust: but the appetite for more was always there. It was as if we were living on the edge of a hurricane. We swept forward, blown and buffeted, but hugely exhilarated.

And at the eye of the hurricane, a still calm. She never rushed, never seemed to be aware of time. One Friday night, an urgent minute arrived from one of the members of the Cabinet: should we do something or not – yes or no by midnight? The Private Secretary and I rushed out a memorandum on the pros and cons and hastened to her flat. Up as always, and working on her boxes, she calmly read the minute and the memo. Then the fatal enquiry: why the need for a decision by midnight, or indeed before Monday? In our haste to answer the Minister's question, we had failed to question the question. For all her energy, she hastened slowly enough to see the point we had missed.

When the day came to announce departure, she was to be found in her room at the House of Commons. The response was theatrical. On hearing the news, she sat down, as if to steady herself. One knew, of course, that it was for effect – but how touching that she bothered to put on the effect. A politician to her fingertips, yes – but the Iron Lady had charm.

Happier times. Sitting beside Michael Heseltine at a Conservative Conference.

Nicholas Ridley

CABINET MINISTER 1983–90

Nicholas Ridley was amongst Margaret Thatcher's staunchest supporters and most trusted colleagues. He joined the Cabinet in 1983 as Secretary of State for Transport and went on to become Secretary of State for the Environment and finally for Trade and Industry. Nicholas Ridley died in 1992.

My style of government

MARGARET THATCHER was always immaculately turned out herself. She dressed smartly, was well-groomed and expected other people to be so as well. During the 1987 election Nigel Lawson appeared on television with his hair in need of a trim; he got a complaint from next door. She wanted to set an example of high standards in all things, and for her example to be followed by others. She wanted 10 Downing Street to become renowned as a place of quality entertaining. She arranged for it to be redecorated in the mid 1980s with style and much gold leaf. It was transformed into a very grand and elegant house for entertaining the great and the good. It was adorned with good pictures from the national collections – one room contained a particularly lovely group of Turners. She entertained a lot. She saw to it that the food and wine, the flowers and the service, were of the highest quality. Quality was the keynote – not extravagance. Whenever the programme of a visiting foreign dignitary allowed, she would give a dinner for him. These dinner parties were glittering occasions. Important and interesting people were asked; she also liked to have plenty of pretty and well-dressed women among the guests. She expected people to rise to the occasion, and they did. Her speech after the dinner was always a model of fluency, erudition and courtesy. She was a master of the impromptu speech. Some of her speeches when the East European leaders came to London were particularly moving. It seemed to cause her no nervousness or bother when she had to make a speech after dinner. This was not the case with some of her principal guests. I remember being fortunate enough to sit next to President Havel of Czechoslovakia when he dined there. Margaret Thatcher was on his left, and she talked to him for most of the meal. When my turn came, he hastily picked up his speech notes to make last-minute improvements. My attempts to engage him in conversation were dashed by Margaret Thatcher saying to me across him, 'Can't you see, Nick, he's trying to finish his speech.'

In addition to official dinners, she gave frequent receptions – for party workers, or a visiting overseas delegation, or for scientists, artists, musicians or entrepreneurs. She also held lunch and dinner parties at Chequers at weekends, particularly when an overseas visitor was staying there. I remember one particular lunch, given for Lech Walesa, the Polish Leader of Solidarity. He was very conscious of Poland's debt to her and of all her help and encouragement. But that didn't stop him calling for a lot more in his very effective after-luncheon speech. There was a strange affinity between the fiery Polish shipyard trade unionist and the high-principled British Tory Prime Minister – two people as different as they could be. It was because they both believed in freedom and in democracy with an

You can strike your way down, but you have to work your way up.

equal passion that they were in alliance; not so much friendship, as a common cause to fight.

Sometimes groups of colleagues would be invited to lunch. It was after some such lunch that she resolved, after a long conversation with Nigel Lawson, Patrick Jenkin and myself, that another attempt must be made to replace the domestic rates. This was the day that she decided to start the studies which eventually led to the Community Charge.

She held a Boxing Day lunch every year to which family, friends and loyal supporters, both inside and outside politics, were bidden. It became a little too famous, and the press would find out who was there and who was not, trying to speculate as to who was 'in' and who was 'out'. It was difficult for her to keep any part of her life private. She always used to ask to this and other parties those acquaintances who had been widowed, or had been ill, or had suffered some misfortune, as well as her friends.

She was neither an egalitarian nor a puritan. From the way she entertained, it could hardly be said that she believed in a 'classless society'. She believed in equal opportunity for anyone to qualify to receive an invitation to one of her dinners; but once achieved, this was a distinction in a class of its own.

She liked to drink a little, although never too much. She preferred whisky and rarely did justice to the excellent wines that adorned the Number 10 dinner table. Government hospitality over the years had procured for Number 10 wines from the finest vineyards of France, and her predecessors cannot have done much damage to the stocks. The wine was always both excellent and adequate in quantity. She was entirely tolerant of those who had had one too many, unless they were proposing to drive themselves home. She often asked people before they had a drink whether or not they were driving and was very strict about this. One evening she unexpectedly visited the Whips Office in the Commons late at night. One of the Whips in the Lords happened to be there. He was considerably inebriated but thought he would go undetected if he stayed put where he was standing and hung onto the table firmly. 'Why don't you sit down,' she said. 'You look far too drunk to stand up.'

'From the way she entertained, it could hardly be said that she believed in a "classless society". She believed in equal opportunity for anyone to qualify to receive an invitation to one of her dinners; but once achieved, this was a distinction in a class of its own.'

Nicholas Ridley

With Polish President Lech Walesa.

Overleaf: Pictured in 1990, trying to spot her enemies?

Mikhail Gorbachev

PRESIDENT OF THE SOVIET UNION 1985–91

Mikhail Gorbachev was the last President of the Soviet Union. He presided over a period of intense change in his country and is credited with the introduction of the modernising policies of *perestroika* and *glasnost*. He famously attempted to foster peace between the superpowers and received the Nobel Peace Prize in 1990.

A woman I could do business with

AT MY FIRST MEETING WITH MRS THATCHER in late 1984, we had established what proved to be a good and lasting relationship. We both appreciated the contact and got on very well. This first meeting might be the reason why the Soviet–British dialogue made such a good start on my taking the helm of the Soviet Union in 1985 – although British policy towards us during the first years of *perestroika* was not exactly what you would call friendly. Great Britain was the first Western country to support the American Strategic Defense Initiative and to participate officially in its development. Margaret Thatcher viewed the Reykjavik meeting as a failure and fully supported Ronald Reagan's position, blaming the Soviet Union for the lack of an agreement. The British Government made a big show of expelling a group of Soviet officials, accusing them all of being agents of the KGB.

But at the same time the British spoke out in favour of a 'constructive long-term dialogue' with the Soviet Union. It is revealing that Margaret Thatcher took the initiative in visiting the Soviet Union after my election as General Secretary. She was a frequent guest in Washington, and it seemed as if she intended to represent Western European interests in the dialogue between the superpowers.

Mrs Thatcher came to Moscow in late March 1987. Our talks took place in the Kremlin, in the presence only of our personal assistants and interpreters. Stressing the significance of her visit, I remarked that the last high-level visit to the Soviet Union by a British Prime Minister had taken place more than twelve years earlier. She corrected me immediately, saying that the last British Conservative Prime Minister had visited the Soviet Union more than twenty years before.

Before getting down to business, I expressed my astonishment at a speech she had made in Torquay only a week before leaving for Moscow, delivered in the spirit of Reagan's anti-communist crusade. I said that we even had the impression that she might cancel her visit.

Mrs Thatcher had maintained that the Soviet Union aspired to 'establish communism and domination worldwide' and that 'Moscow's hand' could be seen in virtually every conflict in the world. Obviously I could not leave it at that and replied that much of her speech in Torquay as well as most of the accusations she had made were Conservative stereotypes going back to the 1940s and 1950s. But Mrs Thatcher stood her ground: 'You are supplying weapons to the Third World countries,' she rejoined, 'while the West supplies the food and aid in addition to helping establish democratic institutions.' The discussion became very heated.

Looking back I must admit (and it seems to me that I have already done so) that our policy towards developing countries had been highly ideological and that, to

Communism never sleeps, never changes its objectives. Nor must we.

a certain extent, Mrs Thatcher had been right in her criticisms. However, it was well known that the West had always been the prime supplier of weapons to the Third World and thus supported authoritarian and even totalitarian regimes, working on the principle that 'that dictator is a son of a bitch, but he is our son of a bitch'.

Our discussion had reached a point where I considered it necessary to say: 'We have frankly expressed our respective views on the world in which we live. But we have not succeeded in bringing our standpoints any closer. It seems to me that our disagreements have not become less after this conversation.'

My partner struck a more conciliatory note. Suddenly changing the course of our conversation, she said: 'We follow your activity with great interest and we fully appreciate your attempts to improve the life of your people. I acknowledge your right to have your own system and security, just as we have the right to ours, and we suggest taking this as a basis for our debate. In spite of all the differences between our systems,' she added, 'we can still exchange some useful experiences. We are deeply impressed by the vigorous policy of reform you are trying to implement. We have a common problem here – how to manage change.'

We went on to discuss our main topic, arms control. At the time Soviet–American talks on strategic arms were being held in Geneva. I went on the offensive, asking Mrs Thatcher directly: 'Is the West ready for real disarmament or have you been forced into negotiations under pressure from public opinion in your countries? I would appreciate it if you could clarify your position.'

Mrs Thatcher advanced the familiar argument that nuclear weapons represented the best guarantee for peace and that there could be no other guarantee in present conditions. 'We believe in nuclear deterrence,' she continued, 'and we do not consider the elimination of nuclear weapons practicable.'

In reply I delivered quite a long harangue, the gist of which was that the West did not want a solution, but was only interested in complicating the issue. I

With Raisa and Mikhail Gorbachev.

concluded: 'Today, we are closer than ever before to making a first step towards genuine disarmament. But the moment we were given this opportunity, you hit the panic button. Is the Tory policy exclusively aimed at hindering disarmament and the reduction of the level of confrontation in the world? It is amazing that Great Britain should feel comfortable in such a position.'

Mrs Thatcher seemed somewhat taken aback by my tirade. 'That's what I call a speech!' she exclaimed. 'I don't even know where to start.' And she assured me that the West did not in any way intend to make life difficult for us or complicate reform in the Soviet Union by rejecting disarmament.

Again and again, Margaret Thatcher repeated her main argument: nuclear weapons are the only means to ensure the security of Great Britain in the event of a conventional war in Europe. For this reason, Britain did not intend to commit itself to limiting in any way its nuclear arsenal. In short, our conversation was going round in circles. In an attempt to ease the tension, Margaret Thatcher told me about a 'funny occurrence', as she put it, which happened during a meeting with Hua Guofeng. The meeting was scheduled to last one hour. The Chinese leader spoke for forty-five minutes, and when Mrs Thatcher asked one single question, he continued his monologue for another twenty minutes. Seeing this, Lord Carrington (the British Foreign Secretary) handed the Prime Minister a written note: 'Madam, you tend to speak too much.'

Mrs Thatcher came to Moscow in June 1990. I had returned from my trip to the United States and Canada on 5 June, a few days before her arrival. She seemed greatly impressed by the results of the visit and complimented me on the 'extraordinarily successful meeting' with George Bush. Indeed the talks with the American President had dispelled a number of mutual concerns, including issues we had often discussed with Margaret Thatcher.

During our first conversation, she remarked that she believed it was essential to emphasise the positive aspects in our relations and to point out our convergent views on a number of issues at our joint press conference. 'Journalists tend to highlight negative aspects,' she said, 'and we must therefore concentrate on the positive achievements. It seems to me that many people, including many of the press, have not yet fully grasped how far we have come and how much the summit meetings contributed to this.'

'In 1986 my idea of a nuclear-free world was perceived as wishful thinking,' I reminded Mrs Thatcher. 'Today we are about to conclude an agreement with the Americans on a 50 per cent cut in strategic nuclear arms, and we have agreed on the elimination of our chemical weapons stockpiles. We have made much headway in only three years! Or, to take another example, the idea of a political settlement of regional conflicts was seen as another utopia. Today, the process has begun. And I must say that you personally have greatly contributed to this.'

My last meeting with Margaret Thatcher in her capacity as Prime Minister took place in Paris on 20 November, on the occasion of the European conference. We concentrated on the situation in the Gulf. I had discussed the issue with Mr Bush on the eve of our meeting, and Margaret Thatcher 'OK'd' our exchange of ideas. However, she admitted that she did not believe that a political settlement

'Madam, you tend to speak too much.'

Lord Carrington

With Soviet Premier Mikhail Gorbachev in 1985.

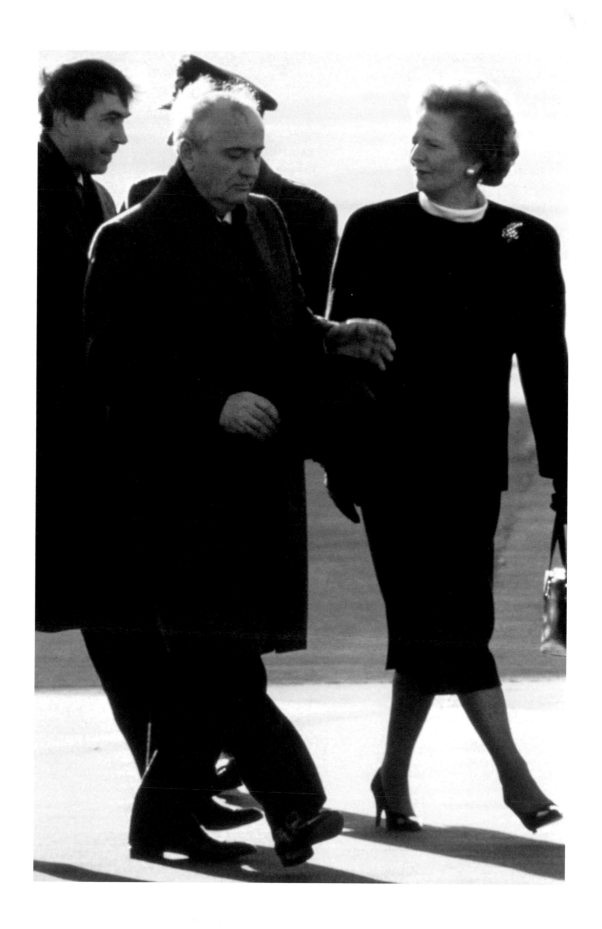

was possible and thought the use of force was inevitable. Hence she proposed that the next UN Security Council resolution (we had discussed it with George Bush) should be formulated in more severe terms, complaining that the Americans seemed to be 'somewhat over-cautious'. Needless to say, we also talked about the situation in the Soviet Union. The British Prime Minister did not hide her concern – she was an experienced politician and she perceived the dangers. We bade farewell at the entrance to my residence. 'God bless you!' she said in a soft voice.

The elections to the leadership of the British Conservative Party took place in Mrs Thatcher's absence. She failed to obtain the necessary majority on first ballot. She had told me that she had enemies – in eleven and a half years at the helm, this is virtually unavoidable. Yet she seemed to have no intention of capitulating. In Paris, when she was informed of the result of the election, she declared to the waiting press that she was 'going to show them' back home. Upon her return to London, however, she announced that she would resign. It was a noble act. Nonetheless, I regretted it.

Margaret Thatcher did much to support our *perestroika*. Needless to say she had her own views on the reforms, perceiving them as winning the Soviet Union over to Western positions, as a Soviet version of 'Thatcherism'. Nonetheless, she genuinely wanted to help us and to mobilise the efforts of the Western countries in support of our policies. During the August 1991 coup, she spoke out in defence of the Soviet President and his family.

One must give her credit for her services to her country. Mrs Thatcher took over at a time when the United Kingdom was lagging behind the other Western nations, and she succeeded in radically changing both the domestic and international situation of Great Britain. However Mrs Thatcher's tough methods and her inherent authoritarianism soured even her closest supporters, not to speak of the opposition, and eventually led to conflict situations. I had the impression that, in order to work with her, you had to accept her style and character unconditionally. Her authoritarianism and her penchant for forceful methods were manifest in British foreign policy. In crisis situations, she spoke out in favour of military sanctions. Even after her resignation as Prime Minister, we would occasionally receive information that 'Mrs Thatcher is suggesting air raids'. She was particularly tough in her approach to the Gulf crisis.

Margaret Thatcher was not an easy partner for us, and her fierce anti-communism would often hinder her from taking a more realistic view on various issues. Still, one must admit that in a number of cases, she was able to substantiate her charges with facts, which eventually led us to review and criticise some of our approaches. She was indeed a strong advocate of Western interests and values.

Margaret Thatcher had much of what I would call the 'Old English Spirit', at least as we Russians usually imagine it, which shows in her commitment to traditions and 'tried and tested' values. During our official meetings she was always very considerate and courteous. We eventually came to know each other better and she showed genuine warmth towards me and Raisa Maksimovna – despite the differences in our views and our political arguments.

Bob Hawke

PRIME MINISTER OF AUSTRALIA 1983–91

The trades unionist and Labour politician Bob Hawke is amongst the most influential figures in Australian politics. He became Prime Minister of Australia in 1983, remaining in that position until 1991.

Sneaking admiration

ON SATURDAY AFTERNOON at Lyford Cay the forty-nine Commonwealth heads met without officials. The meeting followed a plenary on that morning where heated argument had erupted over Margaret Thatcher's lone opposition to sanctions. Debate was at times bitter and the atmosphere spilled over into the afternoon. Margaret was implacable as she fought back against attacks by a number of the speakers. She had a terribly rough time, and although I repudiated her stance, I sympathised with her for the enormous physical and emotional strain she was under.

The afternoon session delegated to a committee of seven (Prime Minister Lyndon Pindling of the Bahamas, Margaret Thatcher, Rajiv Gandhi, Brian Mulroney and myself, with Presidents Robert Mugabe of Zimbabwe and Kenneth Kaunda of Zambia) the Herculean task of trying to reach some common ground on the sanctions issue. The seven of us met that evening, with Robert and Kenneth preferring, literally, to sit on the sidelines. We were to witness a vintage Thatcher performance, Margaret at her best and worst.

Margaret Thatcher was the hardest working head of government I ever met. Her application was prodigious and she was always extraordinarily well briefed for every meeting. Whatever the subject, she could press her sometimes jarring and belligerent viewpoints with great authority, and for that I deeply respected her. But while she had first-class application, she did not always display a first-class mind. In argument she often seemed to be playing catch-up. She sought to buy time while exchanging views so that she could more easily absorb contrary positions and give

I'm not hard, I'm frightfully soft. But I will not be hounded. I will not be driven anywhere against my will.

Margaret Thatcher with fellow world leaders at the Houston Economic Summit, 9 July 1990.

herself room to marshal her thoughts and responses.

In my experience she had two techniques for stalling debate. First she was an inveterate interrupter. I never dealt with a leader who interrupted other speakers so often. It was a cause for irritation among many of those with whom she dealt. Her other technique for slowing the pace of discussion was what I called her delay-by-parenthesis approach. If a leader was unwise enough to attach a parenthetical observation to the main thrust of his argument, Margaret was away. She would grab hold of the parenthesis like a terrier with a bone, tearing into it and worrying it to a degree that often made her interlocutor and the rest of us wild with impatience.

A bizarre example of this technique surfaced in the Lyford Cay committee meeting. We were discussing the Eminent Persons Group and the stage-by-stage concept of sanctions. Brian Mulroney was developing his main argument in support of Rajiv's and my attempt to persuade Margaret to come in behind the idea. Brian was unwise enough to refer to an aside she had made during the afternoon's discussions: 'Margaret, when you said that, I thought that the fat was really in the fire.'

At that her eyes blazed and she pulled herself erect in the chair. 'What do you mean the fat was really in the fire? Just what do you mean? What fat? What fire?' she asked imperiously. 'Brian, I was brought up to mean what I say, and to say what I mean. What do you mean, the fat was really in the fire?'

'My God!' I thought. I couldn't refrain from jumping in: 'Margaret! for Christ's sake! Forget the bloody fat and the bloody fire, it's got nothing to do with anything. Just listen to what Brian's saying, will you.' Margaret looked at me in some astonishment but, to her great credit, she copped it. Then I turned to my friend Mulroney and said: 'Brian, get on with it, and leave the fat out of the fire.'

Margaret could also, I thought, be a little less than straightforward at times. There was one occasion when she seemed, to me, to almost deliberately misunderstand a proposition. One of the proposed sanctions included the proposition that governments would agree not to enter into contracts with majority-owned South African companies. In our private discussion Margaret said she couldn't agree to that because in South Africa there were so many companies with whom Britain had to deal. 'Margaret, we're not talking about in South Africa, we're talking about in our countries. The Australian Government won't have a contract with a majority-owned South African company, you there in the United Kingdom shouldn't deal with such a majority-owned company,' I explained to her. 'Oh, I see,' she replied.

But the very next day she did not see and in our discussion she went off on the same thing again. I thought she was being a little slippery. I do not intend these comments to disguise the fact that I have a certain admiration for Margaret Thatcher. There is so much of her philosophical approach to domestic and international politics that I cannot share, but she is a formidable and remarkable person – applied, committed, dogged, dogmatic, determined and certainly courageous.

Michael Howard
LEADER OF THE CONSERVATIVE PARTY 2003–5

Michael Howard is Conservative MP for Folkestone & Hythe. He joined Margaret
Thatcher's Cabinet in January 1990 as Secretary of State for Employment and served
in the Cabinet until April 1997. He became Leader of the Conservative Party in
November 2003.

Obeying the leader

I FIRST SAW MARGARET THATCHER in action when, as Secretary of State for
Education in the Heath Government, she addressed a dinner at the Coningsby
Club, a Conservative dining club of which I was Chairman. She was very
impressive, in complete command of her subject and, I thought, radiating
authority.

Even so, I am not sure that I then saw her as a future Prime Minister. But,
following events from outside the House of Commons, I was delighted when she
was elected Leader of the Conservative Party in 1975.

People forget the state of the country at that time and in the years which led
up to 1979. The air of defeatism which was the prevailing climate of the time was
the economic and social equivalent of Munich. I remember hearing Peter Jay,
then regarded as the rising guru of his generation, analyse: 'Either', he said, 'we
shall have a government determined to tackle the causes of their weakness, in
which case it will have to take such unpopular measures that it will never be elected
for a second term, or we shall have a government not prepared to take these
measures in which case weakness and failure will continue and accelerate.'

The measures which Margaret Thatcher took were certainly unpopular. But
from the beginning she displayed the resolve and determination which made her,
to my mind, the peacetime counterpart of Churchill. I had relatively little contact
with her after that first encounter, even after I entered Parliament in 1983.

She was then at the height of her powers with a majority of 144 and an
Opposition that appeared to be in terminal decline. Her encounters with Neil
Kinnock were so one-sided as to be embarrassing.

* * * * *

My first job was as Patrick Mayhew's PPS, when Paddy was Solicitor-General.
One evening, Paddy asked me to join him and his wife, Jean, for a quick bite in
the House of Commons canteen. As I was queuing for my supper, I spotted
Margaret having dinner with her PPS, the late and much-lamented Michael
Alison. It was actually the only time I ever saw her in the Members' canteen. As
I made way towards Paddy and Jean, Michael came up to me and asked me to
join him and the Prime Minister.

'I'm so sorry,' I said, 'I am eating with Paddy and Jean.'

'I'm so sorry,' said Michael, 'The Prime Minister would like you to join her.'
Further argument would obviously be futile.

So I dutifully went off and joined the Prime Minister. I was a very new boy.
She had lots to say. And I sat there – wholly in awe – aware that this was a great
opportunity to make an impression on the Prime Minister and that I was making

*I don't mind how
much my
Ministers talk – as
long as they do
what I say.*

a total mess of it, miserable at the thought that Paddy and Jean were in the corner thinking I'd stood them up and completely unable to say a word.

Finally, the Prime Minister got up to leave. I, with a half-eaten meal on my tray, got up to leave as well, eager to make my peace with Paddy and Jean.

'Michael,' the Prime Minister said firmly, 'Sit down and finish your supper.'

I never did join Paddy and Jean that night, and I was never very sure that they understood.

* * * * *

And so it was that in September 1985 I was asked to join the Government. That is a moment no one forgets. I was at home in Kent at the time and was asked whether I would be free to take a telephone call from the Prime Minister. Then I received another call and was asked whether I could go to London to see her.

'Why does she want you to go to London?' asked my wife.

'Perhaps her telephone's out of order?' suggested my eight-year-old daughter.

My first job was Minister for Corporate and Consumer Affairs in the DTI. It was there that I began to have first-hand experience of the Prime Minister's interest in, passion for and mastery of detail.

'Margaret,' I said, 'I've never been able to kick the habit of doing exactly what you say.'

Michael Howard

Margaret Thatcher's eye for detail was legendary. Her ministers knew it and usually went to great lengths to prepare for encounters with the Prime Minister. But not even the most thorough preparation was always enough.

I remember as a Minister mugging up on every detail of a piece of forthcoming legislation, before seeing the Prime Minister. Unfortunately, I had missed the footnote on page 93. The Prime Minister hadn't.

I was asked to explain the footnote. I couldn't. I felt mortified.

There is a somewhat similar story for which I personally cannot vouch. But it has the ring of truth to it.

The Prime Minister was due to arrive in a European capital for a European Union Summit. The Ambassador, determined to impress, had spent weeks preparing himself for any possible question the Prime Minister might ask.

In the car on the way from the airport, the Prime Minister asked:

'Do you have much of a garden?'

'Yes, Prime Minister', came the reply.

'And do you take much of an interest in it?'

'Oh yes, Prime Minister.'

'What sort of soil do you have?'

He had fallen at the first fence, and never recovered.

* * * * *

It is always dangerous in politics to have very specific and particular ambitions. But I had one. I desperately wanted to enter the Cabinet while she was still Prime Minister. I only just made it. In January 1990 she made me Employment Secretary. In November of that year she was gone.

I have often been asked, and often thought, about the fateful events of that November. The advice I gave her and my thoughts and emotions have been

Margaret Thatcher with Michael and Sandra Howard at London's Savoy Hotel at a dinner to mark the twenty-fifth anniversary of her election as Conservative Party Leader.

described in full elsewhere. I told her that if she decided to fight on I would fight with her to the last ditch. But I also expressed my view that she would lose in the second ballot, possibly by a large margin.

I still think that honest advice was right though, of course, we shall never know. But I do not share the view of those who say that even if she had survived she could never have won a fourth general election. I think she would have won again and we can all speculate endlessly on the difference that might have made to the history of the last ten years.

For my part I shall always regard it as a great privilege to have served, for five years, as one of her Ministers.

Margaret Thatcher cuts a cake at the 300 Club luncheon on 18 June 1990. The 300 Club was established to encourage more women to stand for Parliament.

Ruud Lubbers

FORMER PRIME MINISTER OF THE NETHERLANDS

Ruud Lubbers was elected Prime Minister of the Netherlands in November 1982 and led three successive governments through to August 1994. During his terms he was instrumental in introducing the 'Dutch Model', which led to the successful turnaround of the Dutch economy.

A Ruud shock

IN 1989 I CELEBRATED MY 50TH BIRTHDAY. My wife put together a marvellous video of world leaders who wished me a happy birthday who included George Bush, Helmut Kohl, Rajiv Gandhi and Margaret Thatcher. Now, sixteen years later, I am delighted to record my own personal tribute to Margaret.

Although we met before she became Prime Minister, when I was leader of the Dutch Christian Democrats, our first meaningful meetings began at the end of 1982. I remember the European Council in Copenhagen where I had to mediate between President Mitterrand, who represented continental Europe and Margaret, the Atlanticist. It worked surprisingly well.

In the autumn of 1983, Margaret visited me in The Hague. She said jokingly that I should not ruin her reputation. This was an allusion to the nickname of Ruud Shock, which the press had given me. We started to work together on the INF deployment in response to the Soviet SS20 missiles. It was still the time of Ronald Reagan and we all worked towards the achievements at Reykjavik.

On the stairs at Central Office on election night, June 1987.

I admired Margaret for what she did for her own country, but I was really impressed at how she combined a strong anti-Soviet posture with excellent personal relations – even mutual admiration – with Mikhail Gorbachev. In 1989 she invited me to Chequers to discuss the European Monetary System. Margaret was adamant in pointing out the advantages of flexibility. But I dared to tell her that I drive my car in a more relaxed manner when I use seat belts. We were together in Paris when the political curtain fell for her. We had lunch one to one and Margaret confided to me that she would resign but not before John Major was sure of replacing her in the driving seat.

Indeed, by then she had done her job in the UK; in the Commonwealth; in Europe – where she and I quarrelled about how to end apartheid, and where we did our bit to end Soviet oppression. Margaret was a wonderful friend and colleague during those years. The chemistry between us surprised many of our colleagues and there was undoubtedly some jealousy. Later we worked together in the Atlantic Initiative and we continued to practise our common values. Gradually – that is life – we spoke to each other less and less but my gratitude to my dearest Margaret remains as strong as ever.

Shimon Peres

FORMER PRIME MINISTER OF ISRAEL

Shimon Peres has served twice as Prime Minister of Israel and twice as Foreign Minister. He is a recipient of the Nobel Peace Prize.

A changing world

WHILE COMMONLY ALLUDED TO AS THE IRON LADY, throughout our acquaintance – and I may even venture to say our friendship – and well before she was made Baroness in recognition of her outstanding accomplishment and achievements, to me, Margaret Thatcher was simply The Lady.

My encounters with Margaret Thatcher were many and each and every one of them was a learning experience that I treasured. Talk by the nature of things centred on a huge tapestry of global issues – terrorism, globalisation and the economy, the collapse of the former Soviet Union, the Falkland Islands, statesmanship and the domestic and international political arena and, of course, the Middle East conflict, and these are just random samples of our discussions. No matter the topic, our exchanges were always intense, never less than stimulating, at all times enlightening. I invariably felt humbled by the razor blade sharpness of her mind, her acute perception of things and the clarity of her thoughts.

It is these very qualities, combined with an unflagging tenacity of purpose, fearlessness in the face of fierce opposition and indomitable faith in her way, which became an infinite source of inspiration to us, her admirers. It is her strength and compassion, free spirit and capacity to champion vital causes, together with her remarkable determination and commitment to her undertakings, that led me to compare her to another formidable leader with whom I had the privilege of closely working: Golda Meir. While Golda was never dubbed The Iron Lady, she was often referred to as 'The only man in the Government!' Because Golda, like Margaret, pierced the glass roof of the government and soared to the very peak of political power, not by a twist of fate, but on the wings of their uniqueness.

The analogy is not random, for both became popular icons not only in the restricted circumference of their own countries, but were the object of admiration among their peers on a global scale, for they were both forged from uncommon fabric, propelled by an undaunted spirit and motivated by an unswerving resolve to build a better tomorrow for their respective people. Albeit in different parts of the world, they both played a major role in turning the direction of events at their most crucial crossroads and indeed, left an indelible mark on history. In their own distinctive manner, and with banners raised high, they fought their battles courageously and uncompromisingly, twentieth-century revolutionaries and the epitome of women of valour.

In a world of change, Margaret Thatcher has helped it change. In a world of globalisation, she was a catalyst in helping it globalise. She made a clean sweep of many old embedded notions and injected new energy into a stagnating situation. Supported by a measure of luck and armed with the strength of her convictions,

The best basis of British foreign policy is what is in Britain's interests.

'It is her strength and compassion, free spirit and capacity to champion vital causes.'

Shimon Peres

Margaret Thatcher at the 'Europe against Cancer' conference in London, 26 January 1989.

Margaret Thatcher viewed her missions pragmatically and judiciously used the tools at her disposal to turn her vision into reality. History and the world owe much to Margaret Thatcher. So do I.

I look forward to sharing her wisdom and enjoying her company for many years to come and believe the time is apt to reciprocate her good wishes to me when I myself turned eighty.

Lord Tebbit of Chingford

FORMER CABINET MINISTER AND CONSERVATIVE PARTY CHAIRMAN

Norman Tebbit served in Margaret Thatcher's Cabinet from 1981 until 1987, most famously as Secretary of State for Employment. In 1985 he became the Chairman of the Conservative Party, a position he held until 1987.

Under pressure

DURING MARGARET THATCHER'S TIME as Leader of the Opposition her twice weekly clashes at Prime Minister's Question Time, first with Harold Wilson, then with Jim Callaghan, often set the political agenda. It was essential in those clashes – in which the Prime Minister holds all the best cards, including the inestimable advantage of the last word – that she, not him, should emerge the winner.

Her success depended in considerable part upon briefing not only on matters of fact but on tactics to wrong foot her adversary. I was privileged to be a member of her briefing team which consisted of Airey Neave, Michael Dobbs – then a Central Office researcher – George Gardiner and from time to time others such as Nigel Lawson. Naturally our existence became known and we were dubbed by a Labour journalist 'The Gang of Four' and the name stuck.

I don't believe people who go on strike in this country have legitimate cause.

Pictured during the 1990 leadership contest.

It was during these years that I came to know and understand Margaret Thatcher. It was a privileged position but it sometimes had its downside.

I doubt if speech writing for anyone is all honey – certainly it was not so in her case. As in most things, Margaret Thatcher is pretty much a perfectionist about speeches and a good many drafts finish in the waste bin before she is satisfied with a script. I soon learned that holding back my preferred phrases or paragraphs improved their chances of finding their way into the speech rather than the bin, but sometimes the writing sessions went on far too late for my liking.

I well remember being approached in the division lobby at 10pm. 'I've just got a draft of a speech – and it's awful – would you be able to look at it for me Norman?' she asked.

'Of course, when is it for?'

'Oh good,' she replied, 'tomorrow lunchtime – do come round to the office.' Somewhat taken aback I followed her to the office where fellow speech-writers were assembling with pads and pens in hand. We were soon at work but it was hard going to hit the right note. Somewhere about three in the morning I was beginning to wilt and was caught in the midst of a great yawn.

'You're not very bright tonight, Norman,' she commented.

'It's not tonight,' I said rather huffily, 'it's tomorrow bloody morning.' Somehow that night we got a decent draft for her and I concluded that, like me, Margaret Thatcher works best under pressure – pressure that causes more discomfort to one's aides than oneself!

Margaret Thatcher with her trusted colleague Norman Tebbit, for whom the phrase 'one of us', could have been invented.

Lord Waddington

CABINET MINISTER 1987–92

Raised to the Peerage in 1990, David Waddington had served in Margaret Thatcher's Cabinet as Chief Whip and then as Home Secretary. In 1990 John Major appointed him Lord Privy Seal. He was Governor of Bermuda from 1992 until 1997.

She was right

IN OCTOBER 1984 AN IRA BOMB in the Grand Hotel, Brighton nearly killed Margaret Thatcher and half her Cabinet. The next morning, at her insistence, the Conservative Conference continued with its business and over lunch I was behind the platform with her as she waited to go on stage to give her keynote speech. She said three bishops had just called in to pray for her and had had her on her knees, but when she added crossly, 'As if I had nothing better to do', I knew the old spirit was there and she would put on a great show. She did.

Moments after arriving at my desk in the Home Office on the morning of 30 July 1990, I received a call from the Police telling me that Ian Gow, Margaret's Parliamentary Private Secretary when she first became Prime Minister, had been blown up in his car. Margaret had been very fond of Ian and he of her, and when I got to Number 10 a few minutes later she was telling her staff, 'Give me work. Cancel no engagements. I have got to keep busy.' And she forced herself to carry on with her normal programme.

On the morning of 22 November 1990 the Prime Minister, visibly distressed, told her Cabinet that after her failure by four votes to be re-elected Leader of the Party she intended to resign. But that afternoon she was in the House of Commons replying to a censure debate and to all appearances enjoyed herself hugely as she laid about her, demolishing the Opposition case. Words seemed to come easily, but she had sat up half the night preparing for that last great occasion.

Margaret Thatcher, still then Leader of the Opposition, came up to help me in the Clitheroe by-election in February 1979, and at lunch my nervous chairman opened the conversation by suggesting it was about time the country adopted proportional representation.

'Well,' said Margaret, 'I suppose it is an excellent idea if [a pause and a sniff] you don't want the Conservative Party to ever win another election.' Save for purposes of consumption my chairman did not open his mouth again.

And she could be intimidating, having little time for those who did not stand up to her and never suffering fools gladly. But she loved an argument which usually took the form of her trying to test to destruction every proposition advanced by others than herself. On most matters she was convinced she was right, but who can blame her? She usually was. Two hundred and eighty-four economists wrote to *The Times* saying her policies would not work. They did; and Britain is benefiting to this day. Many doubted whether the Falklands could be retaken. She said they had to be and they were. Everyone said the Government could not beat the National Union of Mineworkers: Margaret Thatcher knew better. The Treasury told her Britain had to enter the ERM. She felt in her bones it would end in disaster, and it did. She knew that those opposed to her in her Government and

There are too few rich and too few profits.

in her Party were risking the end of Britain as an independent nation state. That was something she was not prepared to countenance, and the fact that she was brought down for that principal reason is something of which she can be immensely proud.

Margaret Thatcher had great qualities of leadership which stood the country in good stead in times of peril, and she was a giant on the world stage. In those days it was somewhat difficult to describe her save in adjectives familiar to the reader of *Jane's Fighting Ships* – Indefatigable, Indomitable, Intrepid, Courageous.

Her determination to resist every threat to peace from the Soviet Bloc, her willingness to face any amount of unpopularity at home if that was necessary in order to see her own country properly defended and the West secure, led to the deployment of the Cruise missile in Britain. That in turn gave her the moral authority to speak for the West and made the Soviets realise that they had no hope with their own far more limited resources of forever preventing democracy in Eastern Europe, let alone extending their particular brand of tyranny further west. Margaret Thatcher deserves much thanks from the British people and all who love Freedom.

It would not be right to finish without a word about her family and Denis in particular. I think it was during the summer of 1988 that I, as Government Chief Whip and Peter Brooke as Party Chairman, were having supper with the Prime Minister in Number 10 to talk about possible ministerial changes. We had just sat down when Margaret said: 'Poor old Denis upstairs in the flat, eating all on his own. He must be very lonely and fed up.' 'Oh!' I said, glancing at Peter and having a good idea which way the wind was blowing, 'we can't have that. He must come down. We want to see him, don't we, Peter?' 'Do you really?', said the Prime Minister. 'I promise you he won't say a word.' Well, it did not work out quite as the Prime Minister promised, but it brought home to me what a marvellous relationship she had with Denis and how much she depended on him. I think he was her great strength in moments of appalling strain. We also owe him a lot.

Turning the tables …

Sir Nicholas Winterton

CONSERVATIVE MP

Sir Nicholas Winterton was elected to Parliament in a by-election in 1971 and has served as MP for Macclesfield ever since. He is a leading member of the 1922 Committee Executive.

Paying the price

I WAS PART OF THE CAMPAIGN GROUP of thirty-three under the inspired leadership of Airey Neave, Norman St John Stevas and Sir Keith Joseph and others which campaigned passionately to achieve the leadership of the Conservative and Unionist Party for Margaret Thatcher in 1975.

It was a truly exciting time and everyone was fully committed because of Margaret's vision, not only for the future of the Conservative Party, but for the future of our country. The commitment to this campaign was total and victory was the sole objective and it was achieved.

I never regretted my involvement as a junior member of the team having come into the House of Commons at a by-election in the autumn of 1971. This is because there is no doubt that Margaret Thatcher's determination and philosophy changed the culture of our country and inspired confidence for the future.

In the early 1980s I became involved in the saga of the DeLorean motor car company in Northern Ireland when I outlined my concerns about the use of the public money provided to the company. My comments were made outside the House as it was in recess at that time. I was subsequently sued by DeLorean through his solicitors for $250 million, the equivalent at the time of £133 million, slightly more than petty cash I have to say. Because of the situation I requested and was granted a meeting with the Prime Minister at Downing Street. I attended the meeting on my own despite the request I had made to bring my solicitor and at the meeting I was faced not only by the Prime Minister but also the Attorney General, Sir Michael Havers and her Parliamentary Private Secretary, Ian Gow MP and her Private Secretary. It was a difficult and uncomfortable meeting and it is one of the few occasions when Margaret gave way to a ministerial colleague to deal with all the matters that I raised, while I suspect and felt that she was not unsympathetic to my situation. In those days backbenchers were exceedingly vulnerable to any comments made outside the Chamber, while Government Ministers were covered by the full resources of the State. This was a time also when there was no House of Commons insurance cover for such matters as there is today.

For me a memorable event was when Margaret Thatcher, accompanied by Denis, visited my constituency shortly after she resigned the leadership of the Conservative Party. I believe it was the first Conservative Association function she attended after she stepped down. It was a dinner held at Titherington Golf and Country Club to the North of Macclesfield and the event was heavily oversubscribed. The Club had in fact to erect a tent extension in order to accommodate the huge number of people. It was an occasion I will remember for the rest of my life. She made an inspired speech to over 350 people and you could hear a pin drop in the room as everyone listened intently to every word she uttered.

I am staying my own sweet reasonable self.

The way that she dealt with questions was amazing and everyone present admired her knowledge and authority. Denis Thatcher's presence added hugely to the occasion and his humour and total support of Margaret were always to be admired.

A particularly inspiring experience for me was when during the country-wide launch of her first book, *The Downing Street Years*, I was asked by the publishers to chair and act as Master of Ceremonies at a launch in the North West in the Gateway Theatre in the heart of the city of Chester. It was an amazing occasion. There were queues to get into the theatre and when the doors opened the theatre filled to capacity and there were people standing around the walls. All came to meet Mrs Thatcher despite the fact that she was no longer Prime Minister. I was in addition the Lead-in Speaker and it was an honour to have been asked to undertake this responsibility. She was cheered to the proverbial rafters.

Many people believe that Margaret Thatcher's decision to step down from the Leadership of the Party at the time when she did was a great error and the Party has in a way been paying the price ever since.

In the Cabinet Room at Number 10.

Sir Malcolm Rifkind

CABINET MINISTER, 1986–97

Sir Malcolm Rifkind served as MP for Edinburgh Pentlands from 1974–97 and is now MP for Kensington & Chelsea. He joined Margaret Thatcher's Cabinet in 1986 as Scottish Secretary. He was a Cabinet Minister throughout John Major's administration, latterly as Foreign Secretary.

Having her way

THOSE WHO WERE PRIVILEGED to serve in Margaret Thatcher's Cabinet will always be grateful for the experience. She had her own distinctive style of Cabinet Government.

For her a Cabinet discussion was a series of bilateral exchanges rather than a collective analysis of the issues of the day. Whereas John Major would keep his own views to himself until his Cabinet colleagues had expressed theirs, Mrs Thatcher would open the discussion by indicating the conclusion that she wished and expected.

On one occasion she sat down at a Cabinet Committee and began by saying, 'I haven't much time, today. Only enough time to explode and have my way.' As each Minister expressed his view she would often engage him in battle before moving on to the next.

While this could be an alarming experience for a new member of the Cabinet it was neither as distressing nor as difficult for the Cabinet as a whole than this introduction might suggest. For all her bossiness and aversion to compromise, Margaret Thatcher was a constitutionalist and a believer in Cabinet Government to her fingertips.

Unlike an American President who is quite entitled to ignore his Cabinet, none of whom, except the Vice-President, having been elected by the nation, a British Prime Minister is *primus inter pares* and often Mrs Thatcher found herself in the minority. This she accepted with varying degrees of enthusiasm but she never challenged the right of her colleagues to decline to accept her wishes. Indeed, when she went into battle she relished an adversary who was prepared to disagree with her as long as he knew what he was talking about. It was John Major's willingness as a mere junior Whip to tell her in front of his colleagues that she was wrong and misguided that first brought him to her attention and led to his ultimate coronation as her successor to the Tory crown.

When Sir Anthony Parsons, our Ambassador at the UN during the Falklands War, was recalled to brief her she kept interrupting him. After the third interruption in so many minutes he remarked: 'Prime Minister, if you didn't interrupt me so often you might find that you didn't need to.' Some months later she appointed him her foreign policy adviser.

As long as she was Prime Minister her natural gut instincts were tempered by the need to carry her colleagues and ensure acceptable government. Since her retirement that has been less of a constraint. One recalls Gladstone's comment on Sir Robert Peel: 'Former Prime Ministers are like great rafts floating untethered in a harbour.'

We must learn again to be one nation, or one day we shall be no nation.

Imitation is the sincerest form of flattery.

Neil Hamilton

CONSERVATIVE MP

Neil Hamilton served as MP for Tatton from 1983 until the 1997 General Election. He was a member of the No Turning Back Group of MPs. Neil Hamilton currently works as a writer and broadcaster.

Getting the joke

CONTRARY TO POPULAR MYTHOLOGY, Margaret is not at all stuffy or narrow-minded and has a good sense of humour. She likes raising a chuckle by acting up to her caricature handbagging image – a joke all the more amusing to observe when played on someone who thinks she is being serious.

But I have to admit that getting her to see the point of someone else's jokes is sometimes no laughing matter – as I occasionally discovered to my cost. After the *Spectator* awarded me the title 'Parliamentary Wit of the Year' in 1988 she engaged me as a resident jokesmith to add some soufflé lightness to the bread-and-butter pudding of a Prime Ministerial speech.

It was no easy task. For example, in October 1989 I was at Chequers helping with her speech for the debate on the Queen's Speech. This annual debate concerns the Government's programme for the year ahead but technically arises on a motion to present a Loyal Address to the Monarch, thanking her for 'her gracious Speech'. The Government chooses two of its own backbenchers for the honour of proposing and seconding the motion – the first, usually an amiable old buffer long past his sell-by date, and the second, usually some oily young man on the make. They are followed immediately by the Prime Minister, who has to shower compliments upon them before getting on with the serious business.

The seconder in 1989 was an amiable young buffer, Jeremy Hanley, then Tory MP for Richmond-upon-Thames. A chartered accountant by training, he was also a member of MENSA, the club for the very brainy. But his roots were more theatrical – his mother being star of stage and screen, Dinah Sheridan; his father, the well-known comedian, Jimmy Hanley. Jeremy was an excellent and amusing raconteur in his own right and could be relied on to rise to the occasion.

What could Margaret say about him? I suggested a mild witticism, combining a reference to his intelligence and amiability: 'He is very clever and amusing but he never allows his brains to go to his head.' The joke seemed pretty obvious to me, but not alas to Margaret, who exploded: 'I can't say that! If his brains aren't in his head, where will people think they are?' We grappled with the abstruse metaphysics of the humour for some time but, try as I might, I could not get her to see the punchline – she was convinced everyone would think she was suggesting his brains were in his backside!

We have become a Grandmother.

On the famous Downing Street staircase, October 1989.

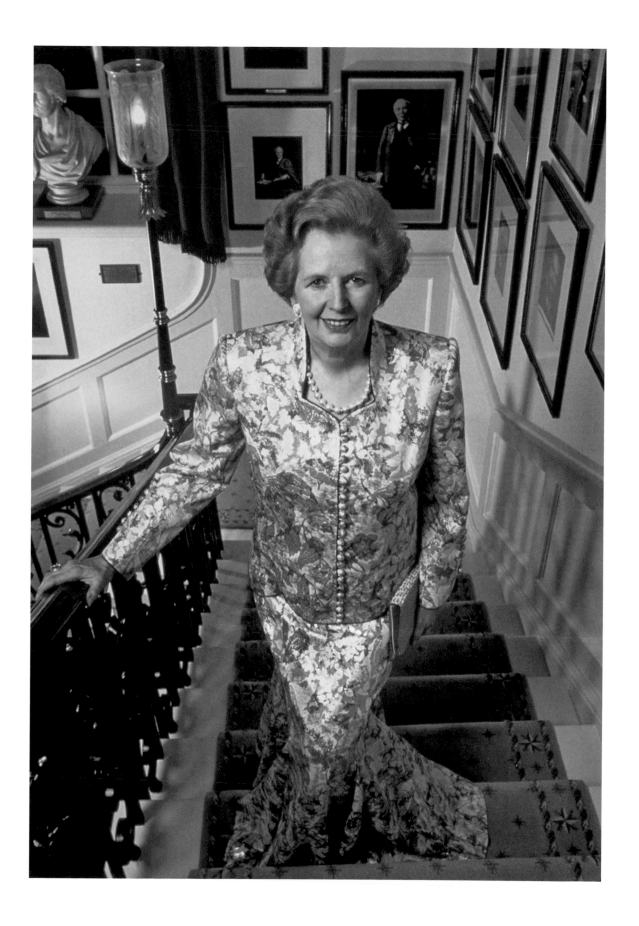

Václav Klaus

PRIME MINISTER OF CZECH REPUBLIC 1992–7

Václav Klaus is one of the foremost politicians of post-communist Eastern Europe. He became Prime Minister of the Czech Republic in 1992 after serving as the Minister for Finance. He has written numerous books on economic policy and has been the recipient of numerous awards for the cause of freedom.

An exceptional woman

ALTHOUGH MARGARET THATCHER AND I have met personally many times in the last decade, I would rather speak briefly of her opinions and attitudes than of personal issues. My view is the view of a politician from Central Europe and from a former communist country. That is probably what makes it somewhat specific.

There were certainly sufficient domestic reasons, motives and arguments, but we may say, with only a slight exaggeration, that the revolution in Central and Eastern Europe which brought about the end of communism was initiated in 1979 by the victory of the Conservative Party in the General Election placing Margaret Thatcher at the head of the British Government. She attacked the ever-expanding state – which represented the dominant tendency throughout the twentieth century. This was a century of socialism with all sorts of adjectives and with a highly varying degree of the humiliation and degradation of the individual – and her fight against socialism was the first example of success. She showed that it was possible to reverse this tendency and return to a liberal political, economic and social system.

Without wishing to be ideological, I cannot but recall that unlike many – more or less – conciliatory Western politicians, Margaret Thatcher understood the dangers of the communist doctrine and it was by her uncompromising attitudes that she contributed immensely to the end of communism.

She did not regard politics as a 'technology of power', but as an instrument for enforcing certain ideas and moral principles. This was the source of her uncompromising stance for which she earned the nickname the 'Iron Lady'. This had nothing in common with her personal characteristics in the way I got to know her. She was not the type of politician who makes compromises. Likewise, her allies either shared her ideas and moral principles or, if they did not, they could not be her allies.

She did not regard freedom as a way to greater efficiency and prosperity. It was a moral principle and the highest value. Therefore, a free society was not just an effective political slogan but a deeply rooted vision, which she continually endeavoured to carry out throughout her life. Those who accused her of being stubborn, persistent or obstinate were people who never really came to understand the real meaning of a 'free society'.

She entered politics at a time when the faith in a 'modern welfare state' and in a 'mixed economy' prevailed. Laissez-faire was considered a relic, belonging to the nineteenth century. Margaret Thatcher opposed these then-dominant opinions, which was, at the end of the 1970s and the beginning of the 1980s, unique. Fortunately, she found an ally in this 'campaign' for the restoration of old

We are the true peace movement.

virtues on the other side of the Atlantic in Ronald Reagan.

Neither could she come to terms with the process of the unification of Europe. She always saw Europe as a community of free and sovereign states connected (or united) by free trade. However, the idea of creating some sort of a 'super state' or a federation of Europe began to prevail on the European continent. The bureaucratisation of European structures, the growing of the 'Eurocracy' and the abandonment of the principles of free trade on a global scale discouraged her and she entered the group of the so-called Euro-sceptics, to which I am honoured to belong as well.

Her attitudes in politics and her conduct in everyday life prove that she is one of the extraordinary figures of the last quarter of the twentieth century. I have met many giants of world politics but none have made such an impression on me as this exceptional woman.

Helmut Kohl

CHANCELLOR OF GERMANY 1982–98

Helmut Kohl was the Chancellor who reunited East and West Germany. He became Leader of the Christian Democratic Union in 1973 and became Chancellor nine years later following the resignation of Helmut Schmidt.

Transforming her country

MARGARET THATCHER can look back on a fulfilled and remarkable life. She served her country with great passion and dedication over many years in a most prominent position. During her time as Prime Minister she transformed and successfully modernised her country in many areas. It is predominantly thanks to the reforms she undertook in the 1980s that Great Britain is today among the most economically successful countries in Europe. Her name will forever be linked with the modernisation of her country.

Whenever I think back to our many discussions, I do so with respect and gratitude – in spite of different views on several issues. She always presented her argument openly and clearly and was fierce in defending them in the face of opposition.

Today Margaret can look back on her life's work with deep satisfaction. She achieved great things for her country.

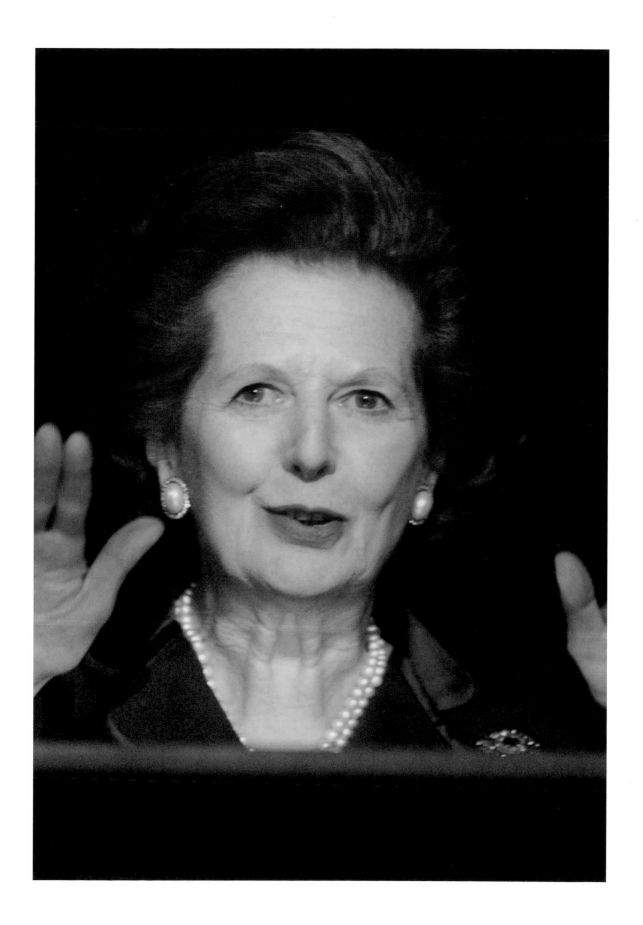

Baroness Trumpington

MINISTER OF STATE AT THE MINISTRY OF AGRICULTURE FISHERIES AND
FOOD 1989–92

Raised to the Peerage in 1980, Baroness Trumpington of Sandwich served as a junior
Minister from 1985 until 1992. Initially a Parliamentary Under Secretary of State at
the DHSS, she took up the same position at the Ministry of Agriculture, becoming the
Minister of State for that department in 1989.

Terrified

I OWE MARGARET THATCHER everything since she made me a Life Peer in her
first Honours List as Prime Minister. That was a huge surprise and I shall never
cease to be grateful to her.

Having said that I am and always shall be terrified of her.

I well remember the first occasion I attended a full Cabinet Meeting in the
place of John MacGregor. I was a brand new MAFF Minister and I had been
instructed to press for a particular professor to be appointed for a job. My only
briefing was given at the last moment and consisted of the bare words that the
Department for Education agreed with this appointment.

When it appeared that my great moment had arrived all I could do was to
repeat the above words, several times, with less and less conviction.

Feeling a total prat and surrounded by the great and the good I subsided in
much sweat.

As the Prime Minister left the Cabinet Room she patted me affectionately on
the shoulder and said, 'Don't worry dear, we will see your professor gets the job.'

The reason I think I am so frightened of her is because I never feel I can say
the sort of thing I would say to my women friends, but always feel I have to ask
her something meaningful about the state of the world. I am sure it's my fault,
and I have never been afraid of sticking to my guns when I felt deeply over any
issue. She never held that against me.

Relaxing with Denis in the
garden of Number 10
Downing Street.

John Whittingdale

CONSERVATIVE MP

John Whittingdale was Margaret Thatcher's Political Secretary from 1988 until 1990 and her Private Secretary from 1990 until 1992. He has been Member of Parliament for Maldon and Chelmsford East since 1992.

This parrot is no more

OF ALL THE DEMANDS on the Prime Minister's time, the one that occupied the most was speech-writing. Every speech went through at least ten drafts and major speeches many more. As Margaret Thatcher's Political Secretary, my job was to co-ordinate the preparation of speeches to Party audiences. My year was divided between fixed points: the Central Council meeting, the Scottish Conference, the Local Government Conference, the Women's Conference and most important of all the Party Conference in October.

Work would start on the Party Conference speech at least a month in advance. At a preliminary meeting, the Prime Minister would set out her ideas as to the areas that the speech should cover. This was usually done in an unbroken flow of raw Thatcher thought which our in-house speech-writing team, and those that I would commission from outside, would have to turn into draft speech form. Subject areas would be allocated between speech-writers and they would then be sent off to prepare paragraphs on each topic for inclusion. Once we had collected a number of contributions, these would be tacked together in a rough structure and the process of refinement and polishing would begin.

It was an immensely time-consuming process and at least once in the preparation of every speech, the Prime Minister would lose confidence in the whole process, tell us that it was all useless and demand that we start again from the beginning. The next few hours would be spent slightly tweaking the sections and then reinserting them while assuring her that they were completely different from the original. At the early stages, we would be meeting once a week. This would then increase to every day and then the whole of the weekend before the Conference would be spent working on the text at Chequers.

Once we got to Blackpool, Bournemouth or Brighton, the whole time would be spent in the Prime Minister's suite surrounded by paper, with a core team which was boosted by those drafted in to make suggestions and improvements. A single critical word at the wrong time could undo weeks of work and my job was as much to keep well-meaning but destructive critics away as it was to bring in and encourage contributors. The average length of a Party Conference speech is about forty minutes. I worked on three and in each case Margaret Thatcher spent at least eighty hours working on the text: two hours for each minute of the speech. Those actually writing the speech spent much more.

The hardest and most important parts of the speech to write were the jokes. Margaret Thatcher is not naturally a joke-teller although she has a dry sense of humour, However, she recognises that without jokes, a speech is flat and dull. A good joke-writer was therefore valued above all others. On our core team, we had two principal joke-writers: the late Sir Ronnie Millar and John O'Sullivan, a journalist and commentator who had been brought in to the Number Ten Policy Unit. They had very different styles and each brought a different kind of humour. However, in each case, Margaret Thatcher frequently required persuasion that what they had written was indeed funny.

In 1990, the Party Conference speech was particularly important. Margaret Thatcher was under heavy attack and had recently suffered the resignation of her Chancellor, Nigel Lawson. Her speech had to be as good as she had ever delivered. A few weeks earlier, the Liberal Democrats had unveiled their new Party symbol. It was supposed to represent a bird taking wing, but in the mind of John O'Sullivan it immediately became a dead parrot. He decided that he would write a section of the speech devoted to mocking the Liberal Democrats and would include a section of Monty Python's Dead Parrot sketch. To anyone familiar with Monty Python it was a terrific idea and very funny. Unfortunately, the Prime Minister had not even heard of Monty Python.

When we came to read through the draft of the speech, Mrs Thatcher paused when she reached the dead parrot section and looked at John O'Sullivan as if he were completely mad. We knew that this would happen and so had prepared our strategy in advance. 'This is', I explained, 'one of the most famous comedy sketches ever written. It will be instantly recognisable to every person in the audience.' I was slightly less certain of this latter point, knowing Conservative audiences, but all of us present insisted to the Prime Minister that it would be the highlight of her speech.

The joke survived that read-through but I knew that she was not convinced. On each subsequent occasion, whenever we reached the parrot section, she stopped and said: 'Are you sure that this is funny?' After about the third or fourth occasion, she tried a new tack. 'I need to see the sketch,' she said. 'If I am to deliver it then I need to get the inflexion absolutely right.' As it happened, I had at home a video of the Python film *And Now for Something Completely Different*, which contains the dead parrot sketch. I therefore brought it into the office the next day.

One of the more surreal moments during my time at Number 10 followed. Sitting in my office watching the dead parrot sketch were Margaret Thatcher, John O'Sullivan, Robin Harris, who was also helping with the speech, Peter Morrison her PPS and myself. At any time, it is a very funny sketch. But the absurdity of the situation made it all the more amusing and I and the three others found it so hilarious that we had tears rolling down our cheeks. Margaret Thatcher, on the other hand, was all the more mystified. It was not her type of humour and she found it difficult to see why we were laughing so much. However, given that we all were, she accepted that it must be funny and so, true professional that she was, she attempted to master the emphasis and inflexion of John Cleese's delivery. She did so brilliantly and was soon able to deliver faultlessly the famous lines: 'This parrot is no more. It has ceased to be. It has expired and gone to meet its maker.'

In the days leading up to the Conference, the Prime Minister required constant reassurance that people would find the lines funny. She was clearly still full of doubt. However, I was able to get to enough people in advance whose opinion she was likely to ask that she was eventually persuaded. Every time we ran through

Being in power is like being a lady. If you have to tell people you are, you aren't.

Society photographer Gemma Levine captures Lady Thatcher at her home, standing before her portrait.

Overleaf: Margaret Thatcher inspects the Guard of Honour at the Guildhall, where she received the Freedom of the City of London, 30 May 1989.

the speech, I found myself laughing at the passage which simply added to the Prime Minister's puzzlement.

Finally, we got to the day of the speech. The text was finished, it had been typed up on to the autocue and we had completed the final rehearsal at which she practised her delivery and the inflexions of the speech. However, as we waited for her to go on to the stage to deliver the speech, she was still worrying about the passage and looking for reasons that it might not work. Just as she was about to go on, another doubt arose in her mind. She looked at me and said anxiously: 'John, Monty Python – are you sure that he is one of us?'

To try to explain to her that Monty Python did not really exist would have been to risk disaster. I therefore did not even try and instead said to her: 'Absolutely, Prime Minister. He is a very good supporter.' Thus reassured, she went on to the platform to give the speech. She did so perfectly and received the biggest laugh of all when she delivered with perfect comic timing the words of the dead parrot sketch.

Margaret and Denis visit a factory during the 1983 election campaign.

John Gummer

CONSERVATIVE MP

John Gummer was elected MP for Lewisham West in 1970 and for Eye in 1979 and has been a Suffolk MP ever since. He was appointed Chairman of the Conservative Party in 1983 and joined the Cabinet in 1989.

Briefing the PM

MINISTERS IN MARGARET THATCHER'S GOVERNMENTS learned there was no point in approaching her on anything if you didn't know your stuff. She would drill down immediately to the heart of the matter and would punish any loose wording or imprecise phrase unmercifully. What was less obvious was that she would change her mind, however inconvenient it was, if she were convinced of your case. She was tough minded and determined but not obstinate or inflexible. She had the stature and the self-confidence to accept that she needed to change course.

My most dramatic memory of that was one evening when I was being briefed by the vets from the Ministry of Agriculture. They were giving me the arguments that I would have to deploy at the next day's meeting of the Council of Ministers in order to defend the British position which sought to restrict the movement of beef because of concern about animal disease. Our partners in the EU were suspicious of our arguments which they thought had more to do with protectionism than a concern with animal health.

Mrs Thatcher had weighed in publicly some weeks earlier to defend the UK position and, as was usual with her, no one could have mistaken her commitment and determination. I began the meeting with the vets with no qualms about our position. I had always taken a strong line on animal health and I was used to arguing from a minority position in the Council of Ministers. The Prime Minister had given me the backing I had wanted and so all seemed set for a good battle but one which I expected to win. Nonetheless, I followed my normal routine which was not to rely upon written submissions but to argue these detailed policies with the experts so that I was fully able to hold my own round the table. It was a procedure I had learned from Michael Heseltine who, rightly, said that it enabled a Minister to ferret out weaknesses and inconsistencies much more effectively than when presented with a sanitised written brief.

On this occasion, I expected no difficulties. This was a long-standing view on which I had no doubts. Then came the shock. As we discussed the issues, the science upon which our position was based seemed less and less certain. The vets became evasive and their answers less precise. Gradually it emerged that our public posture was no longer well-grounded. Fundamental changes in the science had occurred and we had not applied them to our political position. If any one of my fellow EU ministers had been properly briefed they could have shot me down in flames.

It was 7.30 at night. I was due out on the 10.30 plane with a policy that didn't hold water but one that had been recently and publicly commended by the Prime Minister. What was more, if we were shown to be scientifically wrong, a whole raft of other positions would be undermined. Given Mrs Thatcher's position, I

I love argument, I love debate. I don't expect anyone just to sit there and agree with me, that's not their job.

couldn't just change the policy. I had to get her agreement. A phone call fixed an appointment for 7.30 next morning and I set about preparing for the ordeal.

Here was a classically difficult proposition. She was on the record. She had handbagged the European Union. I was to get her to change her view, admit we were wrong and agree with the Commission. Not an enviable task! Worse, it was a very technical matter. I knew from experience that the real problem would be to get enough time to explain the issues logically before she came in with a reprise of her public position. I had to find a way to get the science across before we moved to the politics. There I was on safer ground. Mrs Thatcher was never afraid of facing up to the science even if it were politically inconvenient. I had learned that long before on climate change, where she was the first major political figure to accept the evidence of man's effect on global warming.

So I sent for one of the most astute and trustworthy of my advisers, Simon Dugdale, the Head of Information. Could we, at that time of night, produce five story boards to explain the problem and the solution sufficiently clearly to hold the Prime Minister's undivided attention on this important but very narrow issue? We worked on the wording and one of his graphic staff produced the boards.

At 7.30 next morning, I was ushered into the little study on the first floor at Number 10. The time and the urgency of the meeting meant that there was no private secretary. I launched into the explanation. Mrs T liked the innovation of the story boards. She listened intently, asked some confirmatory questions, then, with a grimace, finally said, 'I'm sorry to say, John, it looks as if you're right. We'll have to change tack. It won't do to be proved factually wrong. But you better be right!' The fierce look in her eye was unmistakeable but so was the fact that she was not the obstinate and inflexible woman that her detractors portrayed. Even on a matter so sensitive, so opposite to what she wanted, so removed from her own instincts, she was willing to change if the facts demanded it. There are few in high office with the self-confidence and commitment to truth who have the guts to let the science prevail. It was that sterling quality of absolute probity that was one of the reasons that she was such a star and such a great woman to work for.

We'll have to change tack. It won't do to be proved factually wrong...

Signing the 1986 Anglo-Irish Agreement with the Irish Taoiseach, Garrett Fitzgerald.

Right: A 1995 photographic portrait by Terence Donovan.

Lord Powell of Bayswater

PRIME MINISTER'S ADVISER ON FOREIGN AFFAIRS AND DEFENCE 1984–91

Charles Powell served as a diplomat in Washington, Bonn and EC Brussels before becoming the Prime Minister's Private Secretary and adviser on foreign affairs and defence, a position that he held from 1984 until 1991.

'My God, that man is so German'

AFTER A PREVIOUS FOREIGN OFFICE CAREER spanning twenty years during most of which Britain's standing and influence in the world steadily declined, I found working for Margaret Thatcher on foreign affairs an exhilarating if sometimes tempestuous experience. Her extraordinary will-power and leadership broke the seemingly endless and inevitable cycle of national decline, restored the nation's confidence and gave us the feeling that Britain once again counted in the world.

It was not exactly a tranquil experience. She was non-stop and so was the turbulence created by her legendary handbag. Foreign visits were invariably conducted at the double: I think our record was seven countries – Malaysia, Singapore, Brunei, Indonesia, Sri Lanka, India and Saudi Arabia – in eight days. Yet only once in twelve years did a slip of the tongue give away that she forgot which country she was in. That had been more of a problem for one of her predecessors, Sir Alec Douglas-Home, whose wife used to follow him down the aircraft steps on foreign visits chanting: 'China, Alec, China' or whatever the country was.

Of course it helped being a woman: that made her more easily identifiable amongst world leaders. But it was the personality and the policies which counted. The strong and unyielding stand against communism, in partnership with Ronald Reagan, which led to the West's triumph in the Cold War: victory in the Falklands: getting 'our money' back from Europe: extricating Rhodesia from illegality to independence: standing by our American allies over Libya when others turned their backs: ensuring a resolute response to Saddam's invasion of Kuwait. All these turned her into a heroic figure, the Iron Lady of legend. She did not win all her battles, with German reunification the prime example. And she fought some unnecessary ones, mainly with her own colleagues in Government. But she indisputably raised Britain's international profile; and whatever the pained expressions and snooty comments of old-style diplomats, she advanced Britain's interests. In the simplest terms, we were taken a lot more seriously in 1990 than in 1980.

Margaret Thatcher was never a diplomat and proud not to be one. She had no time for courtly phrases and carefully drafted compromises. She was ready to go toe to toe with any world leader from Gorbachev to Deng Xiaoping. She had the huge advantage of being unembarrassable, a quality not always shared by her Private Secretary. I recall a meeting with President Mitterrand in Paris during which the President took her for a stroll in the Elysée garden. I sat down in the sun for a blissful moment of peace with my French opposite number, only to be shaken from my reverie by the sight of Mitterrand hurrying back, clutching a blood-stained handkerchief to himself. For a moment of panic I thought: 'she's gone too far this time, she's bitten him!' It turned out to have been an over-enthusiastic

It took us a long time to get rid of the effects of the French Revolution 200 years ago. We don't want another one.

puppy which did the damage, but it was a nasty moment.

She was deeply suspicious of the Foreign Office as an institution, believing that its tribal culture led it to give too much weight to the foreigners and too little to Britain's interests, as well as having its own agenda on European integration. She would gleefully recount the old chestnut of the man asking a policeman in Whitehall during the Second World War black-out, which side the Foreign Office was on and being told: 'the other'. There were some memorable rages, as when she demanded to inspect the gift which the Foreign Office had thoughtfully procured for her to take to Gorbachev and discovered a handsome pair of silver-backed hair-brushes.

'But he's completely bald,' she stormed, and a messenger had to be sent out from London with a replacement gift.

Fortunately the prejudice against the institution was matched by a high regard for many of its most distinguished servants, who were granted a sort of amnesty for the misdeeds – real or imagined – of their alma mater.

Margaret Thatcher's diplomacy was less concerned with making friends than with winning battles. That had a downside in her relationship with Chancellor Kohl, who went to great pains to win her friendship. This extended to inviting her to spend a weekend in his home-town in the Rhineland, including a visit to his favourite tavern to sample his favourite dish of pig's stomach. Margaret Thatcher's appetite seemed mysteriously to fade as Chancellor Kohl went back for seconds and thirds. We moved on to the great crypt of the Romanesque Cathedral of Speyer where Margaret Thatcher was invited to inspect the tombs of Holy Roman Emperors, precursors of earlier attempts at European Union. While she undertook this task without visible enthusiasm, Chancellor Kohl took me behind a pillar: 'now she's seen me here in my own home-town, right at the heart of Europe and on the border with France,' he said, 'surely she will understand that I am not just German, I am European. You must convince her.' I accepted the assignment with trepidation. As soon as we boarded our aircraft for the return to Britain, Margaret Thatcher threw herself into her seat, kicked off her shoes and announced with the finality which was her trade-mark: 'My God, that man is so German.' Gutless, I aborted my mission to persuade her otherwise.

Margaret Thatcher captured the imagination of people outside Britain even more than at home. One only had to witness the rapturous welcome which she received from huge crowds in Poland, Russia, Georgia and Armenia in the late 1980s to realise that she symbolised their hope for relief from communist tyranny. Or to experience her ability to rouse an American audience with her forthright rhetoric on democracy, the rule of law and the need for strong defence. Or to be swept away by the ecstatic welcome of crowds in Africa, despite fatalistic Foreign Office warnings that she would be shunned.

A sometimes embattled but always defiant figure, she invariably stood up for Britain. And just as she galvanised Britain itself, so she galvanised other countries' view of Britain as once again a strong, dependable, worthwhile ally and a country which gives a lead in world affairs. We still benefit from that.

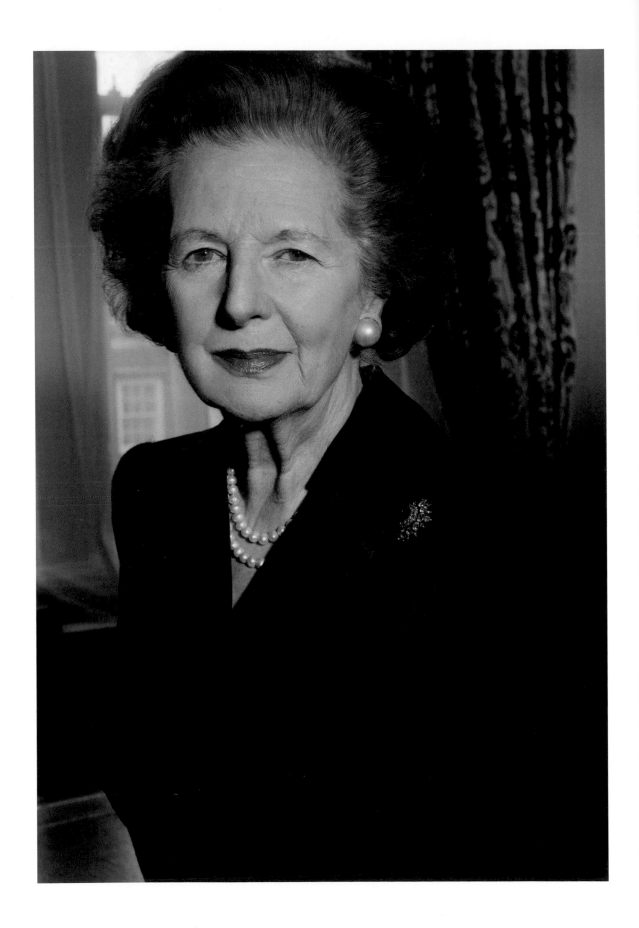

Lord Whitelaw

DEPUTY PRIME MINISTER 1979–88

Willie Whitelaw served as Leader of the House and Secretary of State for Northern Ireland under Edward Heath and as Chairman of the Conservative Party. In Margaret Thatcher's Cabinet he was Home Secretary, Lord President of the Council and Leader of the House of Lords. He served as Deputy Prime Minister under Mrs Thatcher until his retirement in 1998. Lord Whitelaw died in 1999.

Loyalty to the Leader

I HAVE OFTEN WONDERED HOW two such different people managed to get on so well together. Of course, as Prime Minister and Party Leader, it was in her hands to decide how she treated me and used me. I must therefore say at the start that it was her personal kindness and constant understanding which gave me the opportunity to help her. For my part, I hope I always remembered that she was the Leader, who had to face all the ultimate pressures and take the final decisions. Life at the top is very lonely and extremely demanding. Anyone in an immediately subordinate position should never forget the exceptional pressures which a Leader faces, and the personal reactions which they provoke. I believe we both started from these particular positions, and understood them.

Second, we both had a passionate belief in our Party and so in its Government. We probably had somewhat different perceptions of how we would like to see it react in particular circumstances. On such occasions I would certainly have the chance to argue my case, but of course I had to accept that in the final event Margaret Thatcher was the Leader and had the ultimate right to decide. I do not think I ever left her in any doubt that I understood that relationship.

Third, we both knew that we were very different people with varying backgrounds, interests and thus reactions. As a result we had never been close personal friends before we were brought together in this particular political relationship.

I am often asked what it is like serving a woman Leader. In general I would say it is no different from serving a man, except that it would be futile not to appreciate that women are always ready to use their feminine charms, and indeed their feminine qualities, to get their way. Margaret Thatcher is no exception, nor could anyone fail to recognise her great personal charm. Perhaps it was easy for me to work with a woman as I had been brought up by my mother and spent much time alone with her. No one who knew her could deny that my mother was a powerful character.

I was reminded the other day by the hostess who brought my mother and Margaret Thatcher together of their only meeting not long before my mother died. No one knew how it would turn out, since my mother was immensely protective of me and, naturally perhaps, proud of my performance. She was therefore very suspicious of this woman Margaret Thatcher, who had been preferred to her son as Leader of the Conservative Party. In the event, I am told, for I certainly was not present, that they got on famously together. My mother subsequently became an immense fan of Margaret Thatcher, even to the extent

Every Prime Minister needs a Willie.

of upbraiding me for failing to support her more effectively. Alas, she died before she could see Margaret Thatcher as Prime Minister and her son as Home Secretary. I know she would have been far more critical of the latter than the former.

On another topic, I am asked if Margaret Thatcher ever listens to points of view other than her own. This question, with its perception of her, angers me, for it is grossly unfair. I think she probably enjoys an argument more than most people, and the more vigorous it is, the better, as far as she is concerned. She is by nature a conviction politician and so has very strong views, yet she can certainly be swayed and influenced by good arguments in the final event. I wish the critics would realise that no one could have presided over such a successful team as Leader unless they had been prepared to take account of internal discussions. Of course it is not easy to convert her, but that should surely be the case with a powerful Leader. She is certainly the type of chairman who leads from the front and from the start of a discussion makes no secret of her own feelings and views. But all chairmen have their different methods, even if most successful ones like to get their way in the end. I know that I am totally different from Margaret Thatcher in the way that I handle meetings, and that some people regard me as too conciliatory. But I have to acknowledge the truth of the remark which Norman Tebbit alleges that I made to him: 'My image is emollient – and so I am, but only when I am getting my own way.' I suspect too that Margaret Thatcher did not always find me easy to deal with. She had to experience – which I must say she did stoically on occasions – my sudden and unexpected outbursts of rage when crossed in argument. She often accepted, although I imagine she sometimes found it irritating, my cautious approach to parliamentary difficulties and tendency towards compromise. She seldom interfered with my conduct of sensitive Home Office issues, although she must have disliked some of my decisions on the treatment of offenders, and perhaps particularly on broadcasting matters where we have never quite seen eye to eye.

In particular we tended to have different views on the bias of BBC programmes. Naturally, Prime Ministers feel particularly sensitive to criticism which they consider unfair, since they are constantly in the firing line. My feelings about the BBC, on the other hand, were conditioned by my experience in dealing with broadcasting matters as Opposition Chief Whip during the 1960s. When I argued our Party's case at that time I felt that I was treated most fairly by the BBC, sometimes to the intense irritation of Harold Wilson and the then Labour Government.

My experience and so perhaps inevitably my views were very different from those of the Prime Minister and the overwhelming majority of my colleagues. And so when there were controversies over different television or radio programmes, I tended to come out as a defender of the BBC. In addition to my natural instincts, I also felt that as Home Secretary it was my duty to stand up for their point of view. This led to spirited discussions on occasions. As is well known, Margaret is a regular listener to the BBC *Today* programme and, waking early as she does, is extremely well-informed of every detail in the news each morning. So

'I think she probably enjoys an argument more than most people, and the more vigorous it is, the better, as far as she is concerned.'

Lord Whitelaw

she naturally came to some meetings with that day's programme in the forefront of her mind. I have to say that on occasions I wished I had stronger grounds on which to stand up for a BBC programme. I recognise that I had some bad mornings when I abandoned defence of the indefensible. But generally I stood my ground for I felt it was good for me and for my other colleagues, including the Prime Minister, to test our views against each other. Anyway, we probably all rather enjoyed the arguments and perhaps sometimes they did affect subsequent Government reactions.

I suppose the Prime Minister listened to me most on parliamentary and Party matters, where I obviously had a great experience, and least on economic and foreign policy, where I did not claim any special knowledge and where other senior Ministers bore the responsibility.

She was always very generous with her time in giving me opportunities privately to express my feelings on any subject. She also consulted me frequently and kept me fully informed on major issues. I therefore seldom had any reason to argue with her in wider ministerial meetings and usually intervened only if I felt I could be of general assistance.

I can only conclude with a general observation. Margaret Thatcher is a remarkable and powerful Leader in every way. Of course, like everyone in her position, she has her critics and detractors. No doubt she has made mistakes, but no one can deny her incredible achievements, nor should anyone neglect the great contribution that Denis Thatcher made to them, as the country as a whole has increasingly recognised.

After her triumphant speech at the 1988 Conservative Conference. Margaret Thatcher is hugged by her trusted Deputy, Lord Whitelaw.

Overleaf: Lady Thatcher and Sir Denis at the annual Garter ceremony at Windsor Castle, 18 June 2001.

David Amess

CONSERVATIVE MP

David Amess was elected MP for Basildon in 1983, a seat he held until 1997, when he became MP for Southend West.

Where was their backbone?

POLITICALLY I OWE EVERYTHING to Margaret Thatcher. If it had not been for her leadership, I would never have won my seat in Basildon for the first time in 1983 and then retained it in 1987.

For me, Margaret Thatcher was the consummate politician. She had those unique qualities of charisma, enormous courage and determination. She was blessed with first-class skills of leadership and undoubtedly not only changed this country but the world for the better. No one, including myself, had expected to win for the first time in 1983 but all of that was due to the momentum that Margaret Thatcher brought with her in terms of encouraging ordinary working people to support Conservative Party policies. This was yet another great quality she had – common sense and a realisation of the aspirations that ordinary people had for a better life, not only for themselves but also for their children and grandchildren.

I was overwhelmed when I first entered House as a Conservative Member of Parliament and to support a Government led by Margaret Thatcher. She was truly magnificent at Question Time in the House of Commons. When she swept through the lobbies each time we voted, it was as if there was a sort of electric glow round her. She seemed to overshadow everyone.

Throughout those two Parliaments, 1983–1987 and then the one that followed, she faced many crises but never ducked a difficult issue. Debates that she was involved in were very great occasions with magnificent speeches – in stark contrast to the way things are today. I became sickened and disgusted by the whispering campaign that eventually undermined her. I kept thinking to myself, if she really was so awful, what's wrong with these chaps actually not standing up to her. I certainly wouldn't allow myself to be treated as they claimed that they were. Where was their backbone? I am sure Margaret Thatcher had greater respect for those who stood up to her, than those who – as is often described – were walked all over by her and then just complained behind her back. Pathetic. I was appalled when I listened to some of my colleagues, who had everything to thank her for, seemingly becoming concerned about our opinion poll ratings. If anyone should have been concerned, it should have been myself. But I would have much preferred to have lost under Margaret Thatcher's leadership, and I don't believe that would have happened, than to have changed horses midway through a Parliament.

I was angry and inconsolable when the end finally came. And have never really entirely got over the treachery of a number of my colleagues. I actually wrote to one or two and told them to their face what I thought of them. Conservatives should never ever air their dirty linen in public. At the very last minute I and others

'Another great quality she had – common sense and a realisation of the aspirations that ordinary people had for a better life, not only for themselves but also for their children and grandchildren.'

David Amess

Margaret Thatcher meets Nelson Mandela at Number 10 Downing Street shortly after his release from prison in 1990.

were drafted in to try and stiffen the resolve of colleagues but it was too late. I recall being with a number of Margaret's supporters in the room in the Lower Committee corridor thinking that if this was the way the campaign had been run so far, was it any wonder that she was in such a dire position. The effort seemed both complacent and half-hearted.

As I sat round the table going through lists of names of who was going to support who, I just thought it so amateurish and that we shouldn't have to do it at all. That evening, I walked to 10 Downing Street and personally handed a letter in and asked that the Prime Minister be given it. Whether or not she ever received it I don't know, but it was basically telling her not to resign because she still had great support amongst colleagues. As I walked along the road to 10 Downing Street, down Whitehall, there was an air of sick excitement really amongst some of the crowds. These were mainly the people who had been protesting in Trafalgar Square about the Community Charge. I kept thinking to myself that these are the very people who my colleagues are going to give pleasure to by forcing Margaret to stand down.

The next morning when I left home, I was listening to the radio and I can recall Pete Murray saying, 'This news is awful' and then he announced that Margaret Thatcher had resigned as Prime Minister. I was absolutely devastated. I could hardly concentrate on anything. When I arrived at the Commons, I bumped into a colleague who I think was one of the people who had been difficult and when he said to me, 'David, what are you looking so upset about?' I told him why, he said, 'Silly woman, I can't understand why she has resigned,' which for me, basically said it all.

I was inconsolable. I bumped into another colleague, who felt exactly as I did and we both went for a lunchtime drink. I found myself becoming increasingly angry with people. I told the Whips exactly what I thought of them. Just as I told the architect of her defeat exactly what I thought of him – although he certainly showed some guts writing to me directly a few days later.

When I saw Mrs Thatcher behind the Chair, walking to her room, I just said how sorry I was about everything and she put her fingers up indicating just four votes, which is all it was. Absolutely crazy. And I was also sitting behind her when she gave her last performance at Prime Minister's Question Time and she made that fantastic speech. Incredible.

When she left office, it never really seemed the same again. There was the woman who had brought the Conservatives to power, done so much to change the country for the better, now completely cast aside and humiliated on the back-benches. I won a ballot to introduce a topic for debate on a Friday and I chose to do it on Margaret Thatcher's time as Leader of the Conservative Party and Prime Minister.

I am not sure that we will ever see the likes of her again.

Lord Baker of Dorking

CABINET MINISTER 1985–92

A junior Minister in the Conservative Government of 1970–74 and in the early years of the Thatcher administration, Kenneth Baker joined the Cabinet in 1985 as Secretary of State for the Environment. He went on to become Secretary of State for Education and Science, Chancellor of the Duchy of Lancaster and ended his ministerial career in 1992 as Home Secretary. He was raised to the Peerage as Lord Baker of Dorking in 1997.

Contents of the handbag

IN POPULAR MEMORY Prime Ministers are remembered for a characteristic feature. For Disraeli it was the monocle and the small wisp of a beard; for Gladstone, the great shock of white hair; for Chamberlain, the umbrella; for Churchill, the cigar; for Harold Wilson, the Gannex mac; but for Maggie, it would have to be the handbag: she was never without it and it became a formidable weapon. When she joined the Lords there was a cartoon which depicted the Peers cringing away from an empty Front Bench on which was deposited just one handbag.

I have attended meetings where Maggie would 'handbag' a colleague. But in all fairness that colleague usually deserved it. She liked a good argument and she always respected people who would argue strongly and stand up for their corner, as long as they knew their facts and had researched their argument. Woe betide the Minister who was casual or careless – those are the ones who would get the full blaze of her contempt.

But Maggie had another use for the handbag. It contained not only all the things that women carry in their handbags, but also little scraps of paper. At a Cabinet Meeting she would have a brief prepared by the Cabinet Office under the guidance of the Cabinet Secretary. This, you could be assured, was well-read, underlined and marked even to the last page. Then she would have a second brief prepared by her political advisers from the Number Ten Policy Unit and this, too, would be carefully marked. That brief came to her in a separate box which the Civil Servants did not see. These were to arm her for the debate which would take place on the issue under discussion.

The Minister leading the discussion would have no idea what was in either brief but you knew from an early stage what her view was. Her style was not to go around the table like John Major collecting the voices and then coming down upon the side which had the majority. Maggie knew what she wanted but on several occasions she did not get her way.

When Maggie was really up against it and the argument was running against her, she would then pick up her handbag, put it on the Cabinet table and, opening it carefully and slowly, she would take out a piece of well crumpled and thumbed paper. This was the brief that came from no one knows whom – a friend, or someone who had rung her up who had a particular view about the matter in hand. It was unpredictable, sometimes illuminating, at others weird, sometimes an interesting new light, at others a worthless piece of gossip. Whenever she drew out a piece of paper like this the Cabinet Secretary would pale, and the Minister would raise his eyes to the ceiling knowing full well that he was about to be grounded.

When I was Education Secretary, I did discover one of Maggie's private briefers – her hairdresser. He had a child in one of the inner London comprehensive schools and when he was doing the Prime Minister's hair she would hear about his child's poor experiences. The Prime Minister would then tell me and her colleagues that something more had to be done.

Discussions at Cabinet are never predictable. Many are the Ministers who have cursed the contents of that wretched blue handbag.

* * * * *

Early on the morning of 22 November 1990 I was telephoned by Andrew Turnbull from Number 10 and told that the Prime Minister had decided to resign. A great leader of our country, a very great Prime Minister, had been struck down by a collective loss of nerve among her colleagues. It was the end of an era and of a very great Prime Minister.

When I arrived at Number 10 I found my fellow Cabinet colleagues waiting outside the Cabinet Room in a funereal and uneasy silence, not at all keen to catch each other's eye. The Prime Minister came down the stairs a little after nine o'clock, and with head lowered went alone into the Cabinet Room. After a few minutes we were sent in to take our places. Margaret looked very red-eyed and under considerable strain. She began by saying that before the formal business of the Cabinet she wanted to make her position known. She started to read from the paper in front of her, but when she reached the part which said, 'having consulted widely among colleagues', she broke down and could not continue. The words choked in her throat and she wiped away tears from her eyes. She started again falteringly and said, 'I am so sorry.' Cecil Parkinson, sitting next but one to her, suggested that the Lord Chancellor should read the statement. Margaret blew her nose, shook her head and continued, 'I have concluded that the unity of the Party and the prospects of victory in the General Election' – here she paused again and choked on the words, but went on – 'will be better served if I stood down to enable Cabinet colleagues to enter the ballot for the Leadership. I should like to thank all those in Cabinet and outside who have given me such dedicated support.'

David Waddington was dabbing his eyes at this stage, and others were close to tears. Some, while remaining expressionless, must have been relieved. But nobody around that Cabinet table had ever thought they would witness such a scene. Margaret went on, 'It is vital that we stand together. The unity of the Party is crucial and that's why I am giving up. I couldn't bear all the things I have stood for over the past eleven years being rejected. The Cabinet must unite to stop Michael Heseltine.'

Slowly Margaret recovered her composure. It had been a moving scene. Never before had she broken down in front of her colleagues. But at the end she was a real person of flesh and blood, not the cold, unfeeling automaton she was so often portrayed as. Then the Lord Chancellor, James Mackay, read the passage which Robin Butler the Cabinet Secretary had prepared for him, recording the Cabinet's tribute to Margaret's leadership of the country.

It is vital that we stand together. The unity of the Party is crucial and that's why I am giving up.

Enjoying a twirl with Party Chairman Kenneth Baker at the 1987 Party Conference in Blackpool.

'As Party Chairman', I said, 'you have and will always continue to have the love and loyalty of the Party. You have a special place in the heart of the Party. You have led us to victory three times and you would have done so again. Speaking as one of the longest-serving Cabinet Ministers', I added, 'those who have served you recognise that they have been in touch with greatness.' Then Douglas Hurd said he wanted to place on record the superb way in which Margaret had carried herself at the Paris Conference over the last three days, especially with the pressures of the leadership election upon her.

We then turned to other matters, the business of the House and so on. When it came to Foreign Affairs, Margaret gave a spirited, very detailed and long report on her talks with Gorbachev and Bush. She was clearly getting back into her stride. But towards the end of the meeting I could see she was close to tears again.

We were all asked to stay on for coffee, which we then had sitting around the Cabinet table. We talked about the future. Margaret was very keen and insistent that it should be a member of the Cabinet who was elected to succeed her. 'I think the Cabinet will have to do everything it can to ensure this. You will have to work very hard,' she said.

During this meeting I passed a note to Douglas Hurd asking whether he had come to any agreement with John about the candidacy. I had assumed that some time over the last twenty-four hours they must have talked together about this and come to an arrangement. Douglas sent back a note saying they were going to issue a joint statement declaring that they had worked very closely together and would continue to do so but, in all the circumstances, the best way of uniting the Party would be for both to go forward in the next ballot. It would be a friendly contest. Douglas drafted this statement then and there, and passed it to me. It was perfect, a masterly composition. One of Douglas' great gifts is his capacity to draft elegant statements at the drop of a pen. Norman Lamont, who had been promoting John's cause for some time – he had actually canvassed Cecil Parkinson twenty-four hours earlier – could now openly become John's campaign manager. It was clear to me that despite the disavowals of the two protagonists a good deal of preparatory work had already been done by the two camps to marshal their campaign teams.

Cecil was quite scathing about the whole situation. He said both campaigns would be negative if the contestants were going to be friendly. 'If they are going to be friendly, why bother to turn up and vote for them?'

As the meeting broke up I told Cecil and Douglas that as Chairman of the Party I would make a statement to the cameras outside Number 10 on behalf of the Cabinet. I jotted something down outside the Cabinet Room, and then went out to the massed cameras opposite the front door of Number 10 and said, 'This is a typically brave and selfless decision by the Prime Minister. Once again Margaret Thatcher has put her country and the Party's interests before personal considerations. This will allow the Party to elect a new leader to unite the Party and build upon her immense successes. If I could add just a personal note, I am very saddened that our greatest peace-time Prime Minister has left Government. She is an outstanding leader, not only of our country but also of the world – I do not believe we will see her like again.'

I was deeply moved by the events which I had just witnessed. I was very close to tears myself in the Cabinet Room. I had started by being cool about Margaret Thatcher, but over the years I had come to admire her. She has traits of character which can make her not particularly endearing. As Prime Minister she was personally dominant, supremely self-confident, infuriatingly stubborn and held a strange mixture of broad views and narrow prejudices. But Margaret also had a strength of character that made her a natural leader. She was a patriot, always putting the interests of Britain first. She also realised that Britain had to be saved from economic and institutional collapse. No Prime Minister I have known since the War would have seen through that tough Budget of 1981 which deepened the recession we were then going through but proved to be the foundation of the prosperity of the middle and late 1980s. No Prime Minister I have known would have had the courage to launch a sea and land offensive 8,000 miles away to secure the independence of a small group of colonial islands. No Prime Minister since the War would have withstood a miners' strike for over a year. And no Prime Minister since the War would have reduced the power of organised labour in the way that Margaret did.

Time Magazine cover of 3 December 1990, the week after Margaret Thatcher left office.

Alan Clark

CONSERVATIVE MP 1974–92 AND 1997–9

Alan Clark, who died in 1999, was the MP for Plymouth Sutton from 1974 until 1992. He returned to Parliament in 1997 as the MP for Kensington and Chelsea. He served under Margaret Thatcher as Minister for Trade and then Minister of State at the MOD but he is best known for his notoriously indiscreet diaries.

Lovely and haughty

Monday, 19 November 1990

THE WHOLE HOUSE IS IN FERMENT. Little groups, conclaves everywhere. Only in the dining room does some convention seem to have grown up (I presume because no one trusts their dining companions) that we don't talk 'shop'.

'Made your Christmas plans yet?' All that balls. God, the dining room is boring these days, even worse than Pratts'. Big, slow, buffers 'measuring their words' oh-so-firmly; or creepy little narks talking straight out of *Conservative News*.

But in the corridors it is all furtive whispering and glancing over shoulders. The institutional confidence (seen at its most obvious in those who have served a prison term, and which I first noticed in my early days on Warren Street), that special grimacing style of speech out of the corner of the mouth, eyes focusing in another direction, is now it seems the only way of communicating.

Most people are interested – not so much in the result, as in knowing what the result will be in advance, in order to make their own 'dispositions'. To ingratiate oneself with the new regime – *a* new regime, I should say, because the outcome is by no means certain – even as little as a week before it is installed, looks better than joining the stampede afterwards. The issue which can be discussed semi-respectably, is who is most likely to deliver victory at the General Election? But it is packaging, conceals a great basket of bitterness, thwarted personal ambition, and vindictive glee. Talk of country, or loyalty, is dismissed as 'histrionics'.

And there is a strange feeling abroad. Even if the Lady wins – and here I am writing 'even if', pull yourself together Clark, say 'even after she's won' – there will be no escaping the fact that at least one hundred and fifty of her parliamentary colleagues will have rejected her leadership. That's a big chunk. Some people, particularly those who pose as Party Elders, like Tony Grant, are intimating that it might be 'better' if, faced with so blatant a show of No Confidence, she decided to 'heal' the Party by announcing her intention to stand down at a given date (i.e. become a lame duck which the Labour Party could taunt and torment on every occasion, and a busted flush internationally).

And as the savour of a Heseltine victory starts to pervade the crannies and cupboards and committee rooms, so more and more people are 'coming out'. 'Oh, I don't think he'd be so bad, really …' 'He's got such a wide *appeal*.' 'My people just love him, I must say …' 'I know what you mean, but he'd be so good at dealing with …' (fill in particular problem as appropriate).

Most conspicuous in canvassing are Hampson (loonily), Mates (gruffly) and Bill Powell (persuasively). Michael himself is quite shameless in offering all and sundry what they have always wanted. For example, he would probably have got Paul's

Leaving Downing Street for the final time, 28 November 1990.

support anyway, but 'sealed' it with an assurance that Paul would be Speaker in the next House; Soames fell straight away for the 'your talents are long overdue for recognition' line, as did little Nelson and Rhodes James ('you've been treated abominably').

Michael stands in the centre of the Members' lobby, virtually challenging people to wish him good luck. He gives snap 'updates' to journalists, and greets supplicants who are brought along for a short audience by his team. The heavier targets he sees in his room. The Cabinet play their cards close to the chest, although Mellor, apparently, speaks to Michael twice a day on the telephone. Some, like Kenneth Clarke, want her out so badly that they don't need even to blink. And I would guess that there are a fair coterie of Ministers of State and Parly Secs like Sainsbury and Trippier who feel uneasy with the Lady and like the idea of a change.

At the top of the ministerial staircase I ran into Garel Jones. He was bubbling with suppressed excitement. I don't think he actually wants 'Hezzy' as he (spastically) calls him, to win. It would be disruptive of the Blue Chip long-term plan. But he's high on the whole thing.

Tristan said, 'Of course every member of the Cabinet will vote for the Prime Minister in the first round.' Like hell they will.

I said to him, hoping he'd deny it, 'One cannot actually exclude the possibility that Heseltine will score more votes than her on the first ballot.'

'No, I'm afraid one can't.'

'Can one, even, be completely sure that he will not get both the largest total and the necessary margin to win without a second ballot?'

'No, I'm afraid one can't.'

This was really chilling. Apocalypse. Because time is horrendously tight if we have to organise an alternative candidate.

Four working days and a weekend. But if Michael scoops it in one gulp then that is the end of everything.

Maddeningly, I had to return to the Department. Meetings, and an official lunch. Scandinavians.

'I assume that there is no likelihood of Mrs Thatcher being defeated for the position of Prime Minister?'

'Oh no. None whatever. It's just one of these quaint traditions we have in the Conservative Party.'

But the encounter made me realise the enormity of what we're doing – *changing the Prime Minister* – but without any electoral authority so to do. I thought I'd have a talk to Peter, although he doesn't encourage it, and I cancelled my early afternoon engagements and went back over to the House.

I listened outside the door. Silence. I knocked softly, then tried the handle. He was asleep, snoring lightly, in the leather armchair, with his feet resting on the desk.

Drake playing bowls before the Armada and all that, but I didn't like it. This was ten minutes past three in the afternoon of the most critical day of the whole election. I spoke sharply to him. 'Peter.'

He was bleary.

'I assume that there is no likelihood of Mrs Thatcher being defeated for the position of Prime Minister?'

Alan Clark

'I'm sorry to butt in, but I'm really getting a bit worried about the way things are going.'

'Quite all right, old boy, relax.'

'I'm just hearing bad reactions around the place from people where I wouldn't expect it.'

'Look, do you think I'd be like this if I wasn't entirely confident?'

'What's the arithmetic look like?'

'Tight-ish, but OK.'

'Well, what?'

'I've got Michael on 115. It could be 124, at the worst.'

'Look, Peter, I don't think people are being straight with you.'

'I have my ways of checking.'

'Paul?'

'I know about Paul.'

'The Wintertons?'

'The Wintertons, funnily enough, I've got down as 'Don't Know's.'

'What the fuck do you mean, 'Don't Know'? This isn't a fucking street canvas. It's a two-horse race, and each vote affects the relative score by two, unless it's an abstention.'

'Actually, I think there could be quite a few abstentions.'

'Don't you think we should be out there twisting arms?'

'No point. In fact it could be counter-productive. I've got a theory about this. I think some people may abstain on the first ballot in order to give Margaret a fright, then rally to her on the second.' (Balls, I thought, but didn't say.)

'What about the '92? They're completely rotten. They've got a meeting at six. Are you going?'

'No point. But I think *you* should.'

In deep gloom I walked back down Speaker's corridor. It can't really be as bad as this can it? I mean there is absolutely no oomph in her campaign *whatsoever*. Peter is useless, far worse than I thought. When he was pairing Whip he was unpopular, but at least he was crisp. Now he's sozzled. There isn't a single person working for her who cuts any ice at all. I know it's better to be feared than loved. But these people aren't either. And she's in Paris. '*Où est la masse de manoeuvre? – Aucune.*'

I went into the members' tea room. The long table was crowded with Margaret supporters, all nonentities except for Tebbit who was cheering people up. Much shouting and laughter. Blustering reassurance. Norman was saying how unthinkable it was to consider dismissing a Prime Minister during a critical international conference. 'Like Potsdam in 1945,' I said. No one paid any attention. If they heard they didn't, or affected not to understand the allusion.

The crowd thinned out a little and when he got up Norman said that he wanted a word. We went into the Aye lobby and sat at that round table in the centre with all the stationery on it.

'Well … ?'

'It's filthy', I said.

'It could be close. Very close.'

I agreed, '*Fucking* close.'

'If it's like that do you think she should stand in the second ballot?' I simply don't know the answer to this. Governing would be very difficult with half the Party against her. She might have to make concessions to the left. I asked Norman if he thought she would have to bring Heseltine into the Cabinet.

'She'd certainly be under a lot of pressure to do so.'

'Renton.'

'Yeah.'

I said that the key tactic was to get Chris Patten to stand, and draw off the left vote. At least the hard left vote, Charlie Morrison, Bob Hicks, all the wankers. Norman said, 'And Ken Clarke.' I told him no, if you have too many candidates people just get in a muddle and Heseltine walks through them, just as she did in 1975. Norman said that a lot of people now regarded Michael as a right-wing candidate anyway.

'Well, we know different.'

'Too true.'

Norman said, 'If it's open season, I'm dam' well going to put my name in. The right must have a candidate they can vote for.'

'You'd lose.'

'It's likely I would, but at least we'd know our strength. That could be useful in a changed situation.'

'Look, Norman, we want to put additional names in to reduce his total, not ours. I don't think Heseltine has that big a personal vote. It's just an anti-Margaret coalition.'

I could see he was thoughtful. But he didn't want to prolong the conversation, which we were conducting in tones just above a whisper, though still arousing the curious attention of passers-by.

Raising his voice Norman said, 'Well, this time tomorrow everything will be settled,' and gave one of his graveyard cackles.

The '92 meeting was in one of those low-ceilinged rooms on the upper committee room corridor. The mood was tetchy, and apprehensive. There was a kind of fiction running from several (Jill Knight, for example, shockingly), just as Norman had foreseen, that 'Michael' – as defectors call him (supporters of the Prime Minister always refer to him as 'Heseltine'; and this is quite a useful subliminal indicator of how the speaker is going to vote when he or she is being deliberately or defensively opaque) – was 'really' on the right.

The trouble with this club, to which I was elected almost as soon as I arrived here, but with which I have never really felt comfortable, is that it personifies in extreme form two characteristics found in the majority of MPs – stupidity and egomania. It is only the shrewd and subtle guidance of George Gardiner that has prevented them becoming a laughing stock in recent years. But such integrity as they might originally have possessed has been eroded by the inclusion of many from marginal seats. None are quite as awful as Elizabeth Peacock, who spoke squatly and fatly against Margaret – why bother, she won't be here in the next

'It could be close. Very close.'

Norman Tebbit

Parliament anyway – but most are concerned solely with saving their own skins. I spoke loyally and, should have been movingly, of our debt to the PM. But there was a hint of what's-she-ever-done-for-us from the audience and with some justification, so few ministerial appointments having come out of the '92. I tried to make their flesh creep with what Michael would do, got only a subdued ritual cheer when I said Margaret is undefeated, and never will be defeated either in the Country or in this House of Commons. I'm not particularly popular with that lot. They think I'm 'snooty'. Perhaps my boredom threshold shows. But in the ballot tomorrow I'd say they will divide no better than 60/40.

After dinner I had a word with Norman Lamont. He'd just come back from somewhere-or-other. 'I don't like the smell,' he kept saying. 'There's a bad smell to the whole place.' He's right, of course. It's the smell of decay. It's affecting everything, the badge messengers, the police, the drivers. Something nasty is going to happen.

I write this very late, and I am very tired. Perhaps I'm just needlessly depressed. I'd ring the Lady if I could, but she's at a banquet. She's not even coming back for the ballot. Lovely and haughty.

Meeting President Bush and Barbara Bush at the Houston Economic Summit in July 1990.

Lord Parkinson

CHAIRMAN OF THE CONSERVATIVE PARTY, 1981–3

Cecil Parkinson was a Conservative MP from 1970 to 1992, and served in Margaret Thatcher's Falklands War Cabinet. He was Trade and Industry Secretary in 1983 and served again in the Cabinet from 1987 to 1990.

The final hours

Thursday 22 November 1990

AT ABOUT 7.00AM the telephone rang in my London flat. I was surprised to hear the voice of Chris Chope, one of my junior ministers at the Department of Transport. He had some appalling news for me. Margaret Thatcher was almost certain to announce that she would not be a candidate in the second ballot for the leadership of the Conservative Party and would be resigning as Prime Minister. He was telephoning to ask me to make a last-minute appeal to her to change her mind. I was stunned. I had seen her the previous evening at about 6.00pm. At that time she was full of enthusiasm and determined to win on the second ballot. I therefore went out to dinner with my wife and a group of friends feeling sure that with the full and active support of the Cabinet, and with better organization than in the first ballot, she would win well.

We had a very relaxed dinner and got home about midnight. I went straight to bed, and was soon in such a deep sleep that I did not hear the telephone when it rang about 12.45am. My wife answered. It was Trevor Kavanagh, the Political Editor of *The Sun*. He had heard a strong rumour that Margaret was resigning and he wanted to talk to me about it. Ann said that I was asleep, needed the rest and she would not disturb me. She told me about this the next morning after my conversation with Chris Chope.

By 7.10am I was on the telephone to Number 10 and asked to speak to the Prime Minister. The operator asked me to wait. She came back to tell me that the PM was at that moment under the hair dryer and suggested that I telephone again in about half an hour.

I then rang Norman Tebbit to find out what he knew. As usual, he knew a lot. He had been with her until late the night before, working on her speech for the Censure Debate that afternoon, and he was sure that she would be resigning. We agreed that it would be pointless for me to telephone her again.

I left for the office where I was due to meet my ministerial colleagues in Transport for one of our regular early morning prayers. We held them on Tuesdays and Thursdays. Tuesday was 'departmental' and included the Permanent Secretary. Thursday was political and only Ministers, my special adviser, Elizabeth Buchanan, and the desk officer from Conservative Research Department, Perry Miller, attended. We met at 8.30, but before that Chris Chope and Elizabeth Buchanan came in and we pieced together a clear picture of the events of the previous evening and discussed the likely outcome of Cabinet. We were a sombre group.

As a departmental team we had been totally committed to Margaret Thatcher and we were still unanimous in wishing her to carry on as leader. By then, it was

'He was telephoning to ask me to make a last-minute appeal to her to change her mind. I was stunned.'

Lord Parkinson

becoming clear that a group of younger Cabinet Ministers had played a decisive role in persuading her to change her mind. For my part, I did not feel that they were particularly well qualified to interpret the mood of either the Parliamentary Party or the Party in the country to her.

Cabinet had been called for 9.00am and we adjourned our meeting at abut 8.50 so that I could get there. We arranged to meet again at 10.30 so that I could report back to them the outcome of Cabinet.

I left Marsham Street with Elizabeth Buchanan. She was on her way to the meeting of special advisers which took place each week at the same time as Cabinet. It was jokingly called the Shadow Cabinet and those present liked to think that the standard of discussion was of higher quality, possibly than the Cabinet, and certainly than the other Shadow Cabinet.

We were both in a gloomy and angry frame of mind. I arrived at Number 10 unusually early, to find that a number of Cabinet colleagues were already waiting in the anteroom outside the Cabinet room. Most of them were looking grim and saying little. Ken Clarke was the exception. He was telling anybody who cared to listen that if the PM did not resign he would resign before noon that day. He was adamant that she had to go. James Mackay, the Lord Chancellor, was quiet and looked preoccupied. The reason for that became clear a few minutes later.

It was not unusual for Cabinet to start a few minutes late and it did that day. The waiting was almost unbearable and the atmosphere became more tense by the minute. At about 9.10 the door of the Cabinet room was opened and we went in. The Prime Minister was already there, sitting in her usual place, with Sir Robin Butler, the Cabinet Secretary next to her. She had been crying, her eyes were red and swollen and she looked deeply distressed. As we came in I noticed that a carton of tissues had been placed next to her on the Cabinet table. She picked one from the box and wiped away the tears that had welled up into her eyes. There was a deathly silence in the room. In a halting voice she said that she wished to make a statement, following which we would return to normal Cabinet business. She started to read but broke down after a few words. She started a second time and again, she broke down. At this point I spoke, saying 'For God's sake, James, you read it.' This broke the tension. Various colleagues disagreed with me, and in the few seconds this took, the Prime Minister regained her composure and read out the statement. It was the one that was made public later.

I glanced at my colleagues. Most of them could not bring themselves to look at her. They sat staring at the Cabinet table so intently that they looked as if they were trying to drill holes in it with their eyes. Two or three were in tears. I felt deep anger and bitterness that the Prime Minister, who had led us to three election victories, and who only two days earlier had been a pivotal figure at a great international conference in Paris to mark the end of the Cold War, should have been treated so shabbily by her parliamentary colleagues.

James Mackay has obviously been warned in advance and had prepared a statement of his own in which he thanked the Prime Minister on behalf of the Cabinet for her outstanding service to the nation over such a long period. One or two other people added their own tributes, but the Prime Minister brought this to

'She had been crying, her eyes were red and swollen and she looked deeply distressed.'

Lord Parkinson

an early halt with a characteristic remark that she found business easier to cope with than sympathy. By this time she was totally in control of herself and the Cabinet, and we moved on to our normal weekly business.

Cabinet business was despatched quickly that morning and by ten o'clock we had finished. We all realized that this would probably be the last Cabinet meeting over which she would preside, and nobody wanted to be the first to leave. She clearly wanted to talk and suggested that we had coffee. Officials then left the Cabinet room and a rather desultory conversation began. I remember very little of what was said but three things stuck in my mind. The first was a general agreement that the next leader must come from the Cabinet. It should not be Michael Heseltine. The second was that the Cabinet felt both John Major and Douglas Hurd should be put up as candidates in the second ballot since it was not possible to know with any degree of certainty, nor was it possible to find out in the time available which of them was the preferred candidate. The third and most memorable moment came when a colleague said, 'We are going to pin regicide on Heseltine.' The Prime Minister looked puzzled for a moment, and then came the devastating riposte: 'Oh no, it wasn't Heseltine, it was the Cabinet.' It was all the more telling because it was said without the slightest rancour. It was, to her, a simple statement of fact.

With one of her closest political allies, Cecil Parkinson.

Lord Renton
CHIEF WHIP 1990

Tim Renton was Conservative MP for Mid Sussex from 1974 to 1997. He was a member of the Thatcher Government from 1984 to its end and served as Chief Whip from 1989 to 1990. He was raised to the Peerage in 1997. He has written *Chief Whip*, a history of the Whips' office.

Remembering Ian Gow

EVEN IN HER BUSIEST DAYS as Prime Minister, Margaret Thatcher was outstanding in her care and concern for her friends and the tight circle of those who worked directly for her.

It was often said that one reason why Margaret was so slow to accept that interest on house mortgages should cease to be tax free was because one of her private office secretaries told her how hard it would be for her to pay her mortgage if the tax exemption was removed. From my own experience, when a newspaper reported that one of our daughters had been very badly burned on a charity journey across Africa, I received a card from the Prime Minister within hours asking after her, and this was followed by daily enquiries about her progress.

As Margaret Thatcher's last Chief Whip, I never saw this solicitude in greater evidence than on the day of the murder of Ian Gow, the Member of Parliament for Eastbourne. Ian was Margaret's Parliamentary Private Secretary from 1979 to 1983 and then a junior minister who resigned in 1985 rather than vote for the Anglo-Irish agreement.

It was 30 July 1990. We had just completed an extensive ministerial reshuffle following the resignation from the Cabinet of Nick Ridley, one of her closest allies. His departure had already left the Prime Minister feeling isolated in her own Cabinet.

Ian and his wife, Jane, were long-time friends and neighbours in Sussex. The short list for the Eastbourne constituency had had just two names on it, Ian's and mine. Despite police warnings, Ian regularly parked his car overnight in the road outside his house at Hankham, near Eastbourne, and a bomb exploded when he started his car on Monday morning. I heard of his death at ten in the morning and told Number 10 that my wife Alice and I would drive over immediately to be with Jane. We were soon joined by their son, Charles, and his fiancée and by Father Peter, the Bishop of Lewes, and the local priest, Father Jonathan. Alice and Jane went to the local church, where Jane was the organist and Ian a churchwarden. A number of people were there and they came one after the other and hugged Jane, many of them crying, and then went out to leave her alone.

It was a two-hour journey from London and the Prime Minister arrived at Hankham in the early afternoon. She came out of the car up the steps into the garden looking pale, but wholly resolute. I felt enormously for her. Ian had not only been the Parliamentary Secretary to whom she had been closest but he had become a strong and sympathetic supporter. As she said during the course of the day, 'If I was feeling low, Ian would often say to me "Come back and have some supper just with me and Jane." And I often did.' I took her into the house, showed her the room where Jane was and then went out and discussed arrangements with the Sussex Chief Constable, Andrew Turnbull, then the Civil Service Head of her Private Office, and Peter Morrison, her new Parliamentary Private Secretary.

Margaret spent the afternoon comforting and talking to Jane. An impromptu communion service was to be held at 7pm but was moved forward to 6pm so that the Prime Minister could attend before returning to London. The church was almost full and the Prime Minister sat in front on one side, Jane and her two sons on the other. I wrote in my diary for the day that, in church, the Prime Minister 'looked forlorn, withdrawn, quiet and cut off, not her usual vibrant dominating self but almost isolated, quietly miserable'.

The Prime Minister and her small team arrived back in London in the late evening. There were to be no cracks in her armour. Thirty-six hours later she flew to Aspen, Colorado for an International Conference and meetings with President George Bush. That night Iraq invaded Kuwait, oil prices soared, sterling plummeted and Margaret, in the words of her own autobiography, told the President 'my conclusions in the clearest and most straightforward terms'. Three months later a bad-tempered European Community summit took place in Rome. The arguments about economic and monetary union came to a head and this led to the resignation of the Deputy Prime Minister, Geoffrey Howe, on 1 November and Margaret's own, three weeks later, on 22 November.

These storms were public ones and are part of history. I have never forgotten, though, her kindness, her concern and her private resolution on that sunny July day when, amid the peace of the Sussex Downs, brutality and violence took the life of someone whose support she treasured and whose humour she enjoyed.

Margaret Thatcher enjoys a joke with John and Norma Major.

Lord Wakeham

CHIEF WHIP 1983–7

John Wakeham was Conservative MP for Maldon & Colchester South from 1974 to 1992. He joined the Whips' Office in 1979 and was appointed Chief Whip in 1983. In 1987 he became Leader of the House of Commons and was appointed Energy Secretary in 1989. He was elevated to the Peerage in 1992 and became Leader of the House of Lords, a position he relinquished in 1994.

Remembering the achievements

I ENTERED THE HOUSE OF COMMONS IN 1974 – one year before Mrs Thatcher became Leader of the Conservative Party. I left it for the House of Lords barely eighteen months after she left Number 10. My time as an MP was therefore dominated by this giant figure – one of the greatest Prime Ministers this country has ever seen, and probably will ever see.

Tributes elsewhere in this timely volume testify eloquently to the dramatic changes she wrought in British politics – permanently transforming an economy in decline into the powerhouse we have today, and turning us into a nation of owners with stakes for the first time in our businesses, our major industries and, for many, many more, in our own property. Few dispute that success, and the permanent legacy, even among Margaret's detractors.

I do not want to add to this catalogue – but rather to add my own personal memories of the saddest point of Margaret's premiership, her resignation in November 1990.

Those of us who were closest to her knew that a challenge to her leadership from Michael Heseltine was almost inevitable from the moment Geoffrey Howe made his famous speech in the House of Commons. It seemed then a question not of if, but of when.

I had little part in her campaign during the first ballot, because it fell during the climax of the electricity privatisation for which I was responsible. One thing I knew was that the result could never be certain: far too many of my colleagues in the Parliamentary Conservative Party would be telling Margaret's Campaign Managers what they wanted to hear, not how they were really intending to vote.

The result when it came was a great body blow – so near yet so far, with the outcome of a second ballot far from certain.

It was at that point that Margaret asked me to run her campaign for the second ballot. Before we could make any plans, I knew there was one central issue we had to confront. In a Parliamentary system such as ours, no Prime Minister can long remain in office if he or she does not have the support of the Cabinet – and, in this case, that support was regrettably far from clear.

I knew, therefore, that Margaret had to see all the members of the Cabinet to ascertain where they stood. If they were all behind her, there was a very good chance of victory in the second ballot; if they weren't then that victory was far from clear.

On the afternoon of Wednesday 21 November, Margaret gave an accomplished performance in the House of Commons during a statement on the

> *'If they were all behind her, there was a very good chance of victory in the second ballot; if they weren't then that victory was far from clear.'*
>
> Lord Wakeham

Paris summit. After that, she agreed rather reluctantly to see her Cabinet colleagues one by one. She asked each of them their views.

Many Cabinet colleagues said they would stick by her to the end. Some reaffirmed the view expressed by Cranley Onslow, the Chairman of the 1922 Committee, that she should permit the contest to be widened to allow in figures like John Major and Douglas Hurd. At least three warned her that they were prepared to resign if she stayed on. A large number added that they thought, whatever their own decisions, support in Parliament was crumbling away – and that standing again may risk handing victory to Michael Heseltine.

To those who told her they could not see her winning the second ballot, or who themselves refused to support her, she mused that politics was a funny old world. She had won a record three elections; she maintained the overwhelming support of the Conservative Party in the country; she had never lost a motion of confidence in the House of Commons; and the first leadership ballot had shown she still had the support of a substantial majority of Conservative MPs – although not enough to win through the antiquated electoral system that then existed.

Two quite amusing incidents occurred during this round. The first was when Peter Brooke went in to see her and give his support. He was dressed in white tie and tails on his way to a City Dinner and he remarked to me that there was a time in his days at Oxford when white tie and tails was the only appropriate dress in which to make important decisions.

The second came when the late Alan Clark also rushed in without an appointment and said 'Prime Minister, you must fight on – of course you will lose but what a glorious defeat!'

That round of meeting finished at about 8.30pm and Margaret told me she was going back to Number 10 to think things over. She was clearly very depressed – and had to face hours of work on her speech for a Confidence Motion, moved by Neil Kinnock, the next day.

To try and prevent the formation of cabals among Cabinet Ministers and others, it was made clear to colleagues that Margaret was going to sleep on things. The Cabinet meeting was brought forward to 9am to allow decisions to be reached before the formal business began.

By morning – and after consultation with the most important person in her life, Denis – she had decided that it was impossible to carry on and she said so to the Cabinet. It was, understandably, an emotional moment, but composure was soon regained and the meeting ended quite quickly. The rest, as they say – including her bravura final appearance at the Dispatch Box – is history.

I look back many times at that awful week and ponder whether anything different could have been done. Each time, I come up with the same conclusion – against the background of the first ballot, we did everything we possibly could.

Ten years on, the manner of Margaret's departure has, I hope, faded from memory. After all, she deserves to be remembered for all that she achieved for the British people in eleven magnificent years – not for the way it all ended. Those achievements live on, and always will, because she changed Britain for ever. Even so, she would be the first to acknowledge there is still a great deal more to do!

'Prime Minister, you must fight on – of course you will lose but what a glorious defeat!'

Alan Clark

Celebrating the tenth anniversary of her first election victory in May 1989.

Overleaf: William Hague and Margaret Thatcher at an election rally in Plymouth in May 2001.

William Hague

LEADER OF THE CONSERVATIVE PARTY 1997–2001

William Hague became the Leader of the Conservative Party following John Major's resignation in 1997. He had previously served as Minister of State for Social Security and Disabled People and as Secretary of State for Wales.

Maggie's last stand

MANY PEOPLE WILL HAVE MEMORIES about Margaret Thatcher etched indelibly in their political consciousness. Mine has to be the final speech she made in the Commons as Prime Minister in November 1990 following her decision to stand down from the leadership of the Conservative Party.

She had been Prime Minister for eleven years and dominated British politics. She was one of my earliest political heroes and I remember sitting there, as a junior backbencher, watching with a deep sense of sorrow that she was about to bow out.

But what a way to go! Anyone expecting her to be downbeat or subdued by the experiences of recent days was sorely disappointed as she recounted how Britain had been rescued from the spiral of decline and stagnation in which decades of socialism had left it. At one stage Dennis Skinner intervened to suggest she might become Governor of the new European Central Bank. 'What a good idea,' she responded to the hilarity of the House. To Tory cheers, she went on, 'I'm enjoying this.'

It was then that the Conservative backbencher Michael Carttiss spoke for many of us when, pointing across the Chamber, he said 'You can wipe the floor with these people.' It was a magical performance, never to be forgotten by those who saw it.

A few months later I saw her come into the Commons tea room and fall into conversation with Dennis Skinner. On seeing her he had cried out, 'It's not the same without you, love.' Looking across at him she replied, 'How are you, dear?' before the two of them sat together for about forty five minutes in earnest discussion, while the rest of us strained to hear what they were talking about. Whatever people's views of her policies she was held in immense respect right across the spectrum.

I saw that again in my own leadership election in 1997 when she went to the tea room for the first time since leaving the Commons five years earlier – much to the amazement of many new Labour MPs who had never seen her in the flesh before! All the old authority, presence and conviction that she exuded as Prime Minister came back as she handbagged any wavering Conservative MPs.

They were the same qualities that had sustained her through some of her most difficult times as Prime Minister – such as the speech on 22 November 1990. It is hard now to appreciate just how difficult that speech was to make. Yet it turned out to be her grand finale as Prime Minister, worthy of everything she had achieved in eleven years. Moreover, to many of those who were privileged to be there, it was quite simply one of the greatest Parliamentary performances that we had seen, or are ever likely to see.

'You can wipe the floor with these people.'

Michael Carttiss

At a book signing for her second volume of memoirs, *The Path to Power*.

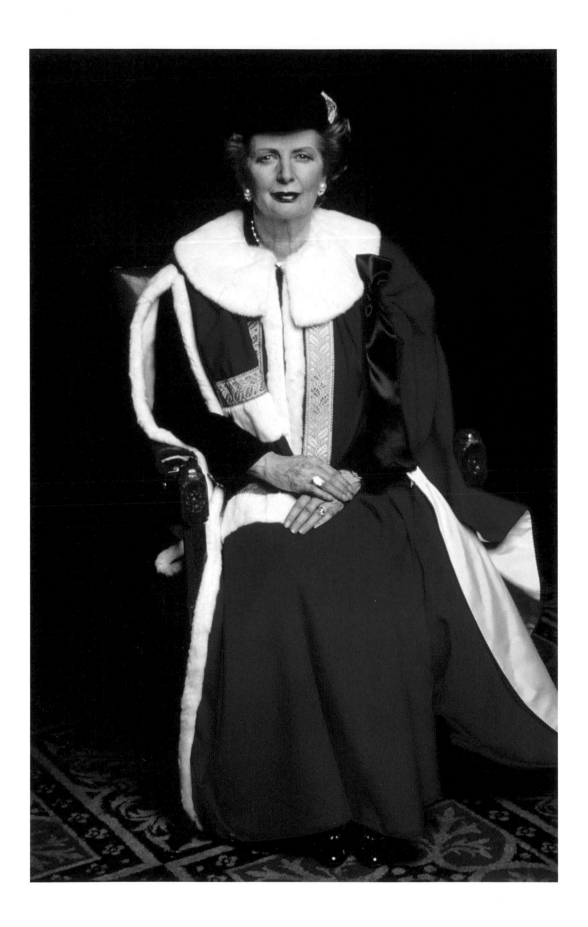

Christine Hamilton

WRITER, BROADCASTER AND BATTLEAXE

The wife of former Conservative MP Neil Hamilton, Christine Hamilton first came to public attention for her vigorous defence of her husband during the 1997 General Election. She capitalised on her image by writing the *Bumper Book of British Battleaxes* and now works as a presenter on radio and television.

Love of chocolate

DURING THE 1992 GENERAL ELECTION Margaret came to speak at a rally for Neil in Knutsford, arriving at our home for supper beforehand. It had been an exciting day. That afternoon she had done a walkabout in Stockport for Tony Favell and had been attacked – fortunately only with a bunch of daffodils. Margaret, of course, carried on with supreme sang-froid but her minders were understandably alarmed by the breach of security.

On arrival with us, all memory of daffodils had been expunged and she beetled in through the front door, reluctantly stepping on the pristine red carpet we had rolled out for the occasion, demanding to know, 'What are the trade figures? What are the trade figures?'

She marched into the drawing-room where Neil steered her to an armchair. Adjacent to this we had carefully placed the cardboard cut-out figure of Margaret which I had bought in Carnaby Street back in the mid 70s which normally sat in our hall to frighten off burglars (very successfully). It was exhilarating to have the real three-dimensional Margaret sitting next to her two-dimensional replica but she affected not to notice, perhaps thinking there was nothing unusual about this and that every home should have one!

Into the dining-room for supper and, amongst a multitude of goodies normally classed in our household as 'forbidden or controlled substances' was a magnificent rich, dark chocolate torte which I had lovingly made. I knew that, although chocolate was one of Margaret's favourite foods, she had given it up for Lent. I assumed, therefore, that she would refuse the proffered delicacy and accept the fruit salad alternative. Not a bit of it! She took a particularly large wedge and rapidly demolished it with gusto. When I gingerly expressed my surprise, she replied in a magisterial tone of mock stern rebuke: 'I have given up chocolate BARS – this is quite different!'

The torte had the desired effect – at the rally, she gave a breathtakingly spectacular tour de force, speaking for over an hour without a single note.

With Governor Arnold Schwarzenegger at the interment of Ronald Reagan at the Reagan Presidential Library in Simi Valley, California on 11 June 2004.

Left: Lady Thatcher poses in her ceremonial robes on her elevation to the House of Lords in 1992. Photographed by Terence Donovan.

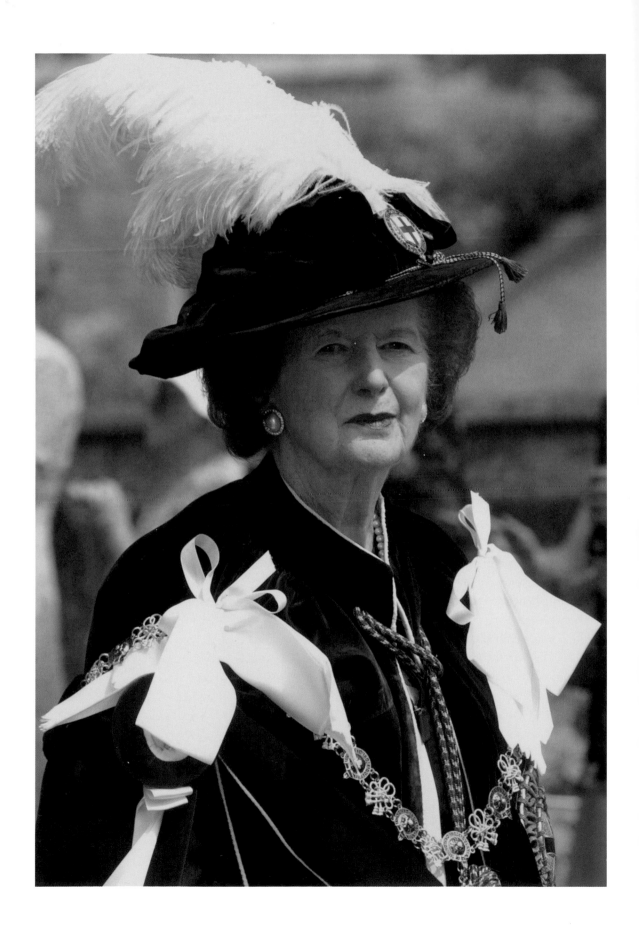

Crispin Blunt

CONSERVATIVE MP

Crispin Blunt has been MP for Reigate since 1997. Prior to that, he was Special Advisor to the Foreign Secretory, Malcom Rifkind.

They're not wet, they're drenched

I FIRST CAME INTO PERSONAL CONTACT with Margaret Thatcher in 1994. I was accompanying Malcolm Rifkind as his Special Adviser who was giving her a private advance briefing on the Front Line First changes to the armed forces. It was an hour's worth of rich political entertainment and one began to appreciate how much her style depended on Ministers who were prepared to stand up to her.

Front Line First was an uncomfortable exercise in budget cuts driven by the Government's wider need to put the UK's finances back on track after the 1990–91 recession. It came on the back of the reductions already in train following the end of the Cold War. Plainly a number of senior defence figures, past and present, had already been to see her to raise their concerns over the state of our defences.

As warm-up training for making the announcement to the House of Commons a week later it could not have been bettered. As a briefing it lasted less than thirty seconds before the avalanche of opinions and questions began to be delivered from Lady Thatcher who was supposed to be receiving the briefing. She ranged over the whole defence portfolio, from the strategic relationship with the USA, to points of detail over infantry overstretch in Northern Ireland to the highly charged emotional ties that accompany much of the politics of defence, in this case on the decision to move the Royal Marines musical training from Deal where they had been bombed by the IRA some years before.

Gradually over the course of an hour her position moved from the inquisitorial, as she satisfied herself that Malcolm's position was sound, to one of offering help with achieving our objectives. The cost savings achieved had more than met their objective, indeed to our surprise we found ourselves able to add to the front line capability of the armed forces and the major capability increase we were after was to place cruise missiles on our hunter killer nuclear-powered submarines. She was well briefed and aware we were having difficulty convincing the Foreign Office of the requirement. The FCO's attitude came as no surprise to the great lady, 'They're not wet, they're drenched.'

Lady Thatcher arrives for the ninety-fifth anniversary birthday party of the Ritz Hotel on 23 May 2001.

Left: Lady Thatcher in procession at the Order of the Garter ceremony at Windsor Castle on 17 June 2002.

Gerald Howarth

CONSERVATIVE MP

Gerald Howarth was elected MP for Cannock in 1983 and served in that capacity until 1987. He became MP for Aldershot in 2001. He is a Conservative front-bench defence spokesman.

La France est morte

IN FEBRUARY 1991, just two months after the pygmies in the Tory Party knifed her, I became *de facto* PPS to Mrs T after her official PPS, Peter Morrison, had turned his attention to other pursuits. I lost my Staffordshire seat of Cannock & Burntwood in June 1992, but continued to call in to see Mrs T at her new office in Chesham Place.

As is well known, she became more and more hostile to the Maastricht Treaty to which John Major ('the man from Coldharbour Lane' as she regularly called him) had signed up. One day, I enquired casually what were her plans for the forthcoming weekend. She replied that she was visiting Paris to dine with French President François Mitterrand.

She continued with that steely, emphatic determination with which so many had already become familiar, 'I am going to tell President Mitterrand that if he signs the Maastricht Treaty "*France est mort*"' – effectively meaning that as a nation state 'France is dead'. My rather limited knowledge of French emboldened me to suggest that '*La France est morte*' would be more grammatically correct and therefore more effective. She then proceeded to rehearse the line.

I was not present at the dinner, but on the following Monday the President of France announced that there would be a referendum on the Maastricht Treaty – eventually approved by a margin of less than 1 per cent. I am sure that the combination of the powerful message conveyed in Mrs T's best French and the deployment of that same feminine charm which won from the King of Saudi Arabia the UK's largest ever defence contract, resulted in France holding the referendum the UK should have had. This year the French people heeded La Dame de Fer's message and rejected the EU Constitution.

With Prime Minister John Major at the 1996 Conservative Party Conference.

Alan Duncan
CONSERVATIVE MP

Alan Duncan has been the MP for Rutland and Melton since 1992. He joined the Conservative front bench in 1998 and is currently a member of the Shadow Cabinet.

Winning the war

IN JUNE 1996, I hosted a summer drinks party in my London garden for the No Turning Back group of Conservative MPs. Mrs T was the guest of honour as President of the NTB group and Michael Portillo, then Secretary of State for Defence, was among the guests.

There was much debate at the time about the review of defence budgets and Mrs T assailed Michael Portillo with questions about what would be left of our defence capability.

Hoping to settle her down by assuring her of our adequate equipment in the future, Michael said: 'Don't worry, Margaret, we have lots of invitations to tender.'

She exploded: 'Invitations to tender – invitations to tender – you cannot win a war with invitations to tender!' and then she paused, quietened down and said: 'I am so sorry, Michael, I must not, I must not.' She then turned around as if to speak to someone else, the conversation having finished and, just as everyone thought that peace had broken out, she swivelled vigorously on her heels, pursed her lips, jabbed her finger right at Michael Portillo and said in a determined and pointed manner: 'Michael, have you ever won a war? I have!'

With John Major and Edward Heath at the Cenotaph on Remembrance Sunday, November 1997.

Hugo Young
POLITICAL JOURNALIST

Hugo Young was Political Editor of the *Sunday Times* from 1973 until 1984 before becoming a columnist for the *Guardian*. His biography of Margaret Thatcher, *One of Us*, is regarded as the one of the definitive accounts of her life. He died in 2003.

Only one of us

MARGARET THATCHER KNEW from the start that I wasn't likely to be One of Us. I worked for the *Sunday Times*, then an independent and liberal paper not under the suzerainty of an owner who was one of her cheer-leaders. I had all the wrong instincts, being neither a Conservative nor someone who believed any political journalist should have other than sceptical connections with politicians. But despite these bad basics, we got on quite well, which was more to her credit than to mine.

It was partly, no doubt, a matter of prudence. The *Sunday Times* was a very big paper with a lot of politically uncommitted readers, and any interview in its pages reached an important audience. I did several of them when she was Prime Minister. The first, I well recall, was preceded by her personal search for Nescafé to get some cups of coffee together. If that happened at Number 10 today, you could be sure there had been a meeting of the spin-doctors beforehand, to assess precisely what impression should be made on this or that journalist who was coming in. Nothing happens by accident now. But the early Thatcher was a cosmetic artefact only when she appeared on television. Her personal coffee-making wasn't, I thought, done for effect. Like her obsession with turning off the Downing Street lights, it was the extension of Grantham housekeeping into the prime ministerial world.

The reason I survived for ten years as an acceptable interviewer, and occasional off-the-record conversationalist, was, I think, twofold.

First, Mrs Thatcher always liked an argument. Although argument was not what this interviewer particularly sought, it was a mode of discourse she found irresistible. Somewhere along the line, the very fact that I was so plainly not in her camp became a virtue. I was bestowed with 'convictions', and even principles. When Matthew Parris left her service as an MP, he once wrote that he was especially counselled to read my stuff as a way of keeping in touch with the world he was deserting, perhaps to know who the enemy was.

Once allotted this label, I never seemed to lose it. One of the things Mrs Thatcher said, intimidatingly, to an early civil servant was that she usually made up her mind about a man in ten seconds – 'and I rarely change it'. So, perhaps, it was with me. One of her attractive virtues was that she never, in those days, showed any side. The grandeur of the post-imperial years was nowhere to be seen. Argument could flow on almost equal terms. She was utterly convinced that, in the course of such discussion, any reasonable person was certain to be persuaded to the way she thought: which is the trait she most specifically shares with Tony Blair.

Her encompassing of me within her invincible power of persuasion was due,

> *'She usually made up her mind about a man in ten seconds.'*
>
> Hugo Young

however, to the second feature of our relationship. I'm sure she never read a word I wrote. I retained my place in the tent of the acceptable because she never knew what I really thought, since she was a stranger to my columns. These became, as the years went by, critical to the point of savagery. I questioned her honesty as much as her wisdom (over Westland, for example). I impugned her motives, ridiculed her judgement and even cast doubt on her sanity. I remained, unread, within the pale: an ambiguous fate, but one which gave me scarcity value at my new employers, the *Guardian*, which otherwise seemed to have no contact of any kind with the Thatcher people.

One thing Mrs Thatcher certainly did not read was my biography of her, *One of Us*. This was an unofficial work in every sense. It drew on my talks with her over the years, but I never asked for a biographical interview. Members of her entourage told me, in due course, that they thought the book rather good. Perhaps because my columns were spiky, they expected a more polemical work between hard covers, and were relieved when that wasn't quite the book I wrote. But from herself – nothing. And after all, why should she? Who would want to read what purported to be a detailed account of their life and thought, when knowing that every nuance, however honestly chronicled, was bound to be not quite how it really was? Besides, by that time, I was permanently excluded from the bunker that had become her residence, the closed world that eventually produced her downfall.

The last time I met her was in what could, nonetheless, be called a biographical context. The occasion was the annual Christmas party given by the American ambassador. A long queue was lining up to shake his hand, and suddenly my wife and I found that Lady Thatcher and her husband had materialised beside us. This wasn't long after she had ceased to be Prime Minister, and she could still not quite credit that she had to queue at all. A frisson of doubt on her face plainly revealed an inner impulse to march up to the front and be greeted without delay. But Denis decided against such a display of amnesia as to who they now were, and the two of them therefore faced ten minutes imprisoned in our company.

The talk, led by her, immediately turned to writing. This was a subject which used to attract little but her scorn. She once asked me in very public company when I was going to get down to some proper work – building wealth, creating jobs etc. – instead of wasting my time with journalism. It was one of the little regrets of my life that I had lacked the presence of mind to say, given such an opportunity: 'After you, Prime Minister'.

But now, she told me, she had just completed the first volume of her memoirs. Naturally, this became the sole subject of our ten-minute shuffle in the queue. She was now a writer. The book had been a great labour, she recalled. But I wouldn't know anything about that, would I? Because I was a professional journalist. I was incredibly lucky, she said with patent reproach. A note of envy was even detectable. It was all so easy for me. She, on the other hand, had had to labour at getting it all down. She had written every line of the first draft herself, she said, although that nice John O'Sullivan had helped her rearrange some of the words into a better order. But it was essentially all her own work. And there would be

'She could still not quite credit that she had to queue at all.'

Hugo Young

Overleaf: Lady Thatcher with Labour Cabinet Ministers Jack Straw and Gordon Brown.

another volume to come, on which her researchers were already hard at work. Meanwhile, what mattered was who owned the copyright to the over-matter in her television interviews. Here Denis stepped in with a commercial reckoning as to the value of what lay, untransmitted, in David Frost's archives. This was serious author talk.

In recent years, she has taken up her life as a politician, albeit surrounded by a court rather than colleagues, and certainly not by journalists invited to give her an argument. Long ago, I resumed my original distance, and she, in more exaggerated form than ever, the delusions of unchallengeable, world-correcting rightness that marked her last months in office. But I bask in the moment when, with ego pumping in a new direction, she was briefly one of us, absolving us writers, just for a year or two, from being One of Them.

A gathering of British Prime Ministers and members of the Royal Family on 27 July 1992.

Tom Utley

WRITER

Tom Utley is a regular columnist for the *Daily Telegraph*.

The funeral of T E Utley

MARGARET THATCHER arrived more than an hour before anybody else for my father's funeral in 1988. She took her place in a pew at the front of the church and sat silently there alone, waiting for the other mourners to arrive and the service to begin. My mother and the rest of us were surprised and terribly touched that the Prime Minister had decided to come. She had just arrived back in London from a summit meeting in Toronto, and she was off to another one in Paris straight after the funeral. It was true that she had known my father fairly well, and he had helped her with some of her speeches. But he was never a prominent public figure, and his friendship with the Prime Minister was not so close as to put her under any sort of obligation to attend his funeral. She had already done more than her duty by my mother by writing her a long and moving letter in her own hand from Toronto on the night of my father's death. It was my father's vicar who told me that the Prime Minister had already been there for more than an hour. I asked him why on earth she had come so early, and I will never forget his reply. 'She told me,' he said, 'that she didn't want to upstage the widow.' Lady Thatcher took no formal part in the service – my brother and I did the readings – and she left with no sort of fuss or fanfare when it was over: just a word with my mother, a handshake for the vicar, a nod to me and my siblings, and she was gone.

Right: Baroness Thatcher of Kesteven takes her seat in the House of Lords.

Three generations of Thatchers, Margaret and Denis, Mark and Diane, Michael and Amanda.

Richard Stone

ARTIST

Richard Stone has painted portraits of the Royal Family for nearly three decades. He has been commissioned to paint two portraits of Lady Thatcher. Prints of Lady Thatcher's portrait have since raised considerable sums for the British Forces Foundation.

Sitting with the Lady

'I DO HOPE that the light in here is all right for you?' enquired Lady Thatcher, extending a hand to greet me. She listened attentively while I explained how I hoped the sittings would progress. It was clear she wanted to give of her best and be a good sitter. With some minor adjustments to the room, a comfortable armchair was positioned to allow the light to fall gently across her face. Coffee was summoned and the first of many enjoyable sittings began.

It was the beginning of a new adventure. Margaret Thatcher had been such an influential Prime Minister, much revered by my family and an inspiration to many of my generation. Her reputation was well known, as was her appearance from countless photographs and caricatures. I started work on the portrait a few days after meeting her for the first time. Not wanting to record just a superficial likeness, I needed to capture something of the strength and determination that a nation has always attributed to her. The trademark blue suit, the ubiquitous handbag not far from her side and the perfect coiffeur succinctly enshrined the public perception of the country's first lady Prime Minister.

With a ramrod straight back and hands neatly clasped in her lap, we gradually broke into conversation. There was talk of the Brighton bombing, the Falklands war, her friendship with Ronald Reagan and most surprisingly, traditional home cooking. Memories of the Falklands took an emotional turn. With a catch in her voice, recalling the lists of casualties brought the reality of the conflict, fought far away, back home. Recollections of the SAS invasion strategy were graphically illustrated over the tea table, with the cups and saucers, sugar bowl, milk jug and teapot used as landmarks to describe the scene.

At times, the conversation was vigorous, with robust opinions expressed giving me moments to see the fire still behind the eyes. Although each sitting would be an hour and a half in length, time would fly as I flung paint on the canvas. Often oblivious to an agitated secretary wanting to draw things to a close, our time together would regularly overrun. On many occasions, when I was tired from the intense concentration, I would be invited to stay on for a drink to relax and continue our conversation. After time, there emerged a softer, more tender aspect to the Iron Lady. She would ask questions and listen carefully to my responses.

It was at moments such as these that I was able to see a more sensitive side that I felt it was necessary to allude to in the portrait. There emerged a different woman, with a kindness, a good humour and indeed a gentleness that was not revealed in the painting. Although the picture was practically finished, I was about

'I needed to capture something of the strength and determination that a nation has always attributed to her. The trademark blue suit, the ubiquitous handbag not far from her side and the perfect coiffeur.'

Richard Stone

A portrait by Richard Stone.

Overleaf: Baroness Thatcher sitting for her portrait by the artist Nelson Shanks.

ready to start all over again, as I now felt I knew her as she really was.

Whilst I had invited Lady Thatcher to view the work as it evolved, she made it clear that she would prefer to see it only on completion. When the work was finished, she stood quietly contemplating her image. Placing a hand up to her pearl necklace and considering her words carefully, she remarked, 'It is how one would like to be remembered.'

Nancy Reagan

FIRST LADY

Nancy Reagan was First Lady of the United States from 1981 to 1989.

Happy Birthday, Margaret.

ABOUT A YEAR AFTER RONNIE DIED, I returned to London for the first time in many years. I had so many great plans for all the people and places I would visit and the events I would attend. But the one appointment I looked forward to the most was with Baroness Thatcher. I wouldn't have missed seeing Margaret for the world. We had the most wonderful afternoon, talking of old times.

Most people are aware of the very special relationship between my husband and Margaret Thatcher as leaders of their respective countries during one of the most difficult periods in modern history. In fact, my husband once said that we were living in a time when 'the survival of our nations and the peace of the world are threatened by forces which are willing to exert any pressure, test any will, and destroy any freedom'. He admired Margaret's strength, determination and courage, and called her 'a world leader in every meaning of the word'.

Ronnie and Margaret were political soul-mates, united in their commitment to freedom and resolution to end communism. When Ronnie entered the White House, he inherited similar problems to those Margaret inherited as Prime Minister: a troubled economy, high inflation and diminished national pride. To overcome this, Ronnie said she demonstrated two great qualities. The first was that she had thought seriously about how to revive the British economy and entered office with a clear set of policies to do so. And he said her second great quality was the true grit of a true Brit.

Generous with compliments and always positive, Margaret spoke very highly of my husband's leadership. I will never forget when she credited him with 'ending the Cold War without firing a shot', and I know it meant so much to Ronnie to receive that kind of praise from her.

For eight years as President, my husband never had a closer ally than Margaret Thatcher. But Margaret was not just an ally; she was also a dear and trusted friend. She and Ronnie shared the same values and beliefs, not only with regard to politics but also on a personal level. We were fortunate to see Margaret and her husband, Denis, in an official capacity, and also enjoyed spending time with them on many visits together as friends.

Throughout the final years of my husband's life, Margaret was a constant source of support and inspiration to me. She defied her doctor's orders and insisted on travelling to Washington to attend Ronnie's funeral service, and remained at my side as we flew back across the country to California for the burial ceremony at the Ronald Reagan Presidential Library. Her magnificent eulogy was one of the most heartwarming tributes my husband ever received.

As we prepare to celebrate Baroness Thatcher's 80th birthday – or as my husband would have said, the 41st anniversary of her 39th birthday – I am pleased to join people all over the world in expressing my love and admiration.

Happy Birthday, Margaret!

Index

Picture Credits

BRIDGEMAN ART LIBRARY: 85.

CAMERA PRESS: 4–5, 9, 11, 16–17, 24, 27, 39, 49, 52–53, 56, 59, 63–64, 71–72, 75, 79, 81, 91, 96 below, 103, 105, 107, 113, 118, 119, 125, 129, 131, 133–134, 136–137, 141, 147, 150, 154, 157, 159, 163, 165, 167, 183, 199, 192–193, 197, 204–205, 208, 211, 213, 219, 221–222, 228, 230–231, 234, 238–239, 241, 245, 253, 258, 262–263, 265, 266, 268–269, 271–272, 274–277.

GETTY IMAGES: 12, 13, 15, 18–21 above, 23, 28, 31, 37, 45, 66, 100–101, 145, 149, 151, 161, 169, 172–173, 199, 203, 215, 217, 247, 249, 267.

TREVOR PAYNE: 65.

POPPERFOTO: facing title page.

REX FEATURES: 42–43, 47, 69, 77, 82–83, 99, 102, 121, 128, 142–143, 175–176, 178, 207, 209, 226–227, 261.

TOPFOTO: 14, 21 below, 41, 57, 87, 89, 95, 96 above, 98, 104, 108, 111, 114, 116, 127, 153, 181, 191, 195, 237, 240, 256, 270, 278, 279, 285.

282–83: reproduced courtesy of the artist Nelson Shanks.

First published in Great Britain in 2005 by Weidenfeld & Nicolson

Text copyright © Iain Dale 2005
Design and layout © Weidenfeld & Nicolson 2005

Some essays previously appeared in *Memories of Maggie* edited by Iain Dale.

We are grateful to the following publishers for permission to reproduce extracts: Aurum Press (*A Bastard's Tale* by Sir George Gardiner and *The Whitelaw Memoirs* by William Whitelaw); Random House (*My Style of Government* by Nicholas Ridley; *An American Life* by Ronald Reagan; *Memoirs* by Mikhail Gorbachev); William Heinemann (*The Hawke Memoirs* by Bob Hawke); and Faber & Faber (*The Turbulent Years* by Kenneth Baker).

A CIP catalogue record for this book is available from the British Library.

ISBN 0 297 85115 2

Designed by NIGEL SOPER
Design assistance by JOANNA CANNON
Edited by LUCINDA MCNEILE
Picture research by TOM GRAVES

Printed and bound in England by Butler & Tanner

Weidenfeld & Nicolson
The Orion Publishing Group Ltd
Wellington House
125 Strand
London, WC2R 0BB

www.orionbooks.co.uk